The Dance of
DECEPTION

The Dance of
DECEPTION

～

PRETENDING
AND TRUTH-TELLING
IN WOMEN'S LIVES

Harriet G. Lerner, Ph.D.

HarperPerennial
A Division of HarperCollinsPublishers

HarperCollins books may be purchased for educational, business, or sales promotional use. For information, please write: Special Markets Department, HarperCollins Publishers, Inc., 10 East 53rd Street, New York, NY 10022.

First HarperPerennial edition published 1994.

Designed by Alma Hochhauser Orenstein

The Library of Congress has catalogued the hardcover edition as follows:

Lerner, Harriet Goldhor.
The dance of deception : pretending and truth-telling in women's lives / Harriet Goldhor Lerner.
    p.   cm.
    Includes index.
    ISBN 0-06-016816-1.
    1. Women—Psychology. 2. Deception. 3. Truthfulness and falsehood. I. Title.
HQ1206.L445 1993
155.3'33—dc20   92–53376
ISBN 0-06-092463-2 (pbk.)

95 96 97 98 ❖/RRD 10 9 8 7 6 5 4 3 2

In memory of AUDRE LORDE,
who taught us that women have gained nothing
from silence.

Contents

Acknowledgments   *vii*

1   Tony and the Martians   *1*

2   Deception and Truth-Telling   *9*

3   To Do the Right Thing   *17*

4   In the Name of Privacy   *34*

5   A Funny Thing Happened on the Way to the Orifice   *48*

6   We Are the Stories We Tell   *67*

7   Our Family Legacies   *83*

8   Honesty versus Truth   *102*

9   Just Pretending   *117*

10   Family Secrets: A Disturbance in the Field   *136*

11   An Affair Is a Big Secret   *156*

12   The Body Seeks Truth   *174*

13   Will the Real Me Please Stand?   *198*

Epilogue: When the Lion Learns to Write   *217*

Notes   *221*

Index   *245*

Acknowledgments

The Dance of Deception completes a trilogy. Unlike its predecessors, this book does not fall into the category of "self-help" or "how-to." I have set out to be thought-provoking rather than prescriptive, although where I believe there is a right or better way to go about things, I spell it out.

I discovered early on in writing this book that I didn't want to limit my terrain. My greatest delight was in choosing a subject as vast, multilayered, shifting, and subjective as human experience itself. So the reader should not expect an orderly, comprehensive text, or an airtight argument to think or behave in a particular way. Instead, I hope the reader will feel jolted, shaken up a bit, pushed to think about a rich variety of subjects, and rewarded for the journey.

A book that deals with so large a subject owes a multitude of acknowledgments. I regret that I cannot begin to name all the people who have contributed over many years to my work. Freshest in my memory are the many friends who gave generously of their time and talents while this work was in progress:

My dear friend Jeffrey Ann Goudie cheered me on (and cheered me up) from start to finish. In addition to timely hand holding, she made excellent suggestions throughout the manuscript. Her husband, Thomas Fox Averill, also read the entire draft and offered vital criticism. It is a blessing to have two such splendid friends, both writers themselves, who took time away from their own valuable projects to lend assistance and support.

This book owes its existence to my manager, Jo-Lynne Worley, who pulled me out of my proposed early retirement (I didn't really mean it, anyway) and convinced me that the best was yet to come. Her steady and loving friendship, her abiding belief in my work, and her quiet, remarkable competence in managing everything, allowed me to begin and complete this book. She has extended, enriched, and organized my life in countless ways.

My close friends in the Topeka community critiqued all or parts of this manuscript, talked and thought with me about my subject, or in some way encouraged and helped me along. My love and thanks to Emily Kofron whose work and presence in the world inspires me. Special thanks also to Ellen Safier, Nancy Maxwell, Marianne Ault-Riché, and Judith Koontz. From out of town, Harris E. Weberman and Sherry Levy-Reiner commented on earlier drafts. Countless women I interviewed informally gave me uncompromisingly honest responses to tough questions about deception and truth-telling in their intimate lives.

This is my third book to pass through the (ever-wiser) hands of Janet Goldstein, my terrific editor at Harper-Collins. She has the gift of knowing immediately when something is "off" and the rare talent for making small suggestions that make a big difference. I also appreciate the fastidious copyediting by Ann Adelman and the careful work of others on the staff of HarperCollins who have done a fine job with the production, promotion, and publicity of all my books. It's a privilege these days to find a publisher one wants to stay wedded to. I also want to thank Karen Wald, Lisa Liebman, Stephanie von Hirschberg, and the staff at *New Woman* magazine, where I have the good fortune to write a monthly advice column.

I am blessed with an extraordinary and ever-widening network of feminist friends and colleagues. My heartfelt thanks to Holly Near and Jeanne Marecek for critiquing each chapter with great care, to Patricia Klein Frithiof for encouraging my work and bringing it to Sweden, to Sonia Johnson and Jade Deforest for their love and generous sharing of ideas and themselves, and to Mollie Katzen for responding so enthusiastically to the final draft.

The Menninger Clinic has provided me with a solid home base from which to work. Peter Novotny has affirmed and supported my projects from my earliest years at Menninger and others have joined in along the way, lending the administrative support that made it possible for me to combine writing and clinical work. I'm especially indebted to Mary Ann Clifft whose careful and meticulous editing is unsurpassed. The entire manuscript has had the benefit of her keen eye. Thanks also to the Menninger library staff and to Eleanor Bell for providing editorial help with the chapter notes.

I am deeply grateful to Carolyn Conger, who is, in the fullest sense of the word, a teacher. Her ability to awaken insight, to empower others to connect with their own wisdom and worth, is remarkable. She taught me about truth from a new angle.

My husband Steve Lerner has been, along with everything else, a precious friend and colleague for almost a quarter of a century. From him, and with him, I've learned much about the subject of this book. I'm grateful for his love, encouragement, and his unwavering belief in my work. He has enhanced my life in more ways than I can articulate.

Intellectual Debts

Writers commonly explain that books are the products of many people's ideas and that the intellectual debt an author owes to others cannot be adequately acknowledged. Never before have I felt this to be so true. Because my subject is at the heart of both feminist theory and the practice of psychotherapy, all of my professional training and my education as a feminist have contributed to this work. It is difficult, if not impossible, to sort out the "ownership" or origin of ideas and probably spurious to try. Although I've done my best to acknowledge my intellectual debts in the Chapter Notes, I apologize in advance for the inevitable omissions.

I want to mention certain people up front, particularly where I have drawn directly or heavily from their work: Sisella Bok has written two important books on ethical implications of secrecy and lying; Pauline Bart loaned me her title for Chapter 5; I'm also deeply indebted to the important work of Carolyn Heilbrun (Chapters 5 and 6), Peggy McIntosh (Chapter 6), Evan Imber-Black and Peggy Papp (Chapter 10), Peggy Vaughan (Chapter 11), Rosabeth Moss Kanter and Elizabeth Kamarck Minnich (Chapter 13), and Audre Lorde, Sonia Johnson, and Jean Tait (Chapter 12).

I especially need to thank Adrienne Rich for her classic texts, *Of Woman Born* and *Lies, Secrets, and Silence*, which are pivotal to my subject. I love the way Rich tells the truth and writes about truth-telling—incisively, urgently, uncompromisingly, and passionately. My gratitude for her brilliant work (which includes thirteen books of poetry) is part of my larger debt to the intellectual revolution wrought by feminism. Without the presence in my life of a feminist community, I would be groping around in the dark or writing comfortably and tamely in a voice that was not my own.

I have learned much from my immensely gifted friend Marianne Ault-Riché who generously included me as an equal partner in two vital projects that she originated—our early communication workshops in Topeka ("Talking Straight" and "Fighting Fair") and the "Women in Context" conference series at Menninger. I also want to thank Elizabeth Kamarck Minnich for her enlightening, inclusive, and hopeful vision of democracy, and her husband, Si Kahn, for keeping this vision alive through his organizing and music.

In writing this book I also drew heavily on my experience as a clinical psychologist and psychotherapist. Throughout my professional training I have had many fine teachers of psychoanalytic and family systems theory. I'm particularly indebted to Katherine Glenn Kent for teaching me to "think systems" over our many years of friendship, and for helping me to apply Bowen family systems theory to my life and work. Her influence is reflected in this book, as is the pioneering work of Murray Bowen. I'm also indebted to an excellent paper on deception by Stephanie Ferrera. Of course, my adoption of other people's ideas doesn't mean they like what I did with them. No one I thank shares all my opinions or necessarily agrees with my conclusions. As always, the ultimate responsibility for this book is mine alone.

Many feminist psychoanalytic thinkers have enriched my life, beginning with my friend Teresa Bernardez, who was the first in the mental health field to focus on the subject of women's anger. Jean Baker Miller's classic text, *Toward a New Psychology of Women*, carefully links the subordination of women to dilemmas regarding authenticity and truth. I thank her for this important work and for all that has followed from her visionary efforts.

For assorted assistance and comeradeship thanks to Susan Kraus, Joanie Shoemaker, Georgia Kolias, Jo-Ann Krestan, Claudia Bepko, Elaine Prostak Berland, Jennifer Nell Hofer, Betty Hoppes, Patricia Spiegelberg Hyland, Nancy Jehl, Doris Jane Chediak, my women's group, and my wise and witty long-distance pal, Carol Tavris. My love to my parents, Rose and Archie Goldhor, my sister (and co-author in juvenile publishing) Susan Goldhor, and my dear sons, Matt and Ben Lerner. Finally, thanks to my readers who continue to overwhelm me with messages of affection, gratitude, and thoughtful challenge.

The Dance of
DECEPTION

Except for the friends and family who have given permission to appear in this book, names and identifying characteristics of individuals mentioned have been changed in order to protect their privacy.

1

Tony and the Martians

When I was twelve, I told a lie that grew to epic proportions. I told my friend Marla, who lived across the street from me in Brooklyn, that I had been contacted by a man named Tony who came from another planet. Since first grade, Marla and I had been on-again, off-again best friends.

I told Marla that Tony told me to find a date. Since no one had asked me out yet (and I believed that no one ever would), Marla had to fix me up with a blind date because Tony said that something bad might happen to me otherwise. Marla, who could accomplish almost anything she set her mind to, went about this project with her usual vigor and enthusiasm. The blind date came and went. Tony did not.

A few minor characters from the same planet were added to the drama, as the personality and presence of Tony grew and became part of my deepening friendship with Marla. Tony emerged as a good-hearted, playful fellow who told me funny things that I could tell only Marla—and that she could tell no one. At a time when my other girlfriends were dropping one best friend for another, my special status with

Marla was secure. Tony stabilized our friendship and strengthened our sense of camaraderie and commitment. And I was in charge—an active director and orchestrator of the threesome: Tony and Marla and me.

I don't remember how often Tony visited or how long he stayed around, but I think it was at least a year before I let him drift out of our lives. Years later, when Marla and I were both graduate students in Berkeley, California, I tearfully told her I had made Tony up. Until then, we had both walled off the Tony business, not bothering to reflect on it or even to remember. Marla protected me and our friendship by choosing not to subject this interplanetary drama to close scrutiny. After all, anything is possible. When we finally talked about it, Marla was lighthearted and forgiving, as I hoped she would be with our long history of friendship binding us together.

In the early 1970s I entered psychoanalysis during my post-doctoral training program in clinical psychology and confessed my "Tony story." I half-jokingly voiced my concern that my analyst would downgrade my diagnosis to something either very bad or very sick. My uneasiness was hardly surprising. Although lying is commonplace in both personal and public—especially political—life, the label of "liar" is a profound condemnation in our culture, bringing to mind pathology and sin. I know parents who punish their children more severely for lying to them than for any other behavior. I have heard otherwise calm parents scream at their children, "Don't you *ever* lie to me again!" So heavy are the negative associations of intention and character that it is difficult to think lovingly, or even objectively, about the role that lying plays in the lives of children and adults.

My analyst (coincidentally also named Tony) was, as always, empathic and nonjudgmental. In psychoanalysis—as in the rest of life—insight and self-understanding do not flourish in an atmosphere of self-depreciation or blame. He and I explored Tony in the context of my distant relationship with my father and my related desperation about getting the "blind date" that I first used Tony for with Marla.

Many years later, after the birth of my second son in 1979, I faced a personal crisis, a health scare, that pushed me to learn more about my mother's diagnosis of advanced endometrial cancer when I was twelve. While talking to my parents at this time, I recognized that I had brought Tony into the picture when my mother, then forty-eight, had been given one year to live. Although I was unaware on a conscious level of her diagnosis and prognosis, I am certain that my unconscious knew everything.

As I reconstructed that year, multiple lies emerged, beginning with my mother's harrowing experience with a medical system that did not provide her with facts. After a long period of misdiagnosed vaginal bleeding, my mother hemorrhaged and was hospitalized for an emergency D&C. This procedure led to the unexpected diagnosis of a hitherto unknown invasive cancer. Her physician (who may himself have been reacting to the long period of misdiagnosis and neglect) told my father the facts—but swore him to secrecy. After the initial procedure, my mother was packing her bags to return home when she was told that an additional stay in the hospital was necessary for a second surgery to "stretch her uterus." With this improbable, mystifying explanation, her doctor performed a complete hysterectomy without her knowledge or permission. She awoke from the surgery, confused and disoriented, and suffering from inexplicable, intense pain.

My mother did not confront her doctor until immediately before her discharge from the hospital, when he referred her for radiation treatment. She demanded to know her diagnosis. He did not answer, but instead took her hand and told her to enjoy life and to try to have enjoyable sex in the year to come. He didn't mention cancer and she didn't push it. A part of her, too, must not have wanted to hear the word spoken out loud. With a referral for prolonged radiation treatment, however, my mother knew the name of her problem even though the medical establishment did not voice it.

In the year that followed, the word "cancer" was never spoken in my family. My mother's health was not even discussed. Inexplicably, she did not die, as predicted, and so we have had the opportunity to talk as adults about that traumatic year after her diagnosis. Our conversations have allowed me to appreciate more deeply how helplessly out of control I must have felt when I brought Tony down from another planet.

My mother, the emotional center of the family, seemed to be dying. Susan, my only sibling, had started college at Barnard and would soon be looking for an apartment in the city. She was getting launched, leaving me for her own grown-up life. My mother had quietly made plans for her brother and sister-in-law, then living in a different part of Brooklyn, to take me in after her death because she did not think that my father could care for me by himself. I was on the edge of losing everyone. Into this precarious world, threatening to pull apart at the seams, I brought Tony.

During the year after my mother's diagnosis, my most important relationships had a lie at their center. In my fam-

ily, the lie was perpetuated through silence. There was a survival issue in my family that no one was talking about. Only
once did I give voice to reality, to truth, in an incident that I
myself do not remember. My mother tells me that some time
after she had finished her radiation treatment and had recov-
ered her energy and spirits, she came down with a bad cold
and took to bed—a singularly rare occurrence for her. I
stormed into the bedroom and screamed at her for lying
down. "Get up!" I commanded with the full force of early
adolescent rage. "You'd better not die—do you hear me?—or
I'll never forgive you!" My mother recalls this outburst—
over as suddenly as it began—as our family's only direct
expression of feeling, our only articulation of danger.

Apart from this isolated outburst, I blanketed myself in
denial, screening out my mother's illness and my questions
about how I would be cared for if she died. Reading back
through my diary—my one place to tell the truth—I do not
find a word during that year about my mother being sick or
about my being afraid. I numbed my consciousness, both
language and feeling. But because the unconscious seeks
truth, I acted out all over the place—in trouble at school and
a mess at home.

With Marla, my best friend, the lie was told in words,
not in silence. I constructed, elaborated, and kept alive a narrative, immersing myself so fully in the drama that I did not
experience myself as standing outside it. Only much later did
I piece together enough context to make sense of my behavior, to think more objectively of its meaning.

Perhaps I wanted to be caught. One evening I found
myself in my sister Susan's bedroom, spontaneously telling
her that I had become friends with a man from another
planet. If Susan had taken this revelation seriously, a confrontation about Tony might have pushed us all toward

addressing the deeper issue. But for better or worse, Susan merely listened to my story, perhaps never giving it a second thought.

Thinking about Context

If my behavior with Marla was viewed out of context, an observer might say, "She lied because that's how she is. She is a liar, out for herself, that sort of child." Or a psychological interpretation might be based on a particular notion about human behavior: "Because she is insecure, she needs to manipulate and control—that's why she lies."

In the absence of context, we tend to view particular behaviors as fixed "traits" or as "personality characteristics" that exist within us, rather than as part of a dance happening between and among us. My creation of Tony, for example, could be viewed as evidence of my manipulative, controlling, and deceptive intentions—words that fit with our culture's general description of how women have wielded power. Of course, these *were* my intentions—to manipulate, control, and deceive, just as my intentions were to love, to connect, strengthen, protect, and survive.

Context allows us to put lying—or any other behavior—into perspective. By broadening our view, we are challenged to take a more complex reality into account, to ask questions (rather than provide answers) about where lies begin.

Did the lie begin, in my case, with a frightened adolescent girl who desperately wanted to avoid any further threat of loss by holding on to her best friend by whatever magic possible?

Did it begin with my parents, unable to address, even with each other, a terrifying illness, then handed down as a death sentence? Or did it begin with *their* parents, Russian Jewish immigrants who could not begin to speak about the massive losses and separations they had endured?

Did the lie begin under the hand of patriarchy, with the male-dominated medical system withholding facts from my mother, mystifying and falsifying her experience, denying her deepest instincts, protecting her from essential knowledge "for her own sake," creating for her a situation of unutterable loneliness? Did truth-telling become less possible still when the doctor told my father to keep my mother's condition a secret, for which she did not easily forgive him? And what of my mother's unspoken plan to transfer me to a relative's home upon her death? Was patriarchy (its consequences then hidden, unspoken, denied) at the heart of a mother's felt knowledge or belief that it might be unwise to leave an adolescent daughter alone with an emotionally isolated father?

I was in my thirties before I connected Tony to my mother's diagnosis of cancer, a connection which cast a new perspective on my behavior of twenty years earlier—as did the facts about my mother's hospital experience then, and the culturally enforced silence surrounding any diagnosis of cancer at that time. Deception is larger than the particular individual responsible for it, larger even than a family. We can never know for sure where a lie begins, with whom it originates, or the many factors that sustain it. We can, however, move toward an increasingly accurate and complex understanding of ourselves as we widen our view of a lie, secret, or silence— or any deceptive behavior, for that matter.

This story about Tony illustrates the importance of context, and how empathy and understanding increase with the bigger picture of family, culture, and the addition of more facts. Further, this story illustrates that our most dramatic and colorful lies—the ones we can decide either to keep secret or to confess—are not necessarily at the center of our emotional life and not where we need to focus our primary attention. My lie to Marla was symptomatic of the paralyzing silence in my family surrounding my mother's illness. My family's silence was symptomatic of a culture which placed cancer, as well as other painful subjects, in the realm of the unspeakable. It is the unspoken, all that we cannot name and productively address, that gets us into trouble; lying is merely one expression of that trouble.

In truth, I did not experience myself as a "liar." Or, more accurately, I knew I was lying to Marla about Tony but I told myself I was *pretending*. We were, perhaps, all pretending— the doctors who withheld information from my mother (for her own sake), my parents who withheld information from us children (for our sake), and the children, myself included, who didn't persist in asking questions (for the family's sake). We were a family like any other, with strengths and vulnerabilities, doing our best to stay afloat in the face of massive anxiety about my mother's—and our own—survival.

2

~

Deception and Truth-Telling

Whether our motives are unconscious or intentional, pristine or nefarious, deception is a part of everyday existence. It wears countless faces in daily life and takes on an endless array of forms and functions. Our language itself speaks to the multiplicity of ways that we depart from truth-telling and engage in deceit:

> We say, she fibbed, fabricated, exaggerated, minimized, withheld.
> We say, she told a white lie, a partial truth, a falsehood, a tall tale.
> We say, she embroidered her story, she pulled the wool over our eyes.
> We say, she keeps secrets (and also, she can't keep a secret).
> We say, she covered up, covered over, concealed, misled, misinformed, twisted, distorted, falsified, misrepresented the facts.
> We say, she is false, elusive, evasive, wily, indirect, tricky,

treacherous, manipulative, untrustworthy, unfaithful, sneaky, scheming, calculating, conniving, corrupt.

We say, she is deceitful, deceptive, duplicitous, dishonest.

We say, she is a hypocrite, a cheat, a charlatan, a callous liar, a fraud.

We say, she presented a clever ruse, a bogus deal, an artifice, a pretense, a fiction, a sham, a hoax.

We say, she is phony, artificial, affected.

We say, she is pretending, charading, posturing, faking, holding back, being an imposter, putting up a good front, hiding behind a facade.

We say, she did not own up, come clean, or level with me.

We say, she gaslighted me, messed with my mind, mystified my reality, betrayed and double-crossed me.

We say, she is two-faced; she speaks out of both sides of her mouth.

We say, she speaks falsely.

We say, she cannot face reality; she cannot face the truth; she engages in self-deception.

We say, how brave she was to reveal nothing, how clever to throw them off track.

We say, she acted with discretion.

We say, she lied out of necessity; she lied for the greater good.

We say, she lied with honor.

Our language provides us with incredibly rich possibilities for describing our departures from truth-telling. Different words and phrases evoke varied images of deception, connoting a range of implications about intention and motivation, and the seriousness of harm done. We may have learned to associate some of these words more with women, some more with men. In either case, we have more words to describe the nuances of how we deceive each other than to describe how we love.

Deception is not a "woman's problem" or even a uniquely human phenomenon, for that matter. From viruses to large mammals—from disease-causing microbes to baboons and chimps—deception is continually at play: an African beetle kills a few ants and attaches their carcasses to its body in order to enter an ant colony to feast undetected; a chimp misdirects her group away from a food source, covers up her own movements so that the location of the food can't be traced, and returns later to dine by herself. Many baboons and chimps, when threatened, make themselves appear larger. Deception has played a major role in the evolution of human life. It is interesting to think about the fact that deception and "con games" are a way of life in all species and throughout nature. Organisms that do not improve their ability to deceive—and to detect deception—are less apt to survive.

Do only humans engage in calculated deception? Not according to the finest animal trainers, who attribute a capacity for moral understanding to a number of species other than our own. Trainers, notes Vicki Hearne, distinguish horses who are trustworthy ("Relax, there isn't a tricky bone in that horse's body") from those who are "sneaky" ("Don't worry, he'll come around okay, he's no real criminal, just a juvenile delinquent") and even "irredeemably dishonest." Although such anthropomorphic, morally loaded language is criticized as naive, even heretical, the scientifically minded critics are hopelessly behind the trainers when it comes to engagement in the real world of animal-human encounters.

The subject of deception pertains to every member of our species, but this book speaks directly to women, and undoubtedly to some women more than others. I invite men to read it, too, of course, not just to learn about the women in their lives but also to find themselves in these pages. Much of what follows is "generically human"; where it isn't, it's useful for the reader to define both commonalities and differences. We can all benefit from examing how we hide the real and show the false. Unexamined deception is now threatening our survival far more than enhancing it.

How, specifically, do we engage in deception?

We lie outright, as I did to Marla, with the intention of convincing the other person of what we know is not true, of what we do not even believe ourselves. As our language illustrates, words and phrases which connote deliberate deception tend to condemn, reflecting our feelings about being on the receiving end of deception. When we are the active players, however, we are more likely to experience ourselves as lying to prevent harm, not create it.

We also depart from truth-telling through silence, as my family did, by failing to speak out. We do not ask an essential question or make a comment to clarify the facts. We withhold information from others that would make a difference in their lives. We do not even say, "There are some things I am not telling you."

In contrast to how we react to stated lies, we are slower to pass negative judgment on what is *withheld*. After all, no one can tell "the whole truth" all the time. (A friend commented recently, "Can you imagine what an impossible world it would be if we could all read each other's minds!") Deception through silence or withholding may be excused, even praised: "My daughter is lucky I never told her about her father"; "The doctor was kind enough to spare her the truth about her illness"; "How incredible that she is always cheery for her children when she is feeling so wretched."

When we are silent or withholding about the self, we may call it "privacy," a word suggesting that our failure to disclose is neutral or harmless. We would all agree that we don't have to tell anyone everything, although the more intimate the relationship the greater both the possibility and the longing to tell—and the bigger the emotional consequences of not telling. Privacy differs from deception. But when we say, "This is nobody's business but my own," we may obscure the full meaning and consequences of secrets and silence, of a life in hiding in which we do not allow ourselves to be known.

Then there are lies, secrets, and silences that begin with the self. We are not clear about what we think, feel, and believe. Our priorities and life goals are not really our own; our behavior is not congruent with our stated values and beliefs. On important matters, we give in, go along, buckle under. We may not feel genuine or real. We are not "centered," "grounded," or in touch with ourselves. As a result, we are not fully present in our most important relationships.

Because of the enormous human capacity for self-deception, we may fail to recognize when we are lying—or when we are not living authentically and truly. In any case, we can be no more honest with others than we are with the self.

Pretending and Truth-Telling

In thinking about women's lives, I have come to pay particular attention to the words "pretending" and "truth-telling," words that touch on all of our actions and relationships as well as who we are and what we might become.

"Pretending" is a word that may help us to suspend our moral judgments about what is good or bad, better or worse, so that we can think more objectively about a difficult subject. It also fits more appropriately into the fabric of women's lives. Our failure to live authentically and to speak truly may have little to do with evil or exploitative intentions. Quite the contrary, pretending more frequently reflects a wish, however misguided, to protect others and to ensure the viability of the self as well as our relationships. Pretending reflects deep prohibitions, real and imagined, against a more direct and forthright assertion of self. Pretending stems naturally from the false and constricted definitions of self that women often absorb without question. "Pretending" is so closely associated with "femininity" that it is, quite simply, what the culture teaches women to do.

In some instances, however, we will rightfully be wary of the word "pretending" precisely because (like "privacy") its neutral and benign connotations would have us trivialize and gloss over what does need our attention, if not our moral judgment. It is not useful to sanitize the fact that under patriarchy, women are continually lied to, and that in the struggle for love, sanity, and survival, we continue to tell lies. Sometimes, only a harsh word like "lying" will do.

Truth-telling, the heart of my subject, is a central challenge in women's lives. The term "truth-telling" seems more encompassing, more courageous, and more richly textured in meaning than the word "honesty." When I say "truth-telling" out loud, I think of bold and pioneering acts, as well as enlivened conversation on the headiest of subjects. For example, "What is truth?" "Who defines what is true and what is real for each of us?" "Do women really have a 'true self' to uncover, find, or, alternatively, to invent?" "Whose truth counts?" Under patriarchy, women are well schooled in pretending and deception. We also have developed an extraordinary capacity to tell the truth, or at least to whisper it.

Reflections on this subject remind me of the tendency to organize our world into dichotomous categories: good and evil, masculine and feminine, yin and yang, gay and straight, and now, pretending and truth-telling. People, of course, are far more complex and multifaceted than the polarities or "opposites" we create.

Truth-telling is, on the one hand, closely linked to whatever is most essential in our lives. It is the foundation of authenticity, self-regard, intimacy, integrity, and joy. We know that closeness requires honesty, that lying erodes trust, that the cruelest lies are often "told" in silence.

Yet this perspective is only part of the overall view. In the name of "truth," we may hurt friends and family members, escalate anxiety nonproductively, disregard the different reality of the other person, and generally move the situation from bad to worse. I have watched my clients—and myself—make every variety of error about who to tell, what to tell, when to tell, how much to tell, and how to tell. And, of course, there are situations in which it may be wiser to be strategic than spontaneous. In my early years at the Menninger Clinic, for example, I was the sole identified feminist; I thus made it my job to openly confront every injustice and to raise the consciousness of my colleagues. In my efforts to convince others of "the truth," I quickly became encapsulated in a role that made it impossible for them to hear what I had to say.

In the real world, the seemingly contradictory activities of pretending and truth-telling are not always "opposite" or discrete. Pretending, for example, may be an indirect move toward the truth, rather than a misdirected flight from it. In pretending love or courage, we may discover that it really does exist—or that we can enhance our capacity for it. Sometimes pretending is a form of experimentation or imitation that widens our experience and sense of possibility; it reflects a wish to find ourselves in order to *be* ourselves. Similarly, at a particular time, pretending may be necessary for survival, or we may feel that it is absolutely essential.

My goal, then, is not to create another false polarity, or to try to push the reader along an unexamined, linear path from pretending to truth-telling. Nor will I provide "answers," "how-to" instructions, or reassurance, although my values and beliefs about a "right" course of action will surely come through. What follows are my reflections on aspects of deception and truth-telling that are vital to our lives. My primary focus is on relationships, including one's relationship to the self. My hope is that you will join me in examining how all of us engage in deception and approach truth-telling—a subject that is at the heart of who we are in the world and what kind of world this is.

3

To Do the Right Thing

In 1970, Dr. Robert Wolk and Arthur Henley published a book called *The Right to Lie*, the first "how-to" guide on using deceit in everyday life. The authors provide numerous examples of "constructive" and "worthwhile" lies that purportedly strengthen intimate relationships.

There is the case of Evelyn G., for example, who with her husband consults a doctor after trying unsuccessfully for a year to become pregnant. Following fertility tests, the doctor telephones Evelyn and asks her to visit him privately. He then informs her that her husband is sterile, but asks her to consider whether her husband should be told. The authors continue:

> Evelyn is deeply disappointed. She has an impulse to tell her husband, "See, I'm not to blame! It's all your fault!" But she knows that this will strike at the heart of his self-esteem. The doctor agrees, adding that such an accusation might possibly even make Paul G. impotent.
>
> To preserve her sex life and her husband's sensibilities, Evelyn decides to tell a lie. She takes full blame for her

inability to conceive. It is a "loving" lie, that protects the marriage. As Evelyn had expected, her husband is sympathetic and tells her not to feel badly, that he will be just as happy to adopt a baby. That is **his** loving lie and concludes an even exchange of deceits that strengthens the relationship.

According to the authors, the "constructive lies" that Evelyn and Paul exchange are born of necessity and kindness, and serve to reinforce the loving bond between them. Happily, the specifics of their story is dated, as is my mother's hospital experience around the time of her first cancer. If nothing else, a physician who joins with one spouse to falsify medical facts to the other might fear a malpractice suit. People still justify lying, however, if they believe it serves a protective end or a greater good. What has changed are cultural norms, and we have changed with them. As creatures of culture and context, our beliefs about "constructive lies" shift with the political climate of the day.

I have thought hard about the impact of culture and context, particularly as I watched the televised congressional hearings in 1991 that turned into a painful and outrageous attack on Anita Hill, as she tried to tell the truth about Supreme Court Justice nominee Clarence Thomas. In the midst of the moral outrage I felt on her behalf, I recalled an experience I had in 1962, more than a quarter of a century ago.

I was spending my junior year of college in Delhi, India, in a program sponsored by the University of Wisconsin, where I was an undergraduate. Midway through the year, I moved from Miranda House, a college dorm in Old Delhi, to a room in a nearby hotel. At this same hotel lived a distinguished American, perhaps forty years my senior, who had retired from a high government position. He was, in his own words, "a very important man." Indeed, he was the most important man I had ever encountered close up.

For months he pursued me aggressively and inappropriately for sex. Later that year, when I came down with malaria, he made advances toward a close woman friend who was caring for me at the time, and was also an American student in the program. After my recovery, I was relieved to find that he continued to pursue her rather than me.

I always found this man's advances unwelcome and discomfiting. Yet never for a moment did I question the "right" of so prominent a man—a veritable force in history, as I saw it—to persist in his efforts to get what he wanted. I was always more attuned and vigilantly protective of his feelings than of my own. My friend and I discussed his advances only with each other. We said nothing to the leader of our program in Delhi.

The following year, back in Madison, Wisconsin, my friend and I sat with this same program leader in the cafeteria of the Student Union. He was visiting briefly from Delhi and was about to return there. Suddenly departing from small talk, he told us that a student was currently reporting sexual advances from this same man. He quickly added that this honorable gentleman would never do such a thing. The student could only be mistaken.

"Right?" he said in our direction. It may well have been meant as a question, but I heard it as a declaration or challenge. My friend and I nodded affirmatively and nothing more was said on the subject. It wasn't until 1991, as I watched, in astonishment, the enemies of Anita Hill, that I thought with sorrow and disbelief about my nod and subsequent silence. Why did I leave that brave student, halfway across the world, in a position of isolation and vulnerability?

What was her name? What price did she pay for speaking the truth? Why had I not spoken out? I felt ashamed of myself—particularly because I had felt not the slightest hint of shame at the time.

I'm sure that I lied for many of the usual reasons people lie: to make myself most comfortable at the moment, to escape disapproval and censure, to avoid complexity and complication, to keep at bay my own emotions, which were linked to my earlier experience. My friend and I feared, perhaps rightfully so, that our disclosure might also be discounted or held against us. Our program head was a compassionate and intelligent man, but the cultural climate of the day enforced denial.

More to the point, I thought at the time that I was doing *the right thing*. I believed that it was my responsibility to protect the reputation of this very important man. I figured that the woman, whoever she was, could handle the situation. But the public image (and personal feelings) of an older man of high status was another matter. Like Evelyn G., who lied to protect her husband from injury and impotence, I believed that my lie was "constructive," even honorable.

How could I have thought this way? Or, given that I did think this way, why is my current perspective so radically different? A generous friend explains, "Well, you're obviously much braver now." I share her view that courage, like good taste, is acquired with age. But I was courageous during my college years, and was not one to submit to injunctions that violated my conscience. No, my individual bravery was not the issue here. Rather, the bravery of other women transformed cultural norms.

The first to speak out about abuses of power must be particularly brave or thick-skinned. When I was in college, terms such as "sexual harassment," "date rape," "sexual abuse," and even "sexism" had not yet been invented. The word "patri-archy" wasn't in my vocabulary. We called these things "life," and I never considered the necessity, or even the possibility, of women creating and codifying language. Without the vocabulary, however, I was unable to name, much less protest, what was happening inside and around me. Also, as more women told the truth, my beliefs about what constitutes "honorable lying" changed, and I began to reexamine the question of who needs protection from whom. Watching Anita Hill reminded me of how much—and how little—has changed in the world since my undergraduate days.

If even one heroic male senator had stood up in eloquent outrage at the abusive treatment of Anita Hill, the "ordinary folks" watching television might have been better able to open their eyes to the abuses of our patriarchal fathers. Yet when it comes to interpreting the motivations of others, we can never know the whole story. In protecting the president's nominee, these politicians might also have convinced them-selves that they were engaging in an honorable lie or a noble silence. They might have believed that protecting "a very important man"—and the collective rule of men—served a greater good. Perhaps they believed that they were acting on behalf of higher principles, such as "loyalty" or "solidarity."

Does the epidemic of lying, duplicity, and concealment on the part of "honorable men"—the leaders of our coun-try—make it easier for us to rationalize our own private departures from the truth? Most of us do see our lies in a benevolent light. So how can we decide in our daily lives whether deception in its countless manifestations is right, or harmless, or justified, or necessary, or good for somebody? How accurately do we observe ourselves and take note of the times we are less than honest or forthright, even over the course of a single day?

What's Your HQ?

I recently came across a quiz in a women's magazine that invited readers to assess their "HQ" (Honesty Quotient) by ranking themselves on a scale of 1 to 10 for truthfulness. Obviously, this rating scale—like others of its kind—could not begin to do justice to human experience or the complexity of even a day in the life of a real human being. Real life is complicated, messy, contextual, unquantifiable, full of paradoxes and contradictions. In a single conversation, I may be truthful, untruthful, and sort of truthful, without even noticing the discrepancies.

Consider the scene that followed a talk I had with my younger son, Ben, about the importance of being honest. As we leave the shopping mall, we pass a video arcade and he demands to play a game. I tell Ben that I have no change, and I pull him along with me toward the exit. I probably do have the change, but we're both in a terrible mood and it seems easier to put it this way than to risk a fight. When we get home, the phone rings and I overhear Ben's impatient response: "Why do you keep bothering me? I don't want you to come over!" I'm mad at Ben for this display of tactlessness, and I whisper to him: "Why don't you just tell him you're busy and can't have friends over today?"

On my better days, I behave more solidly. I tell Ben why I'm not giving him money for a video game and I deal directly with his reaction. I approach the subject of his telephone etiquette without coaching him to fib to a friend. This may seem like a small distinction, but perhaps not. True enough, no single trivial lie undermines my integrity or my relationship with my son. But fibbing, including "polite" or social lies, can become part of the daily fabric of living—a way of avoiding conflict and complication that becomes so habitual we fail to notice even the fact of it and its imperceptible erosion of our integrity and our relationships.

In the abstract, people almost unanimously applaud honesty, which, as popular wisdom has it, is "the best policy." If we actually could measure a person's "HQ," we would each aspire to a high score and would strive to surround ourselves with others who rate high on our ten-point scale. Honesty, like authenticity, is one of our culture's most deeply held values. It is always a slur to say, "She is a dishonest woman," or, "This man does not tell the truth." It is always a compliment to speak of someone's honesty and commitment to the truth.

But what happens when we move away from abstract values and focus instead on specific incidents in the lives of real human beings? Then we have Evelyn and Paul exchanging their "loving lies" on the infertility problem; we have me back in my college days nodding my head in the wrong direction to protect "a very important man." Or, more recently, fourteen white, male senators protecting the president's Supreme Court nominee.

Within my own profession, psychologists hold widely divergent views on whether lies harm or benefit their recipients. Some years ago, this news item appeared in the *San Francisco Chronicle*:

A pale, slight 11-year-old boy, injured but alive, was pulled yesterday from the wreckage of a small plane that crashed Sunday in the mountains of Yosemite National Park. The boy had survived days of raging blizzards and nights of sub-zero temperatures at the 11,000-foot-high crash site, swaddled in a down sleeping bag in the rear seat of the snow-buried wreckage. . . . "How is my mom and dad?" asked the dazed fifth-grader. "Are they all right?" Rescuers did not tell the boy that his stepfather and his mother were dead, still strapped into their seats in the airplane's shattered cockpit, only inches from where he lay.

Dr. Paul Ekman, a professor of psychology and noted expert on lying, selected this news item to illustrate "an altruistic lie, benefiting the target, not providing any gains to the rescuers." He stated that few would deny this fact. But when my husband (also a psychologist and family therapist) and I discuss the same news clipping, we imagine that this lie made the rescuers feel more comfortable and perhaps occurred at the expense of the child. Had we been at the scene, we would not have volunteered the facts. But we try to imagine what the rescuers did tell the boy, who undoubtedly feared (or knew) the worst and asked directly for information about his family.

For days after reading that news item, I found myself thinking about the assault on this boy's reality and on his future capacity to trust that adults would tell him the truth. While knowing more details might shift my perspective, I question the same lie that my fellow psychologist applauds.

It has been fascinating for me to listen to women voice their moral judgment on a range of examples of deception and truth-telling. Sometimes there is a predictably shared response, as when a colleague tells how her parents invented a web of lies and trickery to hide a Jewish family in their home from the Nazis. Her story is unarguably one of coura-geous and honorable deception in the service of a higher ideal.

But more commonly, and more interestingly, we differ in our responses to the myriad ways that people deliberately distort or conceal the truth—and to how they reveal it, for that matter. What one woman considers a necessary revelation, another considers an inappropriate disclosure. While one person claims, "He deserves to have the facts," another insists that "he should be protected from the truth." What one woman calls a "healthy venting of true feelings," another labels a "hostile, inappropriate outburst."

In regard to tolerating or even inviting deceit, we also differ. In her book, *Lying*, the philosopher Sissela Bok claims that everyone, even deceivers, wants to avoid being deceived. Yet some of us consistently demand the truth, while others ask to be "spared." Consider some examples of the second option.

The wife of a university professor says to me, "If my husband is sleeping with other women, I don't ever want to know it."

A mother in a family therapy session looks her daughter directly in the eye and says, "If you're on drugs, don't tell me about it. I can't handle it."

A woman who has been sexually abused by two maternal uncles attends a movie with her mother that includes the theme of incest. As they leave the theater, her mother says, "If anything like that ever happened in our family, I wouldn't want to know about it."

A therapy client tells me she is worried that her brother might be suicidal but then adds, "I really don't want to know. There's nothing I can do anyway."

No one *wants* to be tricked, manipulated, or duped. But we may feel, at a particular moment, that we can't handle a more direct confrontation with what we already suspect or know. We are unlikely to seek "more truth" if we feel unable to manage it, or if we are not confident that potentially painful information is ultimately empowering and could lead to productive problem solving, more informed decision making, and a more solid self in relationships. We vary widely in the degree to which we are in touch with our competence to manage painful facts, and our readiness and willingness to move toward them.

We differ, too, in our capacity to detect deception and, more generally, in our ability to observe and name reality. We all repress, deny, project, distort, tune out, and get sleepy. Our knowledge and interpretation of "the truth" is, at best, partial, subjective, and incomplete. But we do have varying capacities for empathy, intuition, reflection, autonomy, objectivity, integrity, maturity, clarity, and courage—all of which enhance our ability to detect deception and incongruity in ourselves and in others.

We also differ from each other in our subjective experience of lying. One friend tells me, "When I don't tell the truth, I feel it in my body. So I don't get off the phone, for example, by making excuses, like someone's at the door or I'm late for an appointment. Telling a big lie, like faking sexual pleasure, would make me physically sick." She adds, "My body keeps me honest, even if my head wants to get away with things."

This friend describes herself as being committed to the principle of veracity at "a cellular level." She seeks an honest way to express herself, no matter how inconsequential the issue or insignificant the interaction. In contrast, another woman tells me that she comfortably engages in every variety of "social" and "face-saving" lie. She reports feeling fine about this behavior "as long as no one is hurt."

Our cultural emphasis on how women differ from men (consider the phrase "the opposite sex") obscures not only human commonalities but also the range of differences *within* our own gender grouping. Of course, women differ from each other. We differ not only in matters of conscience and moral judgment but also in our philosophy about truth-telling, and in our beliefs about what is productive and growth-enhancing in relationships. We differ in our ability to accurately perceive and process information and to detect deception in ourselves and others. And our ideas about lying and truth-telling are colored from birth onward by our race, class, culture, and unique personal history. All of our life experiences combine to shape our philosophy of what is and is not the truth—and when and how we should tell it.

How often do we articulate our differing philosophy on the many rich and complex dimensions of deception and truth-telling, of speaking and holding back? Since the beginning of recorded time, philosophers and scholars from varied disciplines have debated the nature of truth, as well as the moral, ethical, legal, psychological, and evolutionary aspects of deception and the forces that drive it. But despite the profundity, centrality, and immediacy of this subject in everyday private and public life, we may avoid discussing with others our own personal beliefs about it. Perhaps we should initiate and sustain more such conversations. Clarifying our commonalities and differences helps us examine how we are choosing to live in the world and how we are making decisions about doing "the right thing."

Hiding a Life

An attorney named Lena who was flying from Miami to Boston was engaged in friendly conversation with an older woman next to her. They talked about their respective jobs, then the woman showed Lena a photo of her family, which included a new grandson she was visiting for the first time. Midway into their flight, she asked Lena, "Are you married?" "No," Lena responded matter-of-factly, "but I've been living with a woman for five years and we think of ourselves as married." The woman stared at her blankly, so Lena explained further, "I'm a lesbian. My partner, Maria, is a woman." Her flight companion fell silent and kept her eyes riveted to a magazine for the remainder of the flight.

Lena had left a distant, unsatisfactory marriage that had lasted for nine years. When she came out as a lesbian three years later, she decided that she would never again "live a lie." From that time forward, she has been open about her lesbianism, resisting all temptations to pass as a heterosexual. Some of Lena's friends believe she makes herself unnecessarily vulnerable, but this is what Lena chooses, explaining: "If I'm quiet about Maria in any situation where I would have mentioned my husband or son, I'm acting as if my life and loving is shameful and wrong." Lena will have no part in this, no part in hiding or in pretending through silence to be what she is not.

Lena's family "love her anyway," as they collectively put it, which is among the milder of the homophobic responses she has encountered over the years. There have been more dramatic consequences of her dedication to being truthful: Lena's car has been vandalized by high school students, she has been sexually harassed in her neighborhood, and she almost lost custody of her son, who is now eleven. But the ignorance and hatred she has faced have only strengthened her resolve to be more open. Even to avoid the pain of prejudice, Lena says she would no sooner hide her life than would a black civil rights leader pretend to be white. This deeply held value of living without deception or concealment does not allow Lena to hide the honest affections of her good heart.

Lena believes that silence about her sexual orientation constitutes a lie. "It is lying," Lena argues, "because heterosexuals deny not just our right to love openly but the very fact of our existence." Sure, Lena could have said to her flight companion, "No, I'm not married." But that factually correct statement would have been, from Lena's perspective, intended to mislead. "Silence is a lie," Lena insists, "if you are deliberately going along with another person's false belief. In this case, the false belief happens to erase and degrade the lives of ten percent of the population."

Moreover, Lena reminds me, passing for what one is not never involves a solitary lie. As many have observed, it is easy to tell a lie, but it is almost impossible to tell only one. The first lie may need to be protected by others as well. Concealing something important takes attention and emotional energy that could otherwise serve more creative ends. When we must "watch ourselves," even when we do so automatically and seemingly effortlessly, the process dissipates our energy and erodes our integrity. "It also creates a disturbance in the air," Lena tells me. "Before I was out, I'd bring Maria to office parties and I knew everyone was saying behind my back, 'Are they? Aren't they?' Now they know. And they know that I know they know. It's less crazy-making."

As we discuss the airplane conversation, Lena talks about how trivialities add up. One doesn't say, "Oh, my partner is in the same field as your husband!" One doesn't pull out a photo of one's own to show. One doesn't mention, even if asked, that the purpose of one's flight is to attend a concert to benefit gay and lesbian rights. One doesn't step off the plane and freely embrace one's lover. One doesn't hold hands by the baggage claim. Any of these ways of holding back, of not speaking, of not acting, may seem trivial. But the life this adds up to, Lena says, is a life half-lived.

Is She Honest or Crazy?

I asked a group of Lena's friends—all gay, all out of the closet, and all committed to fighting homophobia—about their reaction to the airplane incident. A vast diversity of opinion was expressed among friends bound by common values and politics.

HELENE: If we were all like Lena, it would be our strongest weapon against homophobia. Lena is unflinchingly honest and brave, and I love her for it. And I'm grateful. It's like what Adrienne Rich says—that when a woman tells the truth, she is creating the possibility for more truth around her. Imagine our collective power if ten percent of the population was, every moment, visible and out!

CLARA: I think you're romanticizing Lena's behavior. I don't tell strangers on airplanes that I'm a lesbian. It's none of their business. Personally, I think that she does so partly for shock value. There is some need for privacy and discretion.

ROGER: What Lena calls "honesty" is a failure to protect herself. It's downright crazy. I worry about her a lot. She could get herself killed by some asshole. It would be more honorable if she would choose her battles.

ROSA: I don't approve of Lena's behavior, because it doesn't accomplish anything positive. It's not useful. I'm pretty open about being gay, but I let people get to know me before I tell them. If people have a relationship with you first, it makes a dent in their stereotypes. If they like you, they may open up their hearts or at least confront their own prejudice. But if you just announce that you're gay right up front, it pushes people away. They never give you a chance. They don't even see you as a real person. It's not strategic.

HELENE: Strategic? Life is not a chess game. There comes a time when you have to stop thinking about strategy and what works and who will think what. You have to say, "I won't take this anymore!" You have to be yourself, *now*. That's where Lena is coming from. She's beyond hiding. She's beyond waiting for some hypothetically "just" world to arrive in which we can all be free. She's *creating* that world, by living it now.

MIKE: I think that we shouldn't try to judge Lena's behavior. It's not our place. What she does is right for her—there could be no other way for Lena. But it certainly wouldn't be right for me. I think that the worst thing we do to each other is to make these judgments. We have to respect and validate our differences. It has to be okay for each of us to be in a different place about what we can share and what we can handle.

HELENE: I disagree. If we don't make judgments, we are morally bankrupt. There *are* matters of right and wrong in this world, good and bad. It's wrong to hide. It's bad to be in the closet. We don't have to blame or condemn each other, we can be loving and supportive. But we still need to push each other to stop the hiding and secrecy which is so destructive to ourselves and to the world.

Honesty—the matter of who, what, when, where, how, and why we tell—is a complex business. Even among a small group of generally like-minded friends, important differences emerge. Clara questions the virtue of Lena's motives, while Helene has nothing but respect for Lena's refusal to hide. Roger believes that protecting oneself should take precedence over revealing oneself, particularly considering the real risks involved. Rosa places the highest value on strategy and believes that patience and timing is the best way to change hearts and minds. Helene believes in confronting injustice directly, forcefully, and immediately. Mike emphasizes the importance of respecting differences. In contrast, Helene impatiently views "respect for difference" as a way of condoning inaction, fence-sitting, or a lack of courage and conviction.

But perhaps Lena's friends would concur in placing her at the high end of the "HQ" scale. (That is, if they agree to define honesty as "being oneself.") Then again, they might not rate her openness so highly. True, Lena is boldly and courageously "herself" in refusing to hide her affections and her woman-centered life. But Lena also tends to distance herself from friends and family, and she leaves much unsaid. She has trouble sharing her feelings of vulnerability with those close to her, and she rarely acknowledges her own need for help and support. She describes herself as a "do-it-your-selfer" rather than one who believes in the healing power of confiding in others. Even Lena's best friend, Helene, does not view Lena as one of the more "open" people in their social group.

Fortunately, we don't have to be rated (or to rate others) on a scale that measures our "HQ" because even close friends or colleagues won't necessarily view a specific incident of revelation or concealment in the same light. We might not even agree on the meaning of such terms as "truth" or "authenticity." At times I have felt like throwing up my hands in the face of seemingly endless unravelings.

Yet I don't really believe, or, more to the point, I don't live as if decisions about truth-telling and deception are hopelessly subjective, infinitely complex, and ultimately unquantifiable. Instead, I decide with confidence that some people and some sources of information are more trustworthy than others. I choose with conviction friends whom I think are open, authentic, and real. I make assessments about which contexts—public or private—provide individuals with more (or less) opportunity to discover, invent, and share their own truths. I observe the power of context to shape and limit the stories we tell. But I also observe the power of individuals to transcend and shape context, to create new stories, and to find new meanings in even the most oppressive circumstances. My work as a clinical psychologist and psychotherapist is guided by these convictions.

And sometimes—such as when watching Anita Hill and Clarence Thomas on television—the question of what is right, what is true, and what is real, appears simple and obvious after all.

4

In the Name of Privacy

My friend hates her large, soft breasts. She is so self-conscious about them that she never relaxes with her husband when they are naked together. He loves her body and seems not to sense her feelings of shame or the constraint she feels with him because of it. My friend tells me, "In bed, even if we are just hugging, I make sure that my breasts don't flop around or slide into my armpits. When we're making love, I press my arms against my sides to give them shape. I've been doing this for so long I don't think about it, but yes, I know it interferes with my experience of being physical with him."

Her husband knows nothing of her feelings. "There's no point in telling him all this," my friend explains, "because I'd become even more tense, more self-conscious, and less spontaneous in bed." She goes on to express another fear, that she acknowledges as less rational. "If I tell him, he might notice how floppy and squishy my breasts really are. I'm afraid he'd get turned off if I draw his attention to them."

I comment to my friend that she and I are different—that I couldn't keep such a big secret from my husband. My friend bristles at my choice of the word "secret," because she thinks that I think secrets are a bad thing in a marriage. "No," she corrects me. "I don't keep secrets from my husband. We are speaking here of privacy. I am a more private person than you are." I agree that she is the more private person, but I still think she is keeping a secret from her husband.

Our conversation pushes me to clarify the difference between privacy and secrecy in my own mind. The distinction between the two categories seems apparent in common language. A private path is not a secret path. The upcoming surprise party I am planning for a friend is a private party but a secret from the guest of honor. With those we love, or seek to love, keeping secrets is different from requiring privacy. But what my friend calls a matter of privacy, I consider a matter of secrecy. How do I distinguish between these overlapping and intertwining concepts in my private (not secret) life?

Is It Private . . . or Secret?

Privacy is a human right. My right to privacy includes my right to control access to a certain amount of emotional and physical space that I take—correctly or not—to be "mine." Privacy protects me from intrusion and ensures my separateness as a human being among others. I do not want my mail opened, my journal read, my phone tapped, my behavior monitored, my property searched, my medical records or sexual history published in the local newspaper. I close the door to my home, my office, the bathroom, and the voting booth. I require periods of time each day when I am not spoken to, looked at, or focused on.

I do not seek privacy in order to fool others or engage in acts of deception. Rather, I seek privacy primarily to protect my dignity and ultimate separateness as a human being. Thus, I publically defend my "right to privacy." In contrast, I don't recall ever using the phrase, my "right to secrecy," although surely I have the right to keep some secrets, my own and others. Secrets may, as lies always do, demand justification. In contrast, it is the violation of privacy, not the guarding of it, that demands justification.

My right to privacy also includes my right to protect my body, and any decisions regarding it, from unwanted control and intrusion by others. The possibility that the government could force me to carry a fetus to term, for example, is as terrifying to me as the possibility that the government could order a fetus ripped from my womb. I feel entitled to make personal choices about reproducing, loving, and dying—without state intervention. If I do not control my own body, I do not control my own life, and I am in no position to seek or define my own truths.

There is also a certain amount of physical space *around* my body that I take to be private, or "mine." If I'm standing with someone who violates this space, I step back. Once, when an elegantly dressed woman positioned herself shoulder to shoulder with me in an otherwise empty, spacious elevator, I was startled. I reflexively moved away and recalled an elderly woman from my graduate school days in New York. This woman, who appeared to be psychotic, ritualistically walked the streets of Broadway near Columbia University with a closed umbrella in hand. When someone stepped inside what seemed to be a near-physical boundary surrounding her person, she umbrellaed them out of her territory, shouting, "You're invading my life space!" I affectionately remembered this woman, and for a moment on the elevator I identified with her, although I did not protect my "life space" so colorfully.

Protecting one's personal space occurs both within and between species. One species will flee from another at a particular "flight distance," for example, six feet for a wall lizard. Within species, each animal has a "social distance," a minimal distance that the animal routinely preserves between itself and others of its kind. "Having space" is a critical aspect of privacy and self-preservation.

Alida Brill, who has written a splendid book on privacy, reminds us that privacy is an accorded right, granted to individuals only when others let them have it. No matter how fiercely we tell others, "Keep out!", they may choose not to respect our wishes or even our legal rights. The ability to protect privacy rests firmly on privilege. Brill speculates that the reason that citizens of the former Soviet Union have such a translation problem with the word "privacy" has as much to do with spatial limitations as it does with political ideology. She reminds us that the homeless, engaged in their morning ablutions in public places, rely totally on the kindness of strangers to avert their eyes, in order to maintain the thinnest slice of private life.

Our society's vulnerable groups—the poor, children and the elderly, lesbians and gays, people of color, girls and women, the sick and disabled—are both most in need of privacy and most vulnerable to having their privacy invaded. Disempowered groups can't count on having privacy unless those in power—that is, those not of "their kind"—will grant it to them. For example, the most crucial decisions about what should and should not be private in the lives of women is ultimately decided in legal and political arenas that include few if any women as decision makers.

Because I consider privacy my right, I am neither secretive nor guarded about requesting or defending it. I openly define my privacy needs to others. I say, "Please knock before coming in," or, "Don't read my mail," or, "Move over, I want more space." Or simply, "That's private." In the ultimate of paradoxes, I go public about my abortion (a private matter) to help protect this most basic right of privacy in women's lives. In contrast, I guard not only my secrets but also the fact that I am keeping them.

In her book *Secrets*, Sissela Bok explores the ethics of concealment and revelation and refines the distinctions between privacy and secrecy. Secrecy always involves the intention to hide or conceal information from another person, just as lying always involves the intention to convince another of what we ourselves do not believe to be true. Keeping a secret over time can require energy and intense, active attention. Secrets may be guarded through silence, or they may require constant vigilance and a complex web of new deceits to protect the old. Secrets forge boundaries, create bonds, isolate, connect, and estrange. Secrets produce coalitions, triangles, insiders and outsiders. Keeping a secret can make us feel powerful, superior, special, and loyal—or anxious, burdened, guilty, and ashamed. Secrets can serve the most loving or malevolent of intentions. We may keep secrets about matters that are trivial or lethal, but there is no one who has not guarded secrets—their own and others—or who has not been affected by the secrets of others.

Privacy and secrecy have overlapping functions in our lives. We rely on both to control the flow of separateness and connectedness in relationships, and to provide us with a layer of protection against intrusion, reaction, and encroachment. In personal relationships, both privacy and secrecy reflect the need to create a boundary around the self by exercising some control over what we conceal and reveal to others. Both give us breathing space.

Privacy and secrecy have so many layers of nuance and meaning in private and public life that no single definition could adequately define either concept or distinguish between them in all instances. Both terms are invoked to defend concealment. As I see it, however, privacy shifts into secrecy when an act of deliberate concealment or hiding has a significant impact on a relationship process. Secrecy, as I define it here, is deliberate concealment *that makes a difference.*

Thus, when my friend chooses not to reveal feelings about her breasts to an inquiring neighbor—or to her husband—she is being private and secretive, respectively. With her husband, the person with whom she seeks to have her most intimate emotional and physical relationship, the concealment or revelation of emotionally sensitive information makes a difference.

What difference does it make that she fails to tell him the truth—that she hates her breasts, that she postures herself in bed with him to firm them up, that she can't relax in the process, that she thinks somehow she is fooling him, that he would "see something," or love her less if she let go and allowed her breasts to fall into their natural shape? In telling him, she would initially feel more vulnerable and less in control. Her husband might respond as she most fears. But even if he leapt from the bed, shrieking, "My God! Get those floppy, squishy breasts out of here!", where might the process of openness and truth-telling take them over the course of months, or years, or a lifetime—compared to, say, a decision on her part to reveal nothing?

Secrecy protects my friend from being open to the full range of her husband's reactions and responses to her real self. Indeed, this is the purpose of secrecy. But secrecy ultimately compounds the painful feelings it is meant to deflect. At the very least, it blocks possibility. If my friend can't bring her feelings out in the open, there is no potential for healing and resolution, for self-acceptance and a deeper intimacy. She will ultimately lose sight of what is possible for her in bed, and rightfully attainable. With secrecy, my friend has no chance to receive her husband's comfort, wisdom, and understanding, to relax into his body knowing she is accepted and desired for herself, to laugh and joke with him about her floppy breasts. Until she shares her secret, she can't begin to understand and assimilate its meanings, look it in the eye, cut it down to size, neutralize it, and drain it of its destructive power.

Keeping secrets involves self-deception because we allow ourselves only to be aware of the positive or protective functions that our secrecy serves. We usually keep secrets with the conscious intention to preserve—not fracture—what is precious to us. We keep a particular secret "for a reason," and it may be a good one at that. But we won't know the emotional costs of keeping a secret until *after* we tell it. The impact of secrecy, or any form of deception, is usually obscured until after a process of truth-telling is well under way.

In my friend's case, concealing her feelings about her body was significant because the content had great emotional meaning to her. But secrets can have reverberating consequences through relationship systems even when the information concealed is so trivial that any outside observer might well ask, "Why would anyone go to such trouble to keep *that* a secret?"

Insiders and Outsiders

Vicki came to see me shortly after marrying her second husband, Sam, a kind and attentive man whom she met by placing an ad in the personal section of a Kansas City paper. A year earlier Vicki had extricated herself from an unhappy marriage of almost two decades. She described her first husband, Jim, as a mocking, belittling, and arrogant man, who devalued her without pause. Vicki was ultimately able to leave him, but not to stand up to him, either before or after the divorce.

Vicki had custody of their two daughters, Betty, eighteen, and Joey, sixteen. She described Joey as "her best friend" in the family, while Betty was viewed as immature and problematic. During our first meeting, Vicki joked about the unorthodox way she met Sam. To illustrate her first husband's critical attitude and arrogance, she added, "That's the kind of information Jim would love to get his hands on. If he knew that I met my husband through the personal ads, he'd never hide his criticalness and contempt."

He would not, however, find out. While Joey knew the true story, Betty hadn't been told. "I swore Joey to secrecy," Vicki explained, "and made her promise that she wouldn't share this information with her sister or Jim. I can't tell Betty because she can't be trusted to keep things confidential from her dad."

"What will you tell Betty," I inquired, "if she asks how you and Sam met?"

"She won't ask," replied Vicki. "She doesn't ask about things."

"And if she did?" I pushed.

"I don't know." Vicki stated flatly. "I'd think of something."

Some secrets are dramatic. Many families hide information of critical emotional importance to their members' identity and sense of reality: Father is alcoholic, Mother relinquished a child before marriage, Little Susie is adopted, Grandmother is dying, Uncle Charlie jumped rather than fell to his death from the third-floor window, six-year-old Paula is being abused. The telling and not telling of secrets as large as these may profoundly affect every aspect of family life for generations to come.

In light of the critical truths that families hide, Vicki's secret about meeting her second husband through the personal ads seems hardly noteworthy. In the broader scheme of things, it is a rather minor piece of information that Vicki chooses to selectively withhold and disclose to her daughters and ex-husband. Yet the consequences of concealing even the most "ordinary" information in families can be far-reaching, because the selective sharing and guarding of information is the stuff of which "insiders" and "outsiders" are made in social groups. Sometimes the *relationship process* which evolves with secrecy may be far more important than the content of the information withheld.

Such was the case in Vicki's family: Joey's role as mother's "best friend" was a compelling one for any girl. Although she was the younger of two sisters, she was entrusted not only with the secret about the personal ad but also with other small details of her mother's life that she was asked to keep confidential from her sister, Betty, and her father, Jim. While no single secret carried particular meaning, the process of secrecy took its toll.

At the time I began working with Vicki, and then with Sam and the children, the emotional cost to Betty was immediately apparent. Betty was the "outsider" in the family—the one who didn't know the facts. She was learning not to ask, to look the other way, to discount her own sense of curiosity and reality. Betty also had to struggle increasingly hard to show her competence, when the family treated her as incompetent by failing to include her.

Not surprisingly, Betty sensed Joey's special position with their mother and blamed her sister for her own hurt feelings. Joey, by agreeing to withhold information from her sister, widened the emotional chasm between them.

Joey's connection to her father was deeply affected as well. The accumulating "Don't tell your dad" messages invited Joey to plant herself firmly in her mother's camp at the expense of her relationship with her father. Joey felt she had to be "for her mother," rather than free to be herself in all relationships.

Vicki's growth was also compromised. By placing her younger daughter, Joey, in the middle of issues with her ex-spouse ("Don't tell your father *anything* he could use against me"), she bypassed the challenge of dealing directly with Jim. Her reactivity and helpless behavior in the face of Jim's criticism had not changed following the divorce. Thus, she continued to give him too much power, and she made him too important in the emotional life of her new family. Vicki behaved as if she could find no way to stand up to Jim, to be real with him, to use her wonderful wit and humor to respond directly to whatever arrogant comment he might make about the personal ad or anything else. She was also teaching her daughters that one must hide from a difficult person rather than be oneself—and then manage the response one gets. Until Vicki learned to hold her own with Jim, which she ultimately did, she remained emotionally hooked on him.

Sam's entrance into the family was also contaminated by the personal ad secret, which involved him. At first, Sam was unable to articulate his feelings, beyond sensing that there was "something wrong" with the requirement that he selectively conceal how he met his wife. It wasn't that he felt compelled to share this information or even that it was on his mind. But Sam knew in his bones that the requirement of secrecy kept Jim lurking in the shadows of the new marriage and skewed his new connections with his two stepdaughters, Joey (whom he could tell) and Betty (whom he was instructed not to tell). Although it was a small thing, Sam's complicity with the secret left him feeling that he was starting a new family in a less than straight and legitimate way. To his credit, Sam eventually told Vicki exactly what he felt. He expressed his wish, and later his intention, to be out of the secret-keeping business.

This family had no intention to hurt, divide, or exclude its members. Yet when I first saw them in therapy, each individual was disempowered, each relationship compromised. The keeping of secrets brought some family members closer, but at the expense of other individuals and other family relationships. When we operate at the expense of others, we compromise ourselves, as well.

Is It Privacy or Patriarchy?

I have defined secrecy, as distinguished from privacy, as intentional concealment that makes a difference in a relationship process. When I evaluate whether I am "being private" or "keeping a secret" from, say, my husband, this is the criterion I apply. Yet, when we examine the complexity of real life, this neat distinction between privacy and secrecy collapses. Privacy, too, may involve concealment that makes a difference. In fact, we may invoke the concept of privacy to justify concealment and to pretend that it makes no difference.

Even when we consider a "pure" example of privacy, concealment may still make a difference. In our shame-based culture, women (like my friend with the squishy breasts) do not simply exercise the right to privacy out of free choice and on behalf of the self. When we say to each other or to ourselves, "This is private; It is my business," we express a basic and essential human right. But in so doing, we may also preserve lies that oppress us, rather than lay claim to our individual freedom. In the name of privacy, we withhold from each other our honest experience. We fail to know each other and be known. We fail, individually and collectively, to scrutinize the "personal" or private in ways that would challenge us to seek new truths and revise old ones.

Under patriarchy—which is all we have known—privacy (a legitimized form of silence) is, for women, both necessary and dangerous. Privacy is necessary not only because it is a human need, but because speaking out—and *being* out—can place some of us emotionally and physically at risk. Privacy is dangerous, however, because the failure to share what is most private or personal isolates us, shames us, and keeps us trapped in narrow, false myths about female experience. Feminism taught us that when we share what is most shameful and private, we learn that it is most universal and shared. The commonality of female experience allows us to challenge old lies and create the space for truth.

* * *

Let's look again at my conversation with my friend who hates her breasts. In this exchange, she disclosed feelings to me that she had never before revealed to anyone. She had often complained about her body, but in a funny, bantering way that masked her sorrow and shame. Now she showed real feeling, specificity, and depth.

A particular incident had inspired this shift toward greater truth-telling. Earlier that evening, she attended a lecture I was giving in the city where she lived. My subject was "The Advice-Giving Industry for Women: Is it Hazardous to Your Health?" During this lecture I facetiously credited self-help books with providing us with such wonderful tips as "How to keep your arms tightly at your sides when you're making love, so that your breasts don't disappear or fall into your armpits." At these words, ripples of laughter arose from the audience. Within seconds, women all through the room were laughing unrestrainedly and breaking into applause.

My friend told me later that this comment alone was worth the price of admission. Really, it was not the quip that she valued. Rather, it was the experience of sitting among hundreds of women of all ages, shapes, and sizes, and being part of the shared response that swept through the room. In those moments of contagious laughter, each woman knew she was not alone in "positioning" her breasts—or worrying about them—when she lay down with a lover.

My friend's joy and relief was in having the private made public, the shameful made silly, the personal made political. She was not alone, and certainly not the first to struggle in a particular way with particular feelings. The lessening of shame that always accompanies this recognition of shared experience led her that evening to speak more openly and truthfully. She hadn't yet told her husband and perhaps she will never choose to. But talking openly with me was possibly a move in that direction.

The next step might bring my friend—and all women—to widen the context. Why are so many of us dissatisfied with our breasts? Recognizing a shared experience helps us stop pathologizing ourselves. Instead of maintaining a narrow and singular focus on the question, "What's wrong with me?", we can begin to ask other questions, like "Who says?", "What group of people has created this reality for us?", "How does it serve them?", "What would be different if we stopped believing it?"

Questions such as these begin to create a new context in which each woman can begin to discover what is true about herself and say it out loud. The process is circular and unending. As one woman speaks the truth—from her private or secret self—she widens the space for more truth around her.

5

A Funny Thing Happened on the Way to the Orifice

In the summer of 1970 I sat in a circle of about twenty women in Berkeley, California. We were in the process of trying to form consciousness-raising groups. One of the women asked who among us had never faked an orgasm. I don't know if she was conducting research or merely being curious.

Only a few women raised their hands. At the time, the business of faking orgasms did not strike me as particularly noteworthy. It was simply a matter of women learning what the culture taught about getting and keeping a man—bolstering the male ego, reflecting men at twice their natural size, listening wide-eyed to *his* ideas, no matter how boring.

I was raised to pretend with men. Pretending was as natural as breathing and as ordinary as good manners. In my growing-up years in Brooklyn, I took the task seriously. When a sixth-grade teacher advised us girls that it was endearing to misspell big words in notes to boys, I consulted my dictionary, to be certain of my misspellings.

My teacher's advice, as silly as it sounds today, simply reflected the predominant prefeminist teachings of the day, which urged women to be smart enough to catch a man but never to outsmart him. Women were encouraged to feign weakness, helplessness, and dependency if they were not fortunate enough to possess these traits naturally. To quote one expert in female popularity, Arlene Dahl, whose book *Always Ask a Man* found its way into my personal library:

> The successful female never lets her competence compete with her femininity. Never upstage a man. Don't top his jokes even if you have to bite your tongue to keep from doing it. Never launch loudly into your own opinions on the subject. . . . Instead draw out his ideas to which you can gracefully add your footnotes from time to time. If you smoke, don't carry matches. In a restaurant let your mate or date do the ordering. You may know more about vintage wine than the wine steward but if you are smart you'll let your man do the choosing and be ecstatic over his selection even if it tastes like shampoo.

Faking orgasms, as I viewed the matter in 1970, was hardly separable from, and no more alarming than, biting our tongues or drinking wine that tastes like shampoo (one can glimpse here the excruciating activity behind female "passivity"). These behaviors, I believed, were merely the prescribed etiquette for middle-class white women like myself, to be shed like a false skin after a good relationship was under way.

I failed to appreciate the enormous unconscious power of the paradoxical rule behind these cultural teachings—the rule that women should strengthen men, and our bond with them, by relinquishing our own strength, and that to do otherwise, or simply to be ourselves, was unfeminine, unlovable, castrating, destructive, and, yes, even life-threatening to men.

I did not comprehend the degree to which we women internalized and played out this rule unconsciously in other important relationships, not just with men whom we believed needed proof of their manhood or those who had economic power over us (such as husbands and bosses) but also with our sisters, our mothers, our best friends, our female lovers.

I did not think much about the terrible cost to our lives—and to men's lives, too—when we behaved not as authentic women but as "female impersonators," to use Carolyn Heilbrun's phrase.

And not until some months after the question of faking orgasms was first raised did it again draw my attention, this time as I was beginning to practice psychotherapy.

So, What Do Little Girls Have?

One of my clients, a twenty-two-year-old graduate student named Krista, had something important to tell me that she could not bring herself to say out loud. For years, she had harbored a profound and corrosive feeling of shame about a secret she had carried. As a new therapist, I wanted to help Krista by respecting her own sense of timing about when she was ready to share. Our work together, however, was a time-limited venture, and I ended up pushing her to get it out on the table. I did not know what to expect.

The secret that Krista ultimately revealed was that she could not achieve orgasm during intercourse unless she stimulated her clitoris at the same time. I confess that I had expected a more colorful revelation.

What struck me as interesting, however, about this simple physical need of hers was Krista's feeling of shame. For years she had kept silent about it, had in fact told no one before me—not her women's group, not her male partners, not her closest female friends. Why? I asked her.

For starters, Krista believed that she was the only woman in San Francisco, in the United States, or even on the planet who had to stimulate her clitoris during intercourse to have an orgasm. Here was a woman who faked orgasm with her longstanding partner, because she wasn't going to do *that* while engaged in the romantic act of making love. It would destroy the emotional climate, Krista explained, and furthermore, she feared she might ultimately lose him to a "real woman" who didn't have this regrettable complication.

Second, Krista felt ashamed to say the word "clitoris" out loud because, until the moment she said the word to me (and I said it back to her), she had never heard it spoken. She was not certain how to pronounce it. No one had ever told her she had one. Krista had unconsciously interpreted this peculiar silence to mean that this very real part of her body, which embodied her sexuality, was forbidden, unspeakable, and confusing, perhaps even grotesque.

During the 1970s, the articulation of such feelings was believed by psychoanalysts to reflect "penis envy." But when my supervisor suggested to me that Krista wanted a penis, that she wanted to be a man, I silently disagreed. I thought that Krista wanted permission to be a woman. She wanted most to be herself.

Around this time I began to understand that the widespread female practice of faking orgasms (or pretending greater enthusiasm about intercourse than is felt) is an act with deeper meaning: It reflects cultural pressures for women to be more concerned with the pleasure that we arouse in others than with the pleasure we might feel within ourselves. Faking orgasm is an important example of pretending and self-betrayal in women's lives that bolsters our sexual partners and protects them at the expense of the self. It reflects the myths we have internalized about what men need from women and have a right to expect from us.

Krista's pattern of "faking it" was also linked to her inability to view her clitoris as a valid aspect of her sexuality. Her silence and inauthenticity was not simply evidence of a personal neurosis, but rather reflected the false labeling of female genitals as well as the predominant beliefs of the day. In psychoanaltyic circles, for example, many of my colleagues still considered the clitoris to be a vestigial organ in adult sexuality; women who preferred clitoral to vaginal stimulation were labeled "masculine" or "phallic" (as were those of us who aspired to be mathematicians or engineers), and were diagnosed as manifesting penis envy or sexual immaturity. Although Masters and Johnson's research challenged these views in the sixties (Why didn't they just *ask* us?), Freud's traditional views had great staying power. Krista's sense that her clitoris was not a central or even legitimate aspect of her sexuality was paralleled by expert opinion which held the same.

Psychoanalytic theory has since been appropriately revised, but not much has changed. What's between our legs is still *misnamed* or *not named* by the dominant group culture, and women are still complicitous with this lie. Perhaps, this is where serious pretending begins.

Raising Vulva Consciousness

I was at the local YWCA when I overheard the following conversation:

"That's his penis, isn't it, Mommy?" squealed a preschool girl pointing to a naked baby boy in the locker room. The mother, more amused than embarrassed by her daughter's unabashed curiosity, answered affirmatively.

"And what's *that?*" the girl asked, pointing now to the crotch of a naked little girl standing nearby.

"That's her *vagina*," the mother answered with that false brightness adults reserve for addressing the very young and the very old.

I cleared my throat—but then bit my tongue. The year was 1990, and I wanted to lean over to this mother and say, "Hey, I think I know something that you don't know." Or maybe, "Vagina! You must be kidding! Do you have X-ray vision, lady?" But apart from pestering my good friends, I try to restrain myself in public places from correcting other people's language. Now, more than two decades after working with Krista in psychotherapy, I know that the misuse of the word "vagina" for everything "down there" is still remarkably persistent.

Most of us were raised on some variation of "boys have a penis and girls have a vagina." To quote again from my personal library: "A girl has two ovaries, a uterus, and a vagina which are her sex organs. A boy's sex organs are a penis and testicles. One of the first changes (at puberty) will be *the growth of hair around the vaginal opening of the girl*." Such partial and inaccurate labeling of female genitalia might inspire any pubescent girl to sit on the bathroom floor with a mirror and conclude that she is a freak. Maya Angelou shares just such a traumatic experience in her first autobiographical account of her life, *I Know Why the Caged Bird Sings*.

The widespread practice of mislabeling female genitalia is almost as astounding in its implications as is the silence that surrounds this fact. True, Americans do not excise the clitoris and ablate the labia, as is practiced in other cultures on countless girls and women of color. Instead, we do the job linguistically—a psychic genital mutilation, if you will. Obviously the two crimes are not equivalent. But language can be as sharp and as swift as the surgeon's knife. What is not named does not exist.

How could Krista—or any woman—feel "permission" to be a sexual being when she has been taught from childhood that she has a vagina (which is internal and difficult to examine) but not that she has a vulva which includes the clitoris and labia? What does it mean for a little girl to discover her clitoris as the prime source of sexual stimulation and gratification, but to have no label for or validation of this reality? ("Only boys have something on the 'outside'"). What new meaning might Freud's concept of "penis envy" take on, if we consider the fact that in his lifetime the words "clitoris," "vulva," and "labia" were not included in the dictionary and, in this country, the only word in Webster's dictionary for female genitalia was "vagina"? Who decides what words are included in the dictionary and who decides what is real?

To this very day, my colleagues continue to say "vagina" when they mean "vulva." And so do the scores of mostly white middle-class parents I have informally interviewed over the years since working with Krista. Most people still misuse the word "vagina" to refer to "what girls have," and many educated parents report that they have never heard the word "vulva," including a large number who think the term refers to a Swedish automobile. When my friend, Nancy, was diagnosed with vestibular adonitis—an uncommon disease of the unspeakable parts—she called the National Institutes of Health and presented the facts to the woman in charge of directing her call. "Vulva?" the woman replied querulously. "Vulva? . . . Is that heart and lungs?"

Those who are knowledgeable about the correct words give the most imaginative reasons for not using them: "Telling my daughter about her clitoris is like telling her to go masturbate"; "I can't tell her about something that tiny [her clitoris] and I'm not even sure how to pronounce it"; "Vulva is a medical term, and I don't want to burden her with words that her friends don't know"; "She'll spread the news to her classmates and how will we deal with that?"; "'Vulva' and 'clitoris' are technical terms" (this one from parents who taught their small daughter about ovaries and Fallopian tubes); and (from a particularly forthright father), "I don't want my daughter to become a sex maniac or to grow up thinking that men can be replaced with a vibrator."

It is not simply that privileged men, the creators and codifiers of language, have named women in accordance with their own unconscious wishes, fears, and fantasies. It is also that we are not yet able to muster the clarity and courage to say "vulva" when that is what we mean and to say "vagina" when that is what we mean. This is not just a matter of linguistic precision, but rather of the deepest levels of truth-telling. If we cannot tell our daughters what they have, we are inviting each new generation of women to pretend—to blur language, sensation, and thought.

Of course, the subject of vulvas is one of countless examples of how female experience is distorted, denied, and falsified. This particular example brings us back to the little girl in the locker room who asked her mother, "And what's *that?*"

How would you answer her?

Renaming Krista's Problem

I don't recall providing Krista with any brilliant insights in my work with her so long ago. I do remember encouraging her to come out of the closet with her secret, and she did. When she returned to therapy after her initial self-disclosure, she told me that she had initiated a frank discussion about sex in her women's group and had learned that about half the women needed clitoral stimulation to achieve orgasm during intercourse. I interpreted this fact to mean that each of these women stimulated her clitoris during love-making—or otherwise had her needs met—but I was wrong. Krista went on to explain that these women, like herself, faked orgasm. "What a relief," Krista told me, "to find out that a whole bunch of us have the same problem."

"And what is the problem, as you see it?" I inquired.

"That we can't come in the normal way," Krista answered matter-of-factly.

"And who says what's normal?" I pushed further. I recall this particular exchange because, at the time, I was struck by how even "scientific communications" on female psychology went in circles. Once something was defined as "unfeminine" or "gender inappropiate," the old rules could not easily be challenged. When women differed from the theories, the exceptions only proved rather than probed the rule, and it was the women—not the theories—who were brought into question. Women were still trying to fit themselves to the predominant theories of the day, rather than the other way around.

Perhaps because I was new at the business of psychotherapy, I felt that I was not particularly helpful to Krista. No doubt she inspired my thinking more than I inspired hers. But her women's group took a great leap forward on the orgasm issue when they later began asking, "Who says?"

It was the women's group that helped Krista to rename her problem—a problem that stemmed not from some shameful personal anomaly, but rather from the narrow and false definitions of female sexuality that Krista had accepted without question. Soon Krista could articulate her dilemma without pathologizing herself: Should she be honest with her boyfriend, lay claim to her own legitimate sexual desires, and risk his distancing from her? Or should she continue faking orgasms and protect the status quo? Krista chose to do the latter.

That was 1970. For Krista and for me, the women's movement was just beginning.

Innocent Pretending?

Although sexual lying is considered by many to be an unethical act (as in having an ongoing affair and denying it), "pretending" is not so disparaged. There is a certain lightness or frivolity associated with words such as "pretending," "faking," and "feigning"—words that may evoke images of discretion, ladylike behavior, or even good manners. Women still tell me that they view sexual faking as an inconsequential act, just something women do, and not a bad idea at that. Not so long ago, when my mother was my age, certain gynecological texts advised physicians to instruct their patients to fake orgasm, noting that such "innocent deception" and "innocent simulation" would help women in their wish to please their husbands. Many women still have no concept that their bodies and their sexuality exist for themselves—no concept that their lives can be lived for themselves.

Why do the words "lying" and "pretending" ring so differently in our ears? We think of lying as a self-serving, self-promoting, or self-protective activity. In contrast, pretending may be done in the service of enhancing another person at the expense of the self. Sexual pretending, for example, has changed cultural forms over the years, requiring women to conform to whatever men wanted to hear at that particular period of history.

Thus, the "modern woman" may feign multiple orgasms whereas the Victorian lady denied sexual pleasure by "lying still"—bending to cultural pressure so strong that she might seem, even to herself, as devoid of instinctual life as the sleeping Snow White. Likewise women throughout history have denied erotic and sensuous ties to other women, or have been granted a kind of limited heterosexual freedom—only to be warned not to exercise it. In high school and college, I had my desires acknowledged, but was told not to act on them lest I "spoil" myself for marriage by decreasing my value, worth, and marketability in the eyes of men who prized virginity. Of course, there have always been courageous women who have resisted these societal strictures, refused to be complicitous, disbelieved what men have told them or said about them, insisting instead on uncovering and living their own truths, sexual and otherwise.

Why do we minimize or soften an act of self-betrayal, even placing it within the category of feminine virtue? Why do we fail to take seriously the act of faking orgasm or exaggerating—or denying—sexual desire? Why do we accept rather than refute the ubiquitous practice of misnaming our most intimate places, symbolically erasing and mystifying our sexuality? Throughout history and around the world, women have not simply "pretended" as an act of feminine goodwill, but instead have been forced to tell sexual lies to men as a matter of self-preservation. "Lustful" nuns and "difficult" wives have been subjected to clitoridectomies; unfaithful women, those who chose to live outside male control (especially those who chose to love other women), have been subjected to ridicule, censure, and violence. For married women who would prefer to be left alone in bed, sexual lying is a matter of economic and emotional necessity, since intercourse is still considered a husband's right and a woman's obligation. And for many, pretending has become a way of life, even when nothing obvious is at stake.

We may not be aware that we are pretending out of fear, or that we are pretending at all. When we learn that our bodies are not for ourselves, we stop tuning in to the signals that our bodies give us about our particular sexual desires and rhythms—as well as our lack of interest. Instead, we feel exhausted at bedtime, or question what is wrong with us for "not wanting it." We may "try to get into it," or think of someone or something else while we're "doing it." Pretending becomes habitual, reflexive, and unexamined.

Of course, it is overly simplistic to define lying as "for the self" and pretending as "for the other." Sorting out the two is difficult until after both the lying and the pretending have stopped. Only then can we determine who exactly is being protected and from what. When we are anxious or threatened, we try to get comfortable, which is where lying and pretending may begin.

So Krista did not fake orgasm just "for him," but also as a strategy to keep him. She wanted to protect his feelings, but she also wanted to protect herself from dealing with those feelings. And Krista may have been inhibited by any number of anxieties about sexuality and intimacy that prevented her from being more truthful in bed. Nor was her pretending necessarily "good for him," because her boyfriend might have felt more than slightly shaken that he had been deceived and more than slightly angry that he had been denied the opportunity to develop a more authentic intimacy.

It has long been the woman's job, whether in the bedroom or boardroom, to magnify men, making them seem larger than life by reflecting and mirroring them back to themselves. As early as 1929, in *A Room of One's Own*, Virginia Woolf wrote about this connection between the enforced inferiority of women and their role of enlarging men in all aspects of private and public life:

> For if she begins to tell the truth, the figure in the looking-glass shrinks; his fitness for life is diminished. How is he to go on giving judgments, civilizing natives, making laws, writing books, dressing up and speechifying at banquets, unless he can see himself at breakfast and at dinner at least twice the size he really is?

Krista once said that she played the part of the perfect lover so that her boyfriend would feel like the perfect lover. But Krista's pretending was surely an attempt, however misguided, to protect her own self-esteem, along with his. In a culture that failed to name or validate real or diverse female experience, Krista was trying to conform to how "a real woman" feels and behaves. She was trying to act "like a woman," to be "like other women," because she had learned that her own truths were inadequate, unnatural, not good enough—or else because she did not yet know what her own truths were.

Consciousness Raising: Naming Our Own Truths

I was a graduate student in New York City when the Women's Liberation movement got rolling in the late sixties. Around the country, women like Krista were joining together in consciousness-raising groups to tell their stories, to say, "This is what it is really like for me." Whether the "it" was orgasm, marriage, housework, friendship, fat, or shaving our legs, women began to tell the truth about their experience.

My first reaction to the Women's Liberation movement was one of disinterest. What did it have to do with me? Partially blinded by my arrogance at having "made it" in a man's world, I saw nothing to complain about, and if I wasn't complaining, I didn't see why anyone else should be. After all, *I* had never been discriminated against as a woman. If other women were tired of feeling like glorified scullery maids, why didn't they get out of the kitchen?

Only slowly did I begin to feel uncomfortable and dishonest in the face of my condescension to feminist protests. It was especially difficult for me to confront the fact that I, too, like Krista, had lied about my pleasures and my pain out of my fears of losing approval and privilege, to say nothing of relationships. The truth—or even the fact of patriarchy—did not suddenly reveal itself to me in a single flash of lightning that brightened a previously darkened terrain. Rather, consciousness raising occurred slowly, imperceptibly, as women

around me created new realities that allowed me to stand
back and see the old one.

It was consciousness raising, not psychotherapy or
expert advice, that led countless women to tell the truth
about their lives and to create passionate new visions of self,
of female community, and of a fair world. This happened
because consciousness-raising groups provided a new context in which women gave priority to their own stories and
exchanges over the communications of men. Also, consciousness-raising groups had no leaders. There was no
therapist, no expert, no facilitator who might fit the new
territory to his or her own map, or who was empowered to
"know best" or speak the truth for others in the group. Consciousness-raising groups were not therapy groups. The
purpose of these groups was not to privatize, individualize,
and pathologize "women's problems," but rather to understand these through the lens of gender and the socially constructed fabric of our lives.

This collective sharing of private experience allowed
women to articulate and challenge the doctrines of patriarchy which had been so pervasive as to be accepted as "laws
of nature." Many women broke the silence about male violence in their lives and, for the first time, were heard. The
psychiatrist Judith Lewis Herman writes, "In the protected
environment of the consulting room, women had dared to
speak of rape, but the learned men of science had not
believed them. In the protected environment of consciousness-raising groups, women spoke of rape and other women
believed them."

The outpouring of anger, creativity, intellectual passion,
erotic energy, and political action that this early stage of

modern feminism inspired was simply incalculable. Armed with the credo that "The personal is political," women arose from a collective slumber and began to change ourselves and the world. All this could not have happened had individual women brought their secrets, their self-disclosures, their confessions, to their psychoanalysts or to their husbands or best friends. Nor could it have happened if women had met together to analyze their problems and pain through the narrow explanatory lens of "bad mothers," "toxic parents," and "dysfunctional family systems" (a term reminiscent of broken stereo components). The refusal of women to pathologize and privatize our lives turned truth-telling into a revolutionary act.

Until women collectively articulated authentic experience, feelings of shame, guilt, and inadequacy flourished ("What's wrong with me?"). These feelings, which blocked healthy anger and protest, are inevitable when women are divided and isolated from each other, when we do not have a safe place to discover our commonalities, to explore our differences and diversity, and to understand the particular social-historical context in which these arise.

Of course, some women are more private than others. It is not the way of all women to disclose their selves in a group, or to discuss the intimate details of their lives. Nor do I wish to glorify these early consciousness-raising days when many white, heterosexual, middle-class, mostly young feminists assumed they comprised and could define the category of "women." But despite the problems, a profound transformation occurred when previously isolated women created groups and offered one another the most personal accounts of our lives. Women who felt like monsters for not fitting the available female scripts moved beyond individual guilt to protest popular myths about female experience.

Was There Therapy (or Truth-Telling) Before Feminism?

Feminist scholar Carolyn Heilbrun regrets the passing of consciousness-raising groups and notes that either women will exchange and create new stories in groups, or we will live our lives isolated in the houses and the stories of men. She also wonders how much any individual woman before feminism was helped by therapy or expert advice. I wonder, too. Before feminism, depressed housewives in therapy learned to compromise and adapt. Women who passionately quested for ambition and achievement along with, or in place of, marriage and motherhood, were viewed as envying or imitating men. Women who loved women were similarly pathologized, as were heterosexual women who expressed anger and unhappiness about "being a woman," as being a woman was defined. Mothers were blamed for everything, including their own unhappiness.

Before the recent wave of feminism, many women were so guilty about their unspeakable feelings that they could not voice them, not even to themselves. When I joined the staff of the Menninger Clinic in the early seventies, it was common for an exhausted, unhappy, and isolated mother of small children to begin therapy with the following goal: "Make me a better wife and mother to my husband and children." She had no other story to put forth, no other vision for herself that felt acceptable and rightfully obtainable. Faking motherhood went deeper than faking orgasms; her feelings were a secret she kept even from herself.

But the unconscious, seeking truth, would voice a protest. The woman would develop symptoms which frequently took the form of an unconscious wildcat strike against her "sacred calling": "I am too depressed/fatigued/

confused/sick to run the household and care for my children." The woman herself experienced inordinate guilt and proclaimed her inadequacies with a vengeance in order to protect herself from her unspeakable rage. It was the rage of one who had so accommodated to someone else's program that she had betrayed, if not lost, her own self.

In my prefeminist days, I took as truth the predominant theories of the day regarding how the "good mother" (or "good-enough mother") feels and conducts herself. I didn't challenge the "scientific literature" on motherhood, written by experts who were neither women nor mothers—nor probably even home enough, for that matter, to know much about fathering. Actually, I did register that there was something wrong in much of what I was being taught about female psychology; but before I was part of a supportive network of feminist scholars, I felt too vulnerable and alone to articulate my feelings.

The intentions of mental health professionals, myself included, have always been to expand, not limit, self-knowledge. The goal of psychotherapy or psychoanalysis is to help women clarify their own choices and discover their own truths in a "neutral" and "value-free" emotional climate. But this is not possible, not then, nor ever. Despite good intentions, no therapist is free from the historical particularities of family and culture, of time and place. Therapists could not begin to move beyond the conventional, man-made narratives of a woman's life until women, collectively, did it first. Of course, any interpretation of experience privileges one story, or particular framing of reality, above others, and edges out other meanings and alternative explanations.

Women are wise to maintain a healthy skepticism toward

all experts who would presume to tell us what is true, and to prescribe how we should think, feel, and conduct ourselves. "Expert opinion" often reflects the privileged and dominant voices in our culture who have access to meaning-making and the media to disperse it. As the poet Audre Lorde says, "The master's tools will never dismantle the master's house." Perhaps the most trustworthy experts on women are those who put forth their theories as partial and tentative speculations and those who share the particulars of their own experience, recognizing that their most deeply held "truths" may or may not be useful to an individual woman as she seeks to uncover her own.

Today, women as a group are less obedient. We no longer accept patronizing or guilt-inducing pronouncements about the "good mother," the "true vaginal orgasm," or the "appropriate place" and "true nature" of women. Nor do we accept the suspect status of those of us who are not mothers or choose not to pair up with men. To all of this, we are saying, "Enough!" It is not that we are more courageous than the women who came before us. Women have always been brave. Rather, we are no longer among the first, or the few, to speak out and share authentic experience. Feminism has created the space for more truth-telling and for the restoring and re-storying of our lives.

6

We Are the Stories We Tell

Is there a "true story" of female experience? If so, then surely it cannot be told by experts who have never been women, nor can any one of us speak for all. Each woman is ultimately the best expert on her own self. But to begin to know our own truths, we need to examine our own stories and those of other women. Telling a "true story" about personal experience is not just a matter of being oneself, or even of finding oneself. It is also, as we will see, a matter of *choosing* oneself.

Re-Storying Female Ambition

My friend Sue overheard a telephone call I made to my dad. I was telling him about a recent speaking engagement and he asked, as he always does, how many people came to hear me. "Oh," I responded enthusiastically, "the hall was packed! There must have been close to a thousand women there." My father was pleased.

Actually, I was exaggerating by a couple of hundred women, and Sue called me on it. Boasting is bad enough, she said, without distorting the facts. By her own report, Sue neither lies nor tolerates lying from others. She is firmly in the camp of those philosophers, theologians, and ethicists who argue that lying is never justified, and that it invariably erodes the soul, annihilates human dignity, and exacts a toll, however imperceptible, on relationships. Sue believes that any lie, no matter how seemingly small, fools with the reality of another human being and impedes trust.

The following day, however, Sue behaved in a way that struck me as dishonest. In a crowded coffee shop as we waited in a long, slow-moving line, we chatted at length with two women, both probably in their fifties, from a rural part of western Kansas. When a table for four became available, they asked us to join them and we accepted, glad to continue our conversation. They spoke poignantly about worsening farm problems and then asked what each of us did for work. "I work with children in a hospital," Sue responded. Both women assumed she was a nurse, and referred to her as such in the conversation that followed. Sue, a pediatric surgeon at a New York City hospital, did not correct this misperception.

For as long as I have known Sue, she has denied or minimized her accomplishments and status. Several months earlier, for example, she decided not to tell her mother and sister about an important promotion because "they were both in such difficult places in their lives." Whenever people seem intimidated by Sue's profession as a surgeon, she explains that she is actually a glorified seamstress, and that surgical expertise requires no more complex skill than the precise handwork that women have created for generations. This has been a repetitive theme or pattern in Sue's life. While I

veered from truth-telling by exaggerating my accomplishments to my father, Sue *minimized* hers to the world.

As we talked about the coffee shop incident, Sue
explained why she had described her work in words that concealed her status and then failed to clarify the facts as the
conversation progressed. In her experience, people are often
intimidated to learn she is a doctor; that information creates
distance between her and the people she meets. Sue thought
this barrier might be especially likely to surface with these
two rural Kansas women. Also, these women were having
wrenching financial struggles; given popular stereotypes
about "rich doctors," Sue felt it would be in poor taste to
mention her profession.

While Sue condemned my exaggerating about the workshop attendance, she saw her behavior as "pure." She was
simply trying to make these two women feel comfortable,
and she hadn't actually *said* she was a nurse. More to the
point, Sue viewed downplaying individual accomplishment
as a virtue, but exaggerating as a vice. Thus, I had told a lie,
while she had acted with honor. Such was not my worldview.

Our differing ethnic backgrounds were probably at play
here. Sue's Anglo-Saxon Protestant family thinks it sinful to
boast, even about distinguished ancestors. By contrast, my
Jewish family considers it sinful for children not to give their
parents something to boast about. Sue and her sister were
discouraged from "standing out" or "showing off," while my
sister and I were encouraged to dazzle and shine. In my family, hitting the winning home run was far more important
than being the good team player Sue was expected to be. In a
number of ways, our experiences in our respective families
led us to respond differently to common dilemmas women
face about work.

Claiming Achievement

The small departures from truth-telling that Sue and I encountered in each other may seem insignificant in comparison to faked orgasms, or other more serious deceptions we have all known. But the tension between Sue and me about what constitutes an honest self-presentation in the arena of work and success was neither trivial nor coincidental.

Like love, work is at the center of all human existence. But women seldom tell the truth, even to ourselves, about the meaning of work in our lives. And patriarchal definitions of what it means to be a woman—to have womanly desires and hopes and ambitions—have, until recently, made truth-telling virtually impossible. Before modern feminism, stories of female ambition were silenced or erased; even now, they are told with apology ("Yes, it's a great honor to be a Nobel Prize laureate, but really, what I love best is staying home and being a mother to Kevin and Annie"). In this larger historical context, my critical reaction to Sue took hold and gathered meaning.

Following the prescriptions of culture, Sue failed to lay claim to honest achievement—failed to give the world a narrative of her life that might expand for all women our sense of risk, adventure, curiosity, and possibility. I think our lunch companions would have appreciated knowing that Sue was a surgeon, and I found it unnecessary and insulting to "protect" such sturdy rural women (or anybody, for that matter) from the facts. I would resent such protection myself, I told Sue. Isn't it our responsibility to speak accurately about the diverse realities of our lives? Shouldn't we refuse complicity with the disastrous, feminine prescription to protect and bolster others by denying our ambition and hiding our ability?

Yet, like Sue, I have often felt pulled to act out some variation of this prescribed female script.

Here's one example. About a year ago, I sat down to write a
brief speech in response to being named Woman of the Year
by the local chapter of the National Women's Business Association. I was particularly touched by the recognition I was
about to receive for my contributions to my own community.
In addition, the day of the award ceremony would be proclaimed by both the mayor of Topeka and the governor of
Kansas as "Dr. Harriet Goldhor Lerner Day." In response to
these honors, I wanted to say something significant, especially to the audience that included people I loved. I decided
that I would share my personal reflections on my journey to
successful authorship. I would tell an honest story.

    But once seated before my computer, I found myself
writing a talk that attributed my success to good luck. I
meant it and, in part, it was true. Success does require a large
measure of timing and luck, and is hardly a result of talent
and perseverance alone. Indeed, I could think of countless
women, past and present, whose extraordinary work had not
been recognized or even valued, let alone published, promoted, and prized.

    But I chose not to tell that story. What stopped me short
was Carolyn Heilbrun's book, *Writing a Woman's Life*, which
documents how patriarchial culture defines and limits
women's lives by determining what stories about women will
be told. Helibrun explains that well into the twentieth century, women were unable to claim achievement or admit
ambition in the telling or recording of their own lives. Those
who were able to achieve and recognize their accomplishments often attributed their success either to luck or to the

efforts or generosity of others. This description was not of an outdated phenomenon, but rather one that I observed daily in my consulting room—and in the acceptance speech I wrote and almost presented in my own community.

On reflection, I recognized that I had as much bad luck as good luck in the publishing world. While writing my first book, *The Dance of Anger*, I was fired, rehired, and fired again by my first publisher. Enormous determination, perseverance, and will kept me going, as the book was then rejected by almost every major publishing house in the country. When it miraculously saw the light of day, I did not release it passively into the world like a bottle left to drift aimlessly out to sea. Instead, I promoted it energetically and aggressively, enlisting my large network of friends and colleagues to do the same.

This summary of events was part of the story I ultimately told—a story about luck (both very good and very bad), but mainly about determination and perseverance against great odds. And while I spoke frankly about the unanticipated cost of fame and glory, I stated emphatically that I have found these stresses far preferable to the stresses of having my work undervalued and rejected.

I thought I had made a bold move toward truth-telling when I shifted from publicly attributing my success to "luck," a historically rooted form of female apology and self-disparagement, to telling the true tale of my individual determination and spirit. The "luck story," I had concluded, was a dishonest narrative. It not only reflected historical forces that make women deny ambition, but indicates the forces that keep us feeling illegitimate when we do receive public acclaim. Women, like other marginalized groups, internalize countless messages: we do not belong in important places; we do not really count; we do not really shape history and culture. And so, when we do achieve recognition, we tend to attribute our success to luck, or if not that, then to something, anything, other than our competent and entitled selves.

A decade or so earlier, I could not have told my story as truthfully, without fear of censure and ridicule, without fear of invidious interpretations ("penis envy" was the label once applied glibly in psychoanalytic circles to women for whom ambition and achievement were central), without fear that my very femininity would be suspect. Now, none of this concerned me, not because I had matured with age (although that too), but because feminism had widened the range of stories women could construct and share about our lives. I credit feminism, more than any other force in my life, with allowing me to move toward the truth, toward greater congruence between my private life and public image.

I wanted Sue, too, to be honest about her brilliant career, especially with her family and friends. To me, this had nothing to do with boasting, or arrogance, or insensitivity to the feelings of others. It simply had to do with telling our stories, and particularly with telling the stories that could not be told earlier. It was a matter of telling the truth. Throughout time, accounts of women's lives—those we have told as well as those told for and about us—have suppressed and distorted the truth about female experience, have made it conform to the narrow scripts society has written for us. I did not want Sue to follow this tradition.

Sue saw it differently. Rather than attributing honesty and virtue to my revised acceptance speech, she doubted the veracity of my story. On the one hand, she shared my concern about false and constricting scripts of women's lives and she agreed that women should feel entitled to ambition, recognition, and honor. On the other hand, Sue felt that the last thing women needed was another narrative that spoke to false notions of individual superstars. This was not an authentic way, she felt, to restore and re-story women's lives.

Feeling Like a Fraud:
McIntosh's Double Vision

As I tried to unravel the tension that developed between Sue and me, the work of Peggy McIntosh was pivotal to my understanding. Peggy McIntosh, an associate director of the Wellesley College Center for Research on Women, has written two critically acclaimed papers weaving together the apparently opposed points of view that Sue and I each voiced. In her examination of feeling like a fraud, McIntosh argues both that we shouldn't let the world make us feel like frauds—and we must keep alive in ourselves the wise sense of fraudulence that may overtake us in public places. From her perspective, Sue and I both held positions of integrity, though both should be present in each person.

The first part of the dual consciousness that McIntosh promotes is perhaps the easier to grasp. Women and other disempowered groups must resist feeling fraudulent when these feelings reflect internalized value systems that tell us we don't belong in spheres of power or authority in public life. And so, we can move against our feelings of fraudulence and learn to stand behind the podium or pulpit and "deliver the goods." This perspective was what made me think Harriet Goldhor Lerner Day in Kansas was a terrific idea, and why I refused to apologize for that honor.

But McIntosh also articulates a second perspective, which she hopes we can preserve along with the first. She wants us to keep alive our valid sense of fraudulence because it can help us to spot and critique the fraudulence in the roles we are asked to play. When we feel fraudulent, or even tentative, apologetic, silenced, and self-doubting, it may reflect our honest refusal to internalize the idea that having power, prestige, or public exposure proves merit and authority. Feeling like a fraud in such circumstances may express our awareness that the dominant culture's form of leadership and authority—and the concomitant images—*do* require fraudulent behavior. From this perspective, we may not hate being behind the podium so much as we hate the podium itself, because we wish instead to create alternative, more collaborative, less rigidly hierarchical ways of exchanging ideas.

McIntosh writes:

> We feel fraudulent, I think, partly because we know that usually those who happen to get the high titles and the acclaim and the imagery going with them are not "the best and the brightest," and we don't want to pretend to be so either. When we entertain nagging thoughts about whether we belong or deserve to be at the podium, or in the boardroom, or tenured, or giving an interview to a newspaper, or earning a good salary for what we like to do, we may be deeply wise in feeling anxious and illegitimate and fraudulent in these circumstances. Those men who feel the same way in such settings may be deeply wise as well, for the public forms and institutions tend to demand that one appear to be an authority figure, an expert, "the best." The public forms and institutions insisting on these images do require fraudulent behavior of us, and they will turn us into frauds if we accept the roles as written. The roles are dishonest and people who are still in touch with their humanity and with their frailty will properly feel fraudulent in them.

And so, McIntosh advocates the dual vision of recognizing that it is bad for us to feel like frauds insofar as that feeling *perpetuates* hierarchies, and yet it is good for us to feel like frauds insofar as that feeling may help us to *undermine* hierarchies. When necessary, we can help each other to overcome feeling fraudulent while acknowledging that such a feeling is normal because we're taught it, and not by accident. Our recognition of the feeling of fraudulence can be a guide to developing ways of behaving which feel more authentic to us.

In Sue's case, she knew that being a surgeon was not inherently more valuable than being a highly skilled carpenter, artist, teacher, or conversationalist. And so she felt properly fraudulent when her work was glorified. She knew her ranking in hierarchical structures lent her power and prestige beyond genuine differences in merit, intelligence, and personal excellence. As McIntosh puts it, "People who feel in public like imposters are perhaps more to be trusted than those who have never experienced feelings of fraudulence." She notes that *the ability to feel fraudulent rests on our capacity to be in touch with our own authenticity.* By knowing what is "real" in ourselves, we can recognize when the self is being violated by institutions or roles that ask us to put aside an integral part of ourselves or to pretend to be what we are not.

Both McIntosh's work and Sue's criticism of my acceptance speech raised questions: How do people make it to the top? Who decides whose work is worthy of attention and economic reward and whose is not? Do those who "make it" get there because they are really the hardest workers, the most persevering, the most deserving, and the very best? If I had spoken more honestly, would I have put less emphasis on individual merit and more on privilege—and yes, luck, including the luck of time and place, birth and circumstance?

Did the world really need another narrative that spoke to false notions of individual merit of the "rugged individual"?

Sue wished that I had used Harriet Goldhor Lerner Day to dethrone myself where others had set me up, to challenge the equation of status and merit, and to underscore the importance of creating new definitions of "success" and a less rigidly stratified world. I might have done this, Sue added, not apologetically or self-disparagingly, not out of prescribed feminine modesty or guilt, but rather from a realistic and balanced regard for myself and others.

And what of Sue choosing to "pass" as a nurse? From her perspective, this choice was not an apologetic self-portrayal, as I had interpreted it. There were good reasons why Sue was troubled by the image that accompanied her status as a doctor and the power that accrued to it. Yes, she wanted praise for work well done, and the power to influence decisions in her field that mattered. But she did not want to be glorified, magnified, even deified—which her status seemed to pull for. She did not want to be falsely set apart from or above other human beings.

I had reacted negatively to how she protested one kind of charade with another by misrepresenting herself at the coffee shop. Pretending to be what one is not, or failing to clarify who one is, did not strike me as a good "solution." I wanted Sue to be clear about her professional status, while being the kind of doctor and person she really wanted to be in her public and personal life. But I now understand Sue's behavior in a different, or rather, an additional light. It is not simply that she has succumbed to the pressures exerted by family and culture, which lead women to feel like "imposters" in positions of authority and power. She is also reacting against the divisiveness of hierarchical roles.

The tension between Sue and me developed around the

subject of how we *portray* our success to others. Women often feel phony simply for being successful, without articulating why, as Sue did. We may feel fraudulent in response to any variety of recognition, attention, success, or praise. Beyond crediting luck, or the generous efforts of others, we may feel that we have deceived, tricked, or fooled others, that we are undeserving, and that we are in danger of being "found out."

These feelings are not exclusive to women, but are remarkably common among us, inspiring a growing number of thinkers and writers to pay attention to how women apologize for success on the one hand, or ensure the lack of it, on the other. Feminist therapists, myself included, have viewed this "fear of success syndrome" or "imposter syndrome" as pathological or problematical, something to help women get past, through, or over as we analyze the forces of family and culture that stand in the way. It has been difficult to keep voices like McIntosh's at the center of our attention—voices that identify some roles and rules of success themselves as dishonest and fraudulent.

Choosing Our Stories

These days, I think of Peggy McIntosh's work when I sit through a formal public introduction of myself: "An internationally acclaimed expert on the psychology of women" . . . "One of the most important relationship experts of our times" . . . and so forth. In response to this glorified image, I think, "Who is this person?" and "How intimidating that sounds!" And even, "Is this true?"

This reaction is not a self-depreciative response, for I

believe that I am probably as worthy of such laudatory intro-
ductions as other psychology experts who are similarly
described. But I am also aware that no one in my field is worthy of such an inflated description. Far more remains
unknown than known in the area of human emotional functioning, and all psychotherapists have a partial, subjective,
and incomplete perspective. Such an introduction is not
"me" (or anyone else for that matter), nor, paradoxically,
does such an intimidating list of my achievements begin to
speak to my actual talents as a thinker, therapist, or human
being. Yet I am also hesitant to disclaim an elevated status
that historically has been denied to all women, and I want my
ideas to count as much as those of other "renowned experts"
in my field.

So, what is true? In some settings, I accept and even help
shape the glorified introduction, just as I gave a speech in my
community attributing my success to determination and talent over luck. In other settings, I tell a different story—one
that recognizes the falsity of elevating my talents and
achievements above those of "ordinary women." It is not that
I am chameleonlike in my self-presentation. Rather, there
are multiple ways we can name or frame what is true and
real, and countless ways we can story and re-story our experience. As I share my stories, and listen to the stories of others, I do not only ask myself, "Is this authentic and true?" I
also consider who is served or disempowered by a particular
story or construction of reality.

Of course, there are many stories that I will never begin
to imagine because my context does not evoke or allow for
them, or because one dominant story I tell about myself sup-
presses and marginalizes other truths.

Angela and Jan

Two young women, Angela and Jan, worked as administrative assistants in a nonprofit service organization housed in a renovated brownstone in Philadelphia. Although they rarely socialized outside of their work, they developed a close friendship that later expanded to include several women on the secretarial staff. Despite low pay and little opportunity for learning or advancement, both Angela and Jan felt satisfied with their positions. The atmosphere was warm and relaxed, they enjoyed each other's company, and they liked the organization.

After working alongside Angela for five years, Jan applied for a position in another public service organization that offered better pay and more challenge. She had applied "just for fun," and expressed reservations when she was offered the position. The new job was across town, in a sterile, fluorescent-lit office where Jan would have little chance to interact with anyone other than her boss.

Angela discouraged Jan from making the change, arguing that money and opportunity were a poor substitute for the warm, collaborative atmosphere of their current setting. "Maybe it's because I'm not one of those ambitious women," Angela said over lunch, "but a friendship like ours and a place like this is hard to come by. I guess I put people first. And money just isn't that important to me." After considering Angela's view and weighing the pros and cons, Jan decided to stay put.

Less than a year later, Angela's brother-in-law offered her a position in a private firm that paid well and provided opportunities for training, travel, and advancement. Angela had not been looking for a new job, but when this one fell in her lap, she decided not to turn it down. Jan felt angry and betrayed by Angela's decision; Angela felt torn and guilty, but explained to Jan that she owed it to herself to make the change.

By Angela's last week of work with Jan, their friendship had reached the breaking point, culminating in a fight in which Jan called Angela a "two-faced liar." For a long time to come, Angela would remember Jan's angry words: "You said that you weren't one of those ambitious women—that people came first! Well, given the opportunity, you sure *became* one of those ambitious women very fast, didn't you? Funny, isn't it!"

Jan's assumptions were both right and wrong. She was right that given the opportunity, Angela did become "one of those ambitious women." But she was wrong in concluding that Angela had lied to her. At the moment when Angela had said, "I don't care about money," or, "People are the most important thing to me about a job," or, "I'm not ambitious," she had told the truth. Only *after* Angela had the promise of real opportunity, more money, and greater power did she begin to value them. In her new job, Angela turned out to be very ambitious indeed. As she put it to Jan many months later, "Maybe I just couldn't let myself know how much I wanted something until I really had it."

Perhaps none of us can say with certainty what we do not want, until we have the opportunity to turn it down. Angela's explanation, however, implies that she had always been ambitious and that she had defensively denied that aspect of herself in her first work setting. This may or may not be true. A more parsimonious explanation is that dead-end jobs evoke dead-end dreams, while new opportunities evoke new desires and, ultimately, new stories about our "true self."

We do not create our stories—or ourselves—in a vacuum; we are always shaped by and shaping our context.

Many of the stories we assume to be "true" or "fixed" about ourselves change dramatically when the context changes, and particularly as we gain (or lose) economic and social power. Even more to the point, there is no such thing as a "true story" (or a "true self") that unfolds separate from the influence of family and culture—free from the particular social, political, and economic factors of the time. From the moment we are first wrapped in a pink or blue blanket, we learn what stories we can tell and whether there is an ear to hear them.

7

Our Family Legacies

My friend Liz Hoffmeister movingly describes her first experience with death in these evocative words:

Not yet three years old, I stood at our mother's funeral, a brother on either side, our arms touching. Grown-ups flowed around us, mouthing words. The most clearly remembered are: "Poor little things, they don't know what has happened." We stood there, impassive, their words disallowing us any show of grief. Our faint pressure on each other's arms and our short life with our mother held us up, eyes dry, while they made many empty sounds that day.

At not quite three, to know your mother is in a box that is to be buried; to hear the grown-ups free to cry; to hear them say that you don't know what has happened is a form of still, cold terror. And not quite so simply that you have lost your mother, and not quite so simply that their words will not let you cry, but that at not quite three you can already wonder what kind of world you find yourself in.

The first world we find ourselves in is a family that is not of our choosing. It is our most influential context. In the best of circumstances, children would feel free to speak their own truths, to give voice to their deepest sorrow, and to know that they would be heard and understood by other family members. But, as Liz's words remind us, and as Bea's story will illustrate, this is not the world in which we find ourselves.

"Who Is This Unhappy Girl?" The Story of Bea

Bea came to therapy after ending a five-year relationship with a man she found boring from the start. She was depressed and pessimistic about future relationships. When I asked her how supportive her parents were to her at this difficult time, she said that she told them nothing. "My father and I talk about the weather," Bea explained, "and my mother can't deal with me when I'm depressed. She can't even begin to hear it."

As far back as Bea could remember, her mother, Ruth, had disqualified Bea's sad feelings. Bea, who had an older brother, was "the happy girl" in the family—a role that was rigidly enforced. Whenever Bea got down in the dumps, her mother would approach her with false brightness and say, "Who is this unhappy girl? This is not my Bea! My Bea has a pretty smile on her face! Let's make this sad little girl go away so that my *real* Bea can come back!" Ruth also went to absurd lengths to protect Bea from anything she thought might disturb her. When Bea was five, her mother refused to take her to a birthday party because she'd heard that a girl with severe cerebral palsy would also be among the party guests.

During Bea's adult life, her mother continued to respond

anxiously to any hint of her daughter's unhappiness. Whenever Bea shared a problem, Ruth would reflexively rush in to fix it, or she would offer unsolicited advice or glib admonitions to "look on the bright side" and "keep a positive attitude." In response to her mother's allergic reaction to depression, Bea had long ago stopped sharing real feelings with her.

The ideal family encourages the optimal growth of all its members and provides a safe space where individuals can more or less be themselves. At their best moments, families promote a sense of unity and belonging (the "we"), while respecting the separateness and difference of individual members (the "I"). Parents make and enforce rules that guide a child's behavior, but they do not regulate the child's emotional and intellectual life. Individual family members can feel free to share their honest thoughts and feelings on emotionally loaded subjects, without telling others what to think and feel, and without getting too nervous about differences. No family member has to deny or silence an important aspect of the self in order to belong and be heard.

That's the ideal, but not the reality for most families, including Bea's. As she was growing up, her parents anxiously avoided a wide range of subjects. Bea sensed what topics were not "safe" and automatically avoided these "high-twitch" areas. Like many children, she silenced herself, disavowed her perceptions, and flattened her curiosity about issues that might threaten family harmony or disrupt family relationships. She also concealed important aspects of herself—such as her sadness and vulnerability. As Bea put it, "I just couldn't be real; I couldn't be myself. No one was honest in my family. It was all pretend."

Yet honesty was valued, if not rigidly prized, by Bea's parents. They punished the children not only for lying and cheating, but also for exaggerating and telling tall tales. "My parents were fanatics about honesty," Bea explained. "They wouldn't even let us believe in Santa Claus. My dad was the type who would make us walk a mile in the snow to return an extra dime the store clerk gave us by mistake. And we had to keep our word no matter what. If you said you would do something, it was considered a major crime to change your mind."

So intense were the sanctions against "dishonesty" that Bea was initially taken aback when she viewed the interior of other families. "When I was in fifth grade, I learned that my best friend's mom made long-distance personal calls from her work phone. She also brought office supplies home for the kids, like paper, pens, and Scotch tape. My friend was encouraged to lie about her age to get cheaper movie tickets or bus fares. Her parents accepted the fact that children don't always tell the truth. At first I was shocked because these behaviors would not have been tolerated in my family. But the paradox was, their family *felt* more honest than mine, more relaxed and spontaneous. In my friend's family, they were direct with each other. They actually talked about what was happening in their lives."

In Bea's family, "honesty" meant sticking to the facts, keeping one's word, and playing by the rules. It did not, however, include the honest sharing of feelings and personal experience. "My mother wasn't honest about her life," Bea explained. "When I asked her about herself, she would only tell me what she thought I should hear or what she thought was good for me." There was a striking incongruity between Ruth's upbeat messages, her behavior, and the almost palpable thickness of her unhappiness, which Bea felt "in the air."

Beyond Intentions

We grow up assuming that our parents will not intentionally lie to us, or deliberately conceal information about things that matter. We take on faith the information they give us. We ask, "Where were you born?" or, "How much did our house cost?" or, "Why has Uncle John stopped visiting us?" We expect straight answers, or, if not that, to be told that some things are private and will not be shared or discussed with us. If we are not told the truth, we cannot trust the universe—including our internal universe of thoughts, feelings, and perceptions.

Like all human beings, however, our parents can be no more honest and direct with us than they are with themselves. The discrepancy Bea sensed between her mother's words and her mother's true feelings probably reflected Ruth's own confusion rather than her deceptive intentions or dishonorable character. It isn't easy for mothers to share their personal feelings when they cannot name them and have been taught so many fictions about female experience.

Also, our parents are guided by the ethic of what is "good for us" rather than what is true. Ruth may have withheld or distorted information with the intention of protecting her daughter—that is, "for her own good." To prepare a daughter for a "happy marriage" and to teach her to be a "good mother," mothers pass down all sorts of myths from one generation of women to the next.

Family therapist Betty Carter notes that mothers routinely tell their daughters what they think is helpful rather than conveying their true doubts, fears, struggles, and uncertainties. This, she notes, reflects a mother's effort to fulfill her impossible responsibility of raising perfect children. Carter writes that "Trying desperately to be 'good mothers' and to guide their daughters, mothers withhold their *deepest personal experience* and try to convey to their daughters how *it should have been* and *how they want it to be for their daughters— instead of how it really is or was for them.*" Although the daughter may be angry at her mother for lying, she may also attempt to fulfill her own maternal responsibility by passing down the same myths in turn to her own daughter.

Within the family, women rarely describe their reality to each other with candor. This failure constitutes a tremendous loss, for it is through our stories, which create an authentic connection to other women, that we begin to uncover our deepest truths. It is not enough to exchange stories in a consciousness-raising group, at a women's conference, or with our five closest friends. Our sense of what is real and true suffers when we are unable to do this in our own families. The difficulty of pushing against silence and secrecy in a family depends on the amount of anxiety surrounding a particular subject and the emotional climate of family relationships.

The Family Emotional Climate

When Bea says about her family, "I just couldn't be real; I couldn't be myself," she is referring to the anxious emotional climate in which she was raised. Family members do not intentionally create an anxious climate for themselves or for each other. Nor do they notice it. Like a fish in water, we don't pay attention to the "givens" of our surroundings.

The level of underground anxiety or emotional intensity in a family is a function of multiple factors. It reflects the real stresses that impinge on the family as it moves through the life cycle, and the parents' economic and social resources to deal with these stresses. It also reflects societal stresses and social inequalities that affect the family. It reflects the parents' level of maturity and emotional functioning, which includes their connections to their own families of origin and the unresolved emotional issues they bring from this source. In the history of a family, anxiety accumulates over many years. Painful events that have not been processed in past generations will remain embedded in a family, and will be reenacted with each new generation.

The level of underground anxiety or emotional intensity in a family determines how much freedom individuals have to discover, clarify, and express their own truths—and how accurately they will see themselves and others. Anxiety drives people toward polarities, toward fusion or cut-off, toward glorifying or hating a difference, toward disclosing too much or too little, toward avoiding a subject entirely or focusing on it incessantly. Anxious families deny differences, sweeping them under the rug in a "group think" mentality that compromises individual autonomy, or they exaggerate differences and magnify them out of proportion.

Anxiety drives projections and distortions. People take things too personally and read too much into the other person's responses—or they do the opposite and entirely miss the nuances and subtleties of both the words and the nonverbal communications. Chronically anxious families are characterized by rigid, authoritarian rules—or the family operates like a glob of protoplasm, without clear parental leadership and generational boundaries. Anxious families deny the realities of change and try to hold the clock still—

or family functioning is so fluid and chaotic that there is no consistent, predictable structure to be counted on. Anxiety pushes us to one extreme or the other.

Anxiety drives triangles. As anxiety mounts, people talk about other family members ("I'm just so worried about the way your brother is behaving!") rather than directly *to* them. As tensions escalate, family members take sides, lose objectivity, overfocus on each other in a worried or blaming way, or join one person's camp at the expense of another. Anxiety heightens reactivity, which makes us quick to tell each other off and to try to shape each other up ("I'm so sick of playing games with my mother that I blew up and let her know how she manipulates everyone!"). Family members equate these intense, anxiety-driven confrontations with being honest, then blame the other person for not changing (". . . and then my mother got so defensive! She just can't accept the truth"). In reality, openness and truth-telling don't begin until at least one person calms down, steps out of the soup, and begins to really think rather than to merely react.

Bea's family had all the hallmarks of a chronically anxious system. Family roles were rigid and polarized; the labels applied to individual family members denied both the complexity of human experience and the inevitability of change. Bea was "always happy"; her older brother, Rob, was "the irresponsible one"; Aunt Mary was "selfish and untrustworthy." Information that challenged family myths and labels was disqualified, as if family coherence required that these remain as sure as sunrise and as fixed as the stars.

Whenever "always happy" Bea showed sadness, her mother would push anxiously for the return of the "real Bea." When "irresponsible Rob" acted responsibly, the family held its collective breath, just *knowing* that he would screw up shortly. When Bea violated an unspoken family rule against visiting her "selfish" Aunt Mary—and Aunt Mary responded warmly and generously in return—the rest of the family intensified their criticism, telling Bea that Aunt Mary was only out to "use her." All families have their myths, party lines, and labels, but when these are rigidly fixed, they exert a profound constraint on "realness." Like a pedestal or a prison, fixed labels that are either positive or negative leave one with little space in which to move around.

In Bea's family, the importance of "togetherness" also mandated that significant differences stay beneath the surface. This anxiety-driven fusion (the loss of the separate "I's" within the "We") was particularly intense between mother and daughter, so that if Ruth said "apples," Bea, as a child, felt unable to say "oranges." Later, as she entered adolescence, Bea did the opposite (which is really the same) and felt compelled to say "oranges" every time her mother said "apples." The enforced "togetherness" between them was so great that Bea felt compelled to push the differences. She suffered from what the poet Lynn Sukenick has called "matraphobia"—the fear of being one's mother. When we must be as unlike our mothers as possible, we rule out the opportunity to discover and invent our real selves, just as we do when we feel compelled to be exactly the same as her.

Even in calmer, more flexible families, differences challenge mothers and daughters. With the role of women changing so fast, it is not surprising that a mother may experience her daughter's expression of difference as disloyalty or betrayal, as discontinuity or loss, and as a judgment on the mother's own life and choices. Such tensions are understandable as a mother watches her daughter struggle to find new and different explanations for what it means to be an adult woman compared to what was prescribed over countless generations.

When it came to expressing her real feelings, Bea did no better with her dad, with whom she also could not articulate honest differences. The entrenched distance in their relationship, however, made things appear calmer and less intense. Like many daughters, Bea had learned to expect nothing from her father and everything from her mother. Although she complained that she couldn't be her "true self" with either parent, Bea focused her negative attention on Ruth.

Our Mothers' Daughters

The relationship with the same-sex parent is, of course, particularly pivotal for the development of authenticity and self-regard. As her mother's apprentice, a daughter watches to see what it means to be a wife, a mother, and an adult woman. A daughter is sensitively attuned to the quality of her mother's life and to how her mother conducts her key relationships, including those with her own family of origin. When a daughter senses her mother's unhappiness or sees through her lies and silence, she may volunteer to fill up her mother's empty bucket, fix her depression, live out her thwarted dreams, or wave her mother's banner at the expense of having a relationship with Dad. It is not simply that parents assign their children to a particular role, like "the happy one" or "Mom's best friend." A child may volunteer for such an impossible job in the family without even being asked.

During a summer on Cape Cod, my psychiatrist friend Teresa Bernardez and I taught a seminar on the subject of mothers and daughters. One participant, a social worker, shared the following story: When she was a little girl, she would ride in the back of her parents' car, as children do. On family trips, she invented an "imaginary twin" to sit with her—or, more accurately, an exact duplicate of herself. Even as a small child, she was able to articulate her reasons for inventing this fictitious double. "This way," she told herself, "I can grow up, travel to faraway places, and live a life of fun and adventure. And my twin can stay home and *be for mother.*"

Her story fascinated me because it illustrates how the child consciously and deliberately did what many daughters do with little or no awareness or intention. Women frequently leave a part of themselves at home. That is, we may sacrifice important aspects of the self in an unconscious effort to *be for* our mothers. A daughter senses her mother's hopes, fears, dreams, compromises, losses, and unfulfilled longings. The greater the suffering in the previous generations of women, the more a daughter may find herself unable to carve out a different life plan for herself—one that includes a large measure of joy, ambition, and zest. Or the daughter may feel compelled to succeed for her mother's sake, to express her mother's unacknowledged ambitions, or to prove that the compromises and hardships of previous generations have not been in vain.

For obvious reasons, the father often appears to be the less intense or less anxious parent. Fathers have been exonerated from parenting in any real sense, while mothers, in contrast, are taught that they *are* the child's environment, and that they are singularly responsible for what their children become.

The myth that motherhood is a "career" rather than a

responsibility and a relationship is a particularly disastrous one. Bea complained frequently in therapy, "My mother needed me to have a happy smile so she could show the world what a good mother she was." Well, why not? In our ambitious, competitive, production-oriented society, a mother may naturally want to create a good product—to show herself, the world, and her own mother that she is a "good mother," that she has done her job well.

One Father's Emotional Legacy

Of course, our fathers, too, for an endless variety of unconscious reasons, will need us to be (or not to be) a particular way for their own sakes. Our parents' perceptions and expectations of us are always colored by their unfinished business with their own families of origin and with each other—and by all the emotional issues, past and present, that affect them.

Bea's dad, Frank, for example, went off the deep end whenever Rob and Bea departed from telling the truth, following rules, or keeping their word. All children break rules, test limits, and engage in deception, but Frank had no flexibility to lighten up about even minor transgressions or a simple change of mind. "Once I promised to take a boy in the neighborhood to the circus and then backed down because it turned out to be the day of a big school event," Bea said. "My father reacted as if I had committed a criminal act."

Frank described his own dad, Bea's grandfather, as a "no-good lying drunk" who could not be counted on. His father's colorful behavior increased in proportion to his alcohol consumption, making him a frequent focus of town gossip in their small Oklahoma community. Frank's mother felt helpless to deal directly with her husband or to leave him. By the time Frank was eight, he had assumed the role of his mother's confidant and emotional ally against his dad.

As the firstborn and only son, Frank set about to restore his family's good name through his own exemplary behavior. He was so overcontrolled that the danger of becoming undercontrolled may always have lurked in the shadows of his unconscious. His own "bad" and mutinous impulses must have terrified him, as they suggested he was like his dad and so might betray his mom.

Frank's experience of his parents was so polarized that he could not acknowledge any competence in his "no-good father" or any shortcomings in his "perfect mother," whom he described as a saint. Even after his parents' death, Frank remained "for Mom" and "against Dad," never gaining a broader, more richly textured understanding and integration of family patterns and his part in them. As a man, Frank always knew who the good and bad guys were—and whose side he was on.

This emotional legacy deeply colored his expectations, perceptions, and reactions to his children, particularly to Rob, also a firstborn and only son. Frank's unconscious fear that his son would be like his own father (combined, perhaps, with his wish that Rob would act out the unacceptable impulses that Frank denied in himself) contributed to a particularly anxious emotional climate for father and son.

As Bea learned more about her dad's family, she was able to understand why being "honest" and "rule-abiding," particularly in the eyes of the community, was not just a virtue or a deeply held value to Frank. It was, instead, a rigid, anxiety-driven focus of concern.

* * *

When anxiety is high enough, or lasts long enough, parents can lose the capacity to separate their emotional issues from ours. A woman told the following story at a National Women's Studies Association meeting: When she was a teenager, her mother, a Holocaust survivor, constantly pressured her to eat more and put on weight. Why? Because "in the camps" her mother explained, "those people who had a few extra pounds could survive a few extra days."

How crazy such thinking sounded to an American-born daughter! Yet this mother was doing what parents usually do, even when they have not been traumatized. Parents do not view their children objectively, as separate "real" selves. Rather, our parents see us through the distorting filter of their own history and life circumstances. Indeed, it was to this mother's credit that she could connect her current behavior with a past trauma, thus giving her daughter some context in which to understand her anxious concern about weight. In response to her daughter's challenge, she could have yelled back, "Because this is what we do in this family!" or, "Because you must eat more to stay alive!" When parents get intensely focused on some aspect of a child's behavior, they typically have no clue about what force from their own past is driving them.

Families are not fair, and we do not choose the family we are born into. Our parents, being human, cannot create the perfect climate, like a garden greenhouse, to foster the blossoming of our true, authentic selves. Too much has happened long before we even enter the scene. When viewed over several generations, no family is free from the emotional ripples or, more accurately, the tidal waves that result from anxious events—immigrations, cut-offs, poverty, and untimely losses—that affect a family's functioning over generations.

Nor do we have one "true self" that might unfold in

some ideal "free" environment, unfettered by roles, rules, traditions, and myths of family, culture, and context. The self does not "unfold," but instead is continually reinvented and re-storied through our interactions with others. Depending on a multiplicity of factors, including time, place, and historical circumstance, we have more (or less) space to be open and flexible in this process.

As adults, we can choose how honestly and authentically we navigate relationships with our first family. Moves toward greater truth-telling require us to define ourselves more clearly, to see others more objectively, to talk straight about issues that matter, and to acknowledge in oneself and others the full, shifting range of competencies and vulnerabilities that make us human. This is where honesty, truth-telling, and "realness" begin. Not with the revelation or the uncovering of dramatic deceptions and secrets, but rather with the dailiness of what we call "being oneself."

Adults have the capacity to reshape the emotional climate of family relationships and to be inventive about truth-telling. Children also influence other family members and make their own choices about concealment and disclosure. A child's capacity for thinking and problem solving, however, is limited, and is coupled with a condition of total economic and emotional dependence. Children are the least empowered family members; as such they can afford to take few risks, whether real or imagined, with adults on whom their very survival depends.

Our Mothers' Stories

When I first saw Bea in therapy, she never disclosed anything of emotional significance to her family members. When her mother asked, "How are you?", Bea replied, "Fine." Only much later could Bea venture to say, "Well, I'm not so fine. I just broke off with this guy and I'm feeling terrible." Such a disclosure might not impress us as a bold act of truth-telling, but it was for Bea, who ultimately learned to appreciate her mother's predictable response ("Oh, you're not really sad, honey") as nothing more than *information* about Ruth's way of managing anxiety. Instead of retreating back into silence and blame, Bea found creative ways to continue the conversation.

Sometimes Bea teased Ruth about her avoidant behavior ("Hey, Mom, are you allergic to sadness? Or do you think that I'm not tough enough to handle feeling miserable?"). She also challenged her in a light, caring way ("So, Mom, when did you start working for the American Red Cross? How did you get this job of rushing in to rescue me by changing the subject every time I'm down?"). As Bea felt calmer and more centered in her mother's presence, she began to ask questions that expanded the context surrounding her mother's behavior.

Bea told Ruth that she would be able to get a better grip on her own ups and downs if she could learn something about how other women in the extended family had managed depression and grief. She asked about Aunt Rhonda, Aunt Mary, Grandma Belle, and Great-Grandma Trina. How depressed had the most depressed family member ever gotten? How did other family members respond? In what generation did this allergy to depression start? What was Ruth's "philosophy" on dealing with depression, and how did it differ from Grandma Belle's beliefs? What was the saddest thing that had ever happened in the family over the past two hundred years?

* * *

As Bea became a more skilled questioner, her mother became more disclosing. When I first met Bea, she was too angry and intense to broach an emotionally loaded subject with Ruth. Intensity breeds more intensity, only adding to the anxious emotional climate that blocked truth-telling to begin with. Moves toward truth-telling may require us to maintain a calm, emotional presence in an anxious emotional field. Paradoxically, this translates into being "less real" in order to help create an emotional climate in which people can be "more real." That is, if "being real" is defined as doing what comes naturally, which in Bea's case meant angrily avoiding or confronting Ruth. This kind of "real-ness" or "truth-telling" invariably shuts the lines of communication down even further.

What a huge challenge it is to arrive at a place where our wish to understand the other person is as great as our wish to be understood! Only when Bea had reached that point could her mother begin to share her stories and to reveal her secrets. Bea, who knew only of Ruth's two sisters, learned that her mother had had a twin brother who drowned at the age of three in a lake on family property. Ruth's mother, Grandma Belle, felt overwhelmingly guilty for not having supervised her son more closely. She subsequently drowned in her own grief, never surfacing long enough to breathe fully again. When Grandma Belle died at age sixty-three, all her son's clothes, toys, and possessions were just as they had been on the day he died. Ruth said, "Time stopped for my mother on that day."

In response to their loss, Bea's grandparents were rigidly polarized. Grandmother could do nothing but grieve while Grandfather could do anything but grieve. They blamed each other for their respective coping styles, and a chilly distance settled like fog into the cracks and corners of their household. Marital problems intensified further because Grandma Belle felt certain that her husband's family blamed her for the drowning, although no one spoke directly to the subject of responsibility and blame. Grandma Belle told Ruth she was devastated by her husband's failure to support her, although she could not speak out on her own behalf either, nor even forgive herself. The family drew apart, with no professional or community resources available to help them support each other in their grief so that they could move ahead with the business of living.

No wonder Ruth was at a loss to respond to her daughter's unhappiness, or to know what to do with her own. Ruth grew up with two adults who pushed the extremes in managing depression and vulnerability. Her father's philosophy was to press forward and "get on with things," as he put it. Her mother, for her part, could get on with nothing. Somewhere along the line, Ruth chose her dad's way for herself and for her own daughter as well. Whenever she noticed Bea showing the normal tears and vulnerabilities of childhood, she also saw, at those very moments, her own mother never coming out of grief. It probably didn't help matters that Bea bore a striking physical resemblance to Grandma Belle, for whom she was named.

Ruth never grieved for her lost twin, worried as she was about her mother's relentless sorrow and the climate of bitterness between her parents. Ruth's underreaction was in direct proportion to her mother's overreaction. "I never cried for my dead brother," Ruth said, "and I haven't cried at a funeral since." At a particularly honest moment, Ruth told Bea, "Maybe I can't stand seeing you upset because if I ever let myself cry, I'm afraid I'd never stop." Later, Ruth did cry in conversation with her daughter, and she did stop.

Bea was ultimately able to tell Ruth why her "protectiveness" was problematic. She let her mother know specifically what she found helpful when she was depressed. Ruth was able to tell Bea how "clutchy" she felt when Bea was feeling down, and she also said frankly that worrying was the only way she knew to be close to her daughter. Their conversation continues, I hope, to this day.

8

Honesty versus Truth

Not long ago, I had the privilege to introduce the performing artist Holly Near at a Menninger women's conference. I felt unusually anxious about my role in this event
because Holly is one of my favorite singers, as well as a political heroine and role model in my life. I had sat in the audience at many of her concerts, and here she was, from
Carnegie Hall to the Ramada Inn in Topeka, Kansas. I was as
nervous as I was thrilled to walk on stage and introduce her.

But at the height of my anxiety, a friend pulled me aside
and criticized my behavior earlier that day: I had failed to
make an appropriate introduction and had left her feeling
invisible and unimportant. She was correct about my behavior, but not about my motives. I apologized and explained
that it had been my "spaciness" at work rather than any lack
of love and regard for her. I just hadn't paid attention.

The next day my friend apologized to me for her bad
timing. She knew how anxious I was before this big event
and she also knew, firsthand, the terrors of public speaking.
After confronting me, she later regretted having acted on her

feelings of the moment and wished she had waited a day to reproach me. I appreciated her apology and told her so. I want my friends to be honest and spontaneous with me, but I also want them to consider my feelings. I want to hear their criticisms, but not at moments when I feel the most vulnerable or overloaded.

Most people can probably name countless examples in their own lives when their timing, or someone else's, has been off. Or when a bit of tact might not only have spared someone pain, but might also have maximized the chances that two people would really listen to each other, rather than anxiously *react*. When I was younger, I believed that timing and tact were the opposites of honesty. Now I believe instead that timing and tact are what make truth-telling possible in the most difficult circumstances and in regard to the toughest subjects.

Nor do I feel compelled to tell "the whole truth" to people who aren't important to me. For example, I've turned down repeated lunch invitations from one woman I find obnoxious. When she asked me directly whether I was avoiding her for personal reasons, I said, "I'm so busy these days that I hardly see my close friends." This was true enough, but it begged the question. Had she been important to me, I would have struggled to figure out just what I found "obnoxious" about her, and I would have sought a way to talk with her about it.

Honesty in the Moment

Some of us equate "honesty" and "being ourselves" with the uncensored expression of thoughts and feelings. It is indeed wonderful to have a relationship so relaxed and intimate that we can share anything and everything without first thinking about it. Yet honesty, as so defined, may also block deeper levels of truth-telling. Consider Clark Moustakas's story about his struggle to distinguish between honesty and truth.

Moustakas, a psychotherapist who led encounter groups, was once advised by his colleagues that in order to be effective and to live a full life himself, he should learn to ferret out and evoke expressions of anger and conflict within the group experience. In so doing, he would find his own angry expressions, serving as a model for others. Although this advice suggested an alien path, not in keeping with "being himself" or with how he wanted to live, Moustakas did not want to close himself off from what might be learned by following his colleagues' advice. Still, he was not convinced that spontaneous angry encounters were necessary for authentic living and growing.

Nonetheless, for about six months, Moustakas pushed himself to experiment with the "anger formula" he had been told was essential to the group process. He found that while it took only minutes to express his anger, it took hours to deal with its consequences. The group meetings were lively but troubling. He observed the upheaval and havoc he was causing in the lives of others, particularly since his own communications as group leader carried great weight.

Eventually, Moustakas experienced stomach pains, headaches, and other physical symptoms that he interpreted as a sign the confrontational style of leadership was alienating him from his own values. He began to ask himself questions: What was the real value of honesty? What was happening to him in these emotional encounters? Then he began to consider deeper questions: Who am I? What do I seek in my life with others? What are my values, ideals, desires?

When others had categorized his previously nonconfrontive leadership style as a weakness or a lack, Moustakas had responded with a willingness to experiment. In the process, however, his body signaled its own truths. Ultimately, Moustakas concluded that he had abandoned a vital pattern of being: "I came to see that my body tensions and headaches were a protest against the denial of my own self. Thus while I was being 'honest' in the moment when I angrily confronted other people, my honesty was often a lie in the sense that it denied something essential in me, something rooted in the values and ways of my life."

Like Moustakas, or anyone else, I hold values, beliefs, and goals that may transcend the impulse to "be myself" or to "be honest," without invitation, at any particular moment. I do not, for example, wish to hurt another human being unnecessarily. I value kindness and compassion. Sometimes the very urgency or intensity of my emotions is the red flag that signals me to stop and think, to separate out fleeting reactions from my more enduring and significant feelings.

I also do not want to be "honest" at my own expense. In certain situations, my efforts to be open and frank have led downward in a spiraling process that made me the focus of negative attention or concern. There have been countless instances in my personal and professional life when being strategic rather than spontaneous was the best approach toward deepening levels of knowing and truth-telling.

With honesty, as with all good things, we can have too much. If a casual acquaintance spills out her deepest feelings and darkest secrets at an office party, we may question her maturity rather than admire her openness. As we grow up, we learn to restrain our uncensored selves, and to make thoughtful and informed choices about how and when to tell what to whom.

Is It Our Anxious, or Real, Selves?

During the writing of my previous books on the subjects of anger and intimacy, I struggled with a conceptual tangle regarding momentary honesty and enduring truth-telling. Sometimes I felt as if I were wearing two different hats, or taking my readers in two directions at once.

On the one hand, my goal was to legitimize the open, direct, and forthright expression of female anger and protest. As subordinate group members, women operate under profound injunctions against voicing any thoughts or feelings that might threaten others or disrupt relationship harmony.

On the other hand, my clinical practice was filled with women who were venting their "real feelings" in a manner that *protected* rather than *protested* the status quo. Getting angry was getting nowhere or even making things worse. My clients' efforts to "tell the truth" or to "be honest" often froze relationships rather than moved them forward.

In my efforts to guide my readers, I sometimes felt like the English professor who wrote on a student's composition, "Be yourself!" and then added, "If this is yourself, be someone else."

Some efforts to be truthful reflect a simple failure to protect ourselves. Sally, a teacher of learning-disabled children, consulted with me after receiving a performance evaluation that failed to do justice to the high quality of her work. Her senior supervisor, a distant man who didn't relate well to the students, criticized Sally as being "too emotional" and "over-involved with individual children at the expense of group discipline." In Sally's opinion, her supervisor had little knowledge of her actual work. She was incensed by his criticism, which labeled as a "weakness" what Sally believed to be the very essence of her strength with the children.

At the first opportunity, Sally confronted her supervisor. She began on a reasonably calm note, but when he became defensive and argumentative, Sally responded with interpretations: "I think that *you* have trouble relating to people and that you have a problem with my style. The children really connect with me, and I believe there's an issue of competition in our relationship that you've never dealt with." The next day, a colleague reported her supervisor's reaction: "Sally's immature response to her evaluation only confirms its accuracy."

The situation deteriorated even more as Sally focused tenaciously on convincing her supervisor of the truth, and he, in response, dug in his heels. Sally then turned to her co-workers, criticizing her supervisor and pressing the other teachers to side with her against him. Perhaps they, too, had complaints about him; however, the zealousness with which Sally attacked him led them to respond in his defense. The more Sally voiced her anger, the more the other women denied their own.

It was evident that Sally was contributing to her own isolation and distress. Her attempt to convince other people of her side of things elicited their disapproval and defensiveness rather than their sympathy. This only increased Sally's sense of bitterness and injustice, and a vicious cycle ensued. Yet when Sally first came to see me, she didn't question her own behavior. She believed unequivocally in saying *what* she felt *when* she felt it, particularly when she felt that truth was on

her side. She didn't distinguish between honesty in work situations and honesty in intimate relationships where closeness is the goal.

If, indeed, Sally's first priority was to confront her boss
with the full force of her emotionality, irrespective of his
response, then her behavior was congruent with her values.
From this perspective, she was, indeed, "doing the right
thing." But as Sally felt increasingly unhappy at work, she
began to reconsider what she wanted to accomplish. Did she
simply want to express her feelings to her supervisor? If so,
was it necessary or useful to try to process the underground
issue of competition, or anything else, between them? Or did
she want instead to maximize her chances of being heard and
reevaluated, or evaluated more positively the next time
around?

When Sally decided that she wanted to champion her
own cause more effectively, she shifted gears, interacted
more thoughtfully, and proceeded with greater awareness of
what she wanted to accomplish and how her behavior
affected those around her. She ultimately stood firmly and
assertively behind her position, but without becoming defensive or attacking. Her earlier honesty not only reflected a
failure to protect and regard herself; it also made it more difficult for her supervisor to be objective or to appreciate the
truth of her position.

Truth-telling obviously requires us to "be ourselves." But it
may also require us to exercise restraint, as we consider matters of timing and tact, and what we hope to accomplish in a
relationship. Also, it takes time and effort to clarify for ourselves—no less for others—what we really think and feel, and

where we stand on important issues. At the very moment we lay claim to being "most honest," we may be anxiously reacting to the other person rather than expressing our deepest feelings. Whatever we experience with the greatest emotional intensity may be what we may mistakenly assume to be "most real."

Thinking versus Emoting

Consider, for example, a nineteen-year-old woman, Peg, who has invited her mother, Anna, to join her in therapy sessions with me so that they can "resolve their relationship." Their interactions are colorful and intense; each blames the other for her unhappiness and confronts her with "the truth" as she sees it. A psychiatric resident, who observes several sessions from behind a one-way mirror, tells me he is impressed that "real feelings" are being expressed.

From my perspective, however, there is little exchange of real feelings between this mother and daughter, although I don't doubt the presence of real pain. The contagious reactivity between them is so high that they behave like two nervous systems hooked together. Almost any topic triggers immediate intensity from the other, so that within moments they are rigidly polarized in opposing camps. Neither can identify and address the core issues, hear the other objectively, or take a position without blaming or telling the other what to do.

Anna and Peg are unquestionably honest with each other. Their freedom to give full vent to their emotions may well be a testimony to the durability of their mother-daughter bond. Surely, their fighting keeps them connected. But they are not in a process of truth-telling, of knowing and being known, of refining and deepening their disclosures to one another. To help them move in this direction, I remain a calm presence in this anxious emotional field and begin to ask questions that facilitate thinking rather than emoting.

Multiple sources of anxiety fuel reactivity in any family relationship. As I question Anna, I learn that her younger sister recently died and that Anna's husband has been unsupportive at this difficult time. Also, her daughter Peg, at nineteen, is now the same age that Anna was when her own father abandoned the family. At this time, Anna sacrificed her plans to study art and design, returning home instead to care for her devastated mother. Caretaking became Anna's full-time job until she married and got pregnant with Peg. She never resumed her career plans.

Now Peg is planning to head west to study violin at a conservatory of music. Without consciously knowing Anna's history of loss and self-sacrifice at her age, Peg nonetheless senses her mother's underlying grief. And Peg is nothing short of masterful at pushing her mother's buttons and sustaining a lively, angry engagement that protects her mother from becoming depressed. As therapy progresses, Peg discovers that she prefers dealing with a "bitchy" mother rather than a sad mother. She fears she could lose herself in waves of compassion for her mother's life, and lose sight of her own wishes for independence, making her struggle to pursue her career goals even harder.

This is not to deny the importance, or the necessity, for giving full voice to our immediate and uncensored reactions. We may—in a particular moment of truth—swear, scream, moan, curse the darkness, or otherwise show another person the full force of our rage or pain. I value the raw, unbridled emotional exchanges I have shared with my husband, which are part of knowing each other so deeply and trusting that we can survive almost anything. But I am glad that these are only moments, that they are few and far between, and that we can step back from them to reflect and talk about what they mean. I also value my capacity to withhold or conceal my emotions, and to use both intuition and thinking to make choices about whom to tell what.

No single moment of honesty, self-disclosure, revelation, or emotionality can determine how truth-telling will proceed over time. Truth-telling is a *process*—and one that cannot be sustained in a chronically anxious or distant emotional field. Remember how Bea managed to reconnect with her mother, Ruth, before asking her about the legacy of depression in their family? Rather than confronting her mother in a blaming way, Bea kept the emotional intensity down by teasing her about being allergic to depression. And as Bea learned to interpret her mother's avoidant behaviors as expressions of anxiety, rather than as personal rejection, she was able to "lighten up" around Ruth. She worked slowly over time to create the conditions of safety that ultimately allowed Ruth to reveal the secret of her twin brother's death, and the family's reaction to that loss.

Most family relationships are emotionally intense, although when the intensity is managed by distancing, it gives an appearance of calm. Anna and Peg—like Bea and Ruth—moved forward in the process of truth-telling only after they were able to reflect on the broader context in which their intensity developed. Only then could they listen respectfully (rather than reactively) to each other. And as Peg slowly became genuinely interested in her mother's history, she began to understand that this was her history as well, and thus "about her." As a true exchange of stories took place, they both developed a more accurate and objective picture of themselves and each other.

Truth-telling in families is a slow, bumpy process without end. Each question and each disclosure evokes new questions, new feelings, and new disclosures. The revelation of personal feelings, or previously concealed information, can mark the beginning of future disclosures and uncoverings, or the opposite. Depending on how we define honesty, it may impede or facilitate truth-telling.

My dictionary equates honesty with moral excellence: honesty implies truthfulness, integrity, sincerity, fairness, and an absence of deception or fraud. As so defined, honesty is unarguably—and always—essential to the process of truth-telling. But when people reveal personal examples of "honesty," they typically focus on incidents when they have reacted, sometimes after a long silence. "I finally got up the courage to tell my mother that she's ruining my sister's life," one woman says. Another explains, "I told my boss that he's totally insecure and threatened by competent women." Yet another reveals, "I called my mother on her birthday and said, 'Sit down, Mom, I'm a dyke.'" When one tracks the specific interactional sequences following disclosures like these (who said what, when, and then what), they often result in the relationship shifting from bad to worse. The solution to the problem is not to become less honest, but rather to become better truth-tellers.

Truth-Telling as a Process

During my college year in India, I conducted research on the attitudes of a young group of Harijan ("Untouchable") women toward the caste system. Although the caste system had been legally abolished, its rigid hierarchical structure still pervaded some aspects of Hindu society. Harijan women remained in the lowest position in the social stratum, in essence outside the system. My questions of these women concerned their attitudes toward untouchability and the caste system, and whether they internalized the deep-rooted prejudices against them. I wanted to know how they viewed their lack of status and opportunity. How did they feel about being assigned by birth to the "low and dirty" work of cleaning latrines and sweeping dirt with inadequate brooms? What of value or comfort did they find in their assigned, unalterable roles? What changes did they hope for and how might these come about?

Although these questions were deeply personal, I hoped not to be lied to, or shunned, or viewed with suspicion. To this end, I did not parachute down to their village from the sky, pencil and pad in hand, and begin my soul-searching inquiry. First, I studied the language and culture. I worked with the women daily, cared for their children, and participated with them in major life cycle events such as births, weddings, and funerals. Before asking the more difficult questions that my research required, I talked with each woman about everyday concerns.

Then I formulated my questions with care, so as to minimize any anxiety, shame, or discomfort they might evoke. I also listened with care, suspending all judgment. Still, my research did not always proceed smoothly. My Hindi wasn't good enough to work without a translator. My presence did not always inspire trust. The interviews were not conducted "my way," either. A woman might fail to show up for an interview scheduled at noon, but then arrive in the early evening with five extended family members. Although the process was sometimes frustrating, I learned a great deal. I attributed problems and misunderstandings to cultural differences and my status as an outsider.

In a culture closer to home, such as our own families, however, we are so emotionally hooked into the system that we can easily lose, or never develop, such a process-oriented view of gathering and sharing information. Instead, we may descend on our family with our own agenda, and without having laid any groundwork for truth-telling. We may know next to nothing about our parents' history and culture. We may have maintained only superficial contact, if that, over the years. We may have exerted only minimal effort to attend or even acknowledge important family events. We may have little objective perspective on family patterns and our part in them. We may approach a family secret or "hot issue" in a clumsy or confrontational way.

Then, when we meet with resistance, we may bolt rather than be able to implement a long-term plan for whatever it is we hope to accomplish. As a result, we may be too quick to blame and diagnose the other person ("My father just won't talk about the past") rather than to consider how we, ourselves, might become more skilled and patient in gathering information.

Of course, we will always be more reactive and "twitchy" when we are within a system rather than outside it. That's why therapists and consultants can be invaluable to families, businesses, and other organizations, particularly if they can avoid being drawn into the anxious emotional field they are there to observe. But even in the midst of the problems, even when we're in the soup, we can learn skills for climbing out and getting clearer about the real isues and how best to address difficult truths.

Anthropologists know how much is to be learned before carrrying out research projects like the one I undertook as a college student in India. As a family systems therapist, I know how much is to be learned about opening up conversations within families and other systems where lies, secrets, and silence have prevailed. Whether the "hot issue" is incest, religion, a father's drinking, marital dissatisfaction, or a daughter's responsibility for an aging parent, one theme emerges clearly in my work with families. Doing what comes naturally may just as naturally land us in trouble. In the name of either "honesty" or "truth," we are likely to drive anxiety higher rather than promote the conditions of safety that encourage truth-telling. Much of what we call "telling the truth" involves an unproductive effort to change, convince, or convert another person, rather than an attempt to clarify our own selves.

To discover new truths or reaffirm old ones, we must be willing to experiment with different ways of being in relationships and to persevere in the face of resistance. Issues that cannot be talked about frankly (and relationships in which real talk occurs rarely, if at all) have often been encapsulated in anxiety from generation to generation. It is no surprise that substantive change occurs slowly, with inevitable frustrations and derailments. Our challenge is to approach "high-twitch" subjects in ways that are likely to sustain connection rather than cut-off, and to maximize the opportunity for deepening conversation over time, rather than "hit-and-run" disclosures, revelations, and confrontations.

"Why bother?" That was my response to a friend many years ago who challenged me to open up an emotion-laden issue in my own family—slowly, responsibly, and with care, and with a plan to manage the inevitable resistance evoked by change. Interestingly, it was no bother to me to try steadily yet clumsily to be in conversation with women halfway around the world. Today, my response would be, instead, "Why *not* bother?" There is, perhaps, no more direct route to discovering our own truths than to unearth the stories in our immediate and extended family. The stories of our family members are *our* stories, these stories "are us," and it is in the exchanging and refining of personal experiences that we can come to know our own truths.

9

Just Pretending

"Let's pretend!"

And why not? Pretending can be a creative, even magical act. A child says to her best friend, "Let's pretend we're astronauts." A teacher says to her dance students, "Pretend that you're an animal of your choosing and *be* that animal." Pretending stretches our imagination, enhances empathy, expands our sense of possibility, and provides a vehicle for self-expression and self-discovery.

When pretending involves deception—as it often does—it can still be a playful form of inventiveness and "make-believe." One of my most cherished childhood memories is of riding the train from Brooklyn to Manhattan with my sister, Susan, who was taking me to the fanciest stores on Fifth Avenue. Our parents could only afford to give us subway tokens, but we planned to masquerade as millionaires. Our first stop was Tiffany's: "Do you think we should buy Mother this diamond necklace for her birthday?" I inquired loudly of Susan, pointing to the most expensive item in view and hoping to capture the attention of the well-heeled shoppers nearby. "Oh, don't be silly!" Susan replied in her most grown-up, haughty voice. "Mother has several *exactly* like it, you know." In this way, we spent a happy, memorable afternoon.

But pretending can also be a most serious venture: "I pretended to be sleeping whenever my father came into my room and touched me"; "He escaped the Nazis by pretending he was a crazy man"; "My brother and I tried to pretend that things were normal in our family." When reality is limiting, harsh, or dangerous, pretending is an act of coping, self-preservation, and survival.

Between what is playful and what is desperate, we could name countless forms and functions of pretending in everyday life. Whether the intention is to dazzle or distract, confuse or camouflage, masquerade or malinger, impress or impersonate, pretending is an ever present adaptational strategy throughout all of nature. A particular act of pretending may elicit censure ("Why must she always pretend to have it all together?") or admiration ("I was amazed that she was able to give such an uplifting performance when her heart was breaking"). In either case, the human capacity to hide the real and display the false is truly extraordinary, allowing us to regulate relationships through highly complex choices about how we present ourselves to others.

But how do we distinguish pretending from other forms of deception, such as lying. Interestingly, people do routinely distinguish between the two, at least where their own behavior is concerned. When, for example, I ask friends to provide me with specific examples of lies they have told recently, there is an initial, palpable silence. Not so when I ask the same friends for examples of pretending: "I pretended to be out when my friend called"; "I acted like I was interested in the conversation"; "I pretended that nothing was wrong when I had lunch with my folks"; "When she was telling me about the authors who influenced her work, I kept nodding my head as if I had heard of them."

Not one person asked me to define my terms. People assumed that they knew when they were pretending, and to what end. Unlike other forms of deception, acts of pretending were described without defensiveness or apology, and with conscious recognition of their adaptive value. A young woman called Beth whom I met briefly in Denver described an incident of pretending that highlights how we typically distinguish between pretending and lying.

Beth, an experienced woodswoman, had recently led a group of Girl Scouts on a weekend wilderness trip. A severe and unexpected thunderstorm washed out the main trails and created hazardous conditions. Beth lost her way, and went from feeling nervous to fearing for the survival of the group. Teetering on the edge of panic, Beth "talked herself down," as she put it, and forced herself to act as if she was feeling calm and confident. On top of this deception, she added another: "I pretended to myself that I was an actor, that the group was being filmed for a television show, and that the film crew was just out of sight." In this way, she managed to get a grip on her anxiety and to keep a clear head.

In Beth's situation, pretending had clear adaptational advantages over authenticity. Beth's primary task was to ensure the safety of the group, not share her true feelings. "Fear can be contagious," she explained, "and I didn't want mine spilling over into the group." Feigning courage and calm also helped her muster these qualities in herself. "When I let myself feel fear, I become more fearful," Beth explained. "When I act brave, I'm better able to *be* brave."

There's a postscript to this story. In the Scout meeting that followed this dramatic adventure, Beth encouraged the girls to talk about the experience. Early in the discussion, one girl said to Beth, "You were telling us not to worry, but you looked scared to me." Several other girls nodded in assent. They, too, had picked up on Beth's anxiety but had also pretended not to notice it.

Beth calmly explained that she had, indeed, felt scared, particularly because she was responsible for their safety. To veer from truth-telling at this juncture would have required Beth to lie. The group's primary task now was emotional rather than functional: the job at hand involved processing the frightening experience they had been through together. Beth felt that anything short of the facts would disqualify the girls' perceptions, invalidate their sense of reality, and impair their trust in authority. She intuitively decided how much to share—for example, she didn't describe the morbid images of dead Girl Scouts that flashed through her mind when she was most afraid. But she knew that honesty was essential to helping the group process their experience and move on.

A Definition of Terms

What *are* the distinguishing features of pretending?

First, pretending conveys the possibility—and sometimes even the wish—to fool not only others but also oneself. When Beth, for example, pretended to be calm and courageous, she wanted most of all to convince herself.

Second, this word describes feigning or faking, but not stating a lie. As my younger son Ben put it, "I can pretend that I'm not angry with my friend. But if he says, 'Are you angry at me?' and I say, 'No,' then I'm lying." His example reminded me of my friend Sue, who didn't feel dishonest passing as a nurse because she didn't explicitly lie about her status.

The third and most salient feature of pretending builds on the first two. Like sexual pretending, pretending in general (at least from the pretender's perspective) implies a *mild* act of feigning or faking that neither rattles the conscience nor demands careful examination. We don't typically associate the word with a shattering personal betrayal, a flagrant lie, or an unforgivable breach of trust. Rather, it calls to mind the suggestion that this particular form of insincerity or false appearance is personally okay or culturally sanctioned.

According to one dictionary, pretending is "mild in force" and implies "no evil." The two dictionaries in my library don't even include the words "lie" or "deceive" among the synonyms provided. Pretending is a "soft" verb. As such, it is the form of deception we are least likely to scrutinize. The very word "pretending," like the word "privacy," invites us *not* to pay attention.

And yet, as I listen to women reveal how they pretend in their own personal lives, I hear stories of grave, ongoing deceptions. Of necessity, these must be shored up by lying and self-betrayal: "I pretended that I was in love with him, because I was desperate to get married"; "I pretended to want sex"; "I pretended to enjoy motherhood"; "I pretended to be happy in my marriage." Patriarchy schools women to pretend as a virtual way of life, and then trivializes its eroding effects on ourselves and our partners.

Women's ways of pretending demand our most careful attention. We must take pretending seriously, precisely because we are taught not to. Pretending, by definition, is inconsequential. But this itself is a lie, or at best only a partial truth. If women stopped pretending tomorrow, the world as we know it would also stop. So, too, is the case with "privacy." What is private is by definition nobody's business but our own. But when women collectively came forth and made the private public—then all that we took to be "true" under patriarchy was challenged and reviewed.

Contrary to what the dictionary tells us, pretending is potentially the most serious form of deception because it can involve *living* a lie, rather than telling one. And we are least likely to catch ourselves in the act. When we tell an outright lie, we feel jolted. But pretending is imperceptibly woven into the fabric of daily life and so leads to the construction of a false self. We may not feel any jolts along the way, because we are, after all, "just pretending." In time, we don't notice ourselves doing it at all.

Pretending, patriarchal style, deadens our passion, calcifies our choices, and blocks us from knowing and acting on our own truths. But there are also other types of pretending that can help rather than harm us.

There is pretending that enlightens and enlivens, that leads us to invent and discover new truths, that helps us not only to find but also to choose ourselves. This kind of pretending is illustrated by Beth's comment, "When I act brave, I'm better able to *be* brave." Bold and courageous acts of pretending can help clarify and expand what is real and true about ourselves, just as momentary honesty can impede truth-telling.

Beth's story about feigning courage with her Girl Scouts reminds me of my own efforts at pretense during a time of crisis. Shortly after President George Bush declared war in the Gulf, I was scheduled to present a workshop in Texas. I didn't want to go. I felt despair about living under a government more concerned with profits and power than with human lives, in particular, with lives of color. For the first time in my adult life, I felt that my work made absolutely no difference in the world. My professional focus on individuals and families seemed wildly unimportant.

As I packed for the workshop, I cried about the war and felt hopeless about the world's future. I decided, however, to pretend to feel hope, because I believe that maintaining hope is a moral imperative. As long as we can *feel* hope, there is hope. Also, for me, acting hopeful was perhaps the quickest route to being hopeful.

At the workshop I talked about warring families and warring nations. I focused on the extraordinary challenge of moving from blaming people toward understanding escalating patterns of conflict and our own part in them. I told the participants that my firsthand experience with individuals and families who have successfully met this challenge in the most difficult of circumstances encouraged me to maintain hope. As I stood at the podium and made these comments, I actually felt hopeful. I was no longer pretending, although that had been my starting point.

If I had truly lost all capacity to feel hope at the time of the Gulf war, pretending would have been of no value to me. I have never been able to shake myself free from pain or pessimism with false reassurances that deny a deeper reality. Glib affirmations to "think positively" and "look on the bright side" can alienate us from our bodies and our unconscious, by serving to conceal emotional complexity rather than uncover what is hidden or lost. Sometimes, however, we only learn what is true, or real, or possible, or "still there" by experimenting with pretending and by restraining our so-called true selves.

The Courage to Pretend

An attorney friend of mine, Molly, called me for advice on a family matter. She had just returned from her brother's wedding in Des Moines, where things hadn't gone well. Molly told me that their mother, Ethel, had been narcissistic and self-centered, trying to control the whole show and coldly distancing when things didn't go her way. Ethel disapproved of the non-traditional wedding ceremony, and she sat through it with a look of undisguised exasperation. There were no raised voices during the four-day family gathering, but an unremitting tension had settled between mother and daughter.

Molly's mother, whom I had met briefly on several occasions, was a competent, energetic, "take-charge" person. Although Molly valued her mother's style, she didn't respond well to its more extreme manifestations, which predictably surfaced at anxious times such as family events. I asked Molly whether Ethel would have behaved differently if Molly's father, Sam, had survived his unexpected heart attack fifteen months earlier. As far as Molly knew, he hadn't been mentioned during the ceremony or in any family conversation. Molly's response to my question was, "Thank God he didn't live to see it!" Sam had been a rabbi. The bride had been raised Catholic. The wedding took place in a Unitarian Fellowhip, and the woman marrying them was, as Molly put it, "weird." No wonder, I joked with Molly, that everyone seemed a bit tense.

When Molly returned home to Lawrence, Kansas, her anger at her mother mounted rather than dissipated. She sat down at the computer and wrote her mother a four-page, single-spaced letter. In it she shared her observations of the recent family dynamics, with particular emphasis on Ethel's self-centered behavior and Molly's reactions to it. True to her legalistic background, she documented each point in careful detail. In an attempt to be fair, she also noted the contributions of herself and other family members to the problems. She concluded by saying: "I know we have all contributed to the dysfunction of our family, as well as to the denial of this dysfunction."

Although Molly felt driven to write the letter ("Someone has to tell the truth in this family"), she found herself hesitant to mail it, and called me instead to get a different perspective on the situation. I asked her whether she was aiming for momentary honesty or enduring truth-telling. That is, did she want to share her reactions with her mother, as Sally first did with her supervisor, irrespective of the response she might evoke? If so, then mail the letter. Or did she want to take the hard road and begin to lay the groundwork for greater truth-telling to develop? Molly indicated the second choice.

Molly wanted my reaction to her letter, and she asked specifically what I'd do in her shoes. I told her that I wouldn't mail it. The letter was long and extremely intense. And the content was blaming, even though honesty, not blaming, was Molly's good intention. Since Molly had frequently complained to me in the past that her mother couldn't handle even minor criticism, she didn't need me to predict that Ethel would get defensive reading the letter.

What then, was the "right" way for Molly to proceed? There are undoubtedly many right ways. Molly, however, wanted to know what kind of letter I would write, based on the family systems perspective that guides my work as a therapist. I told her I'd write a shorter, chattier letter to Ethel. I'd keep it low-keyed, because I'd be aiming to reduce anxiety and reactivity, not raise it further. I'd address the family tension in a paragraph or two, rather than in a treatise. And

I'd stick to sharing my own truth rather than criticizing my mother.

"So, after commenting on the weather and the wheat fields, you'd say *what* in this paragraph or two?" Molly insisted. I told her that I would say something like the following:

"Mom, I felt some tension between us when I was home for the wedding. I'd be interested in hearing your thoughts, because I've been trying to sort my feelings out since I returned. I was pretty tense around the time of the wedding and I realize that this was the first time our family has been all together since Dad's death. I think the wedding was a vivid reminder to me that Dad isn't around anymore. I also find myself wondering how Dad would have reacted to the wedding, if he had lived to see it."

Molly said that the "low-keyed part" made sense to her, but that the rest didn't fit because she hadn't thought about her dad during the wedding or since. According to Molly, Sam had been a distant and critical father, whose death left her largely unaffected. As she mulled over our conversation the next day, however, she decided "to pretend," to try it out or "try it on," as she explained, to see what might be learned from such an experiment. She began the letter, but when she started to write the part about her dad, she burst into tears.

Molly's reluctant attempt at pretending ended up evoking real feelings. As she wrote the letter, her grief about her father surfaced, along with genuine curiosity about her mother's experience. What had it been like for Ethel to be at the wedding without Sam? How was she affected by knowing how upset Sam would have been about their son's departure from the family's religious and cultural tradition?

Molly mailed the new letter, and Ethel wrote back the same day that she received it. Molly described her mother's response as a long litany emphasizing how glad she was that Sam died before the wedding because the very thought of how he would have suffered caused Ethel more grief than anyone could imagine. Molly was initially taken aback by her mother's response, since Ethel's "poor me" attitude never failed to push her buttons. As we talked about the letter, however, Molly was able to step back a bit and regain a process-oriented view.

From my perspective, I viewed Ethel's response more positively, as evidence of her willingness to engage with her daughter around emotional subjects. Even if Ethel had failed to respond to Molly's communication, I would not have felt particularly discouraged. Rather, I would have viewed Ethel's distancing as information about her way of managing anxiety, and I would have encouraged Molly to think about where to go from there.

Molly responded to her mother with a note that asked a few empathic rather than critical questions. For example, she expressed interest in how her paternal grandparents had responded to Ethel and Sam's wedding years earlier. Although Molly's grandparents had been orthodox Jews, her parents had been married in a reformed synagogue, thus departing significantly from the traditions of the previous generation. Molly worded her questions respectfully, rather than in her usual legalistic manner. She learned that her paternal grandmother had been too upset to attend the wedding, and that Ethel had never felt accepted by her mother-in-law. This revelation eventually led to her mother disclosing other family stories and secrets that had never been told, nor asked about.

Over time, Molly began to address the question of how differences were managed in their family. She shared with Ethel her observation that many of their family members seemed to have a hard time with differences, and that the problem appeared to be generations in the making. "As I get older," Molly wrote, "I'm realizing that loving my family doesn't mean we all have to be the same." In a subsequent phone call to her mother, Molly mentioned that she felt as if both Sam and Ethel reacted critically whenever she did something differently than Ethel would. And so, her relationship with her mother began to move forward, although with some moves backward. Most importantly, however, Molly began to see more movement forward than backward over time.

We can approach truth-telling as a lifelong process, or as hit-and-run confrontation. We can be focused on our own part in the process, or on "getting" a certain response. Obviously, we will all yo-yo back and forth between reflection and reactivity, but it is useful to think about where we ultimately want to stand.

Truth-telling, as we have seen, is a thing of accumulation. Truths are not "told" but rather enlarged on and refined over time. Like a long-distance run, truth-telling takes endurance, the capacity to push forward in the face of enormous resistance. At the same time, truth-telling requires restraint. It asks us to sit still when we feel fired up to act. Finally, it requires us to develop the wisdom and intuition to know when to do what.

Realistically speaking, we're not wired to take the high road. With Molly, I could easily adopt a thoughtful, process-oriented view of change, because it's not my family and it does fall within my area of professional expertise. Like an anthropologist studying a society to which she does not belong, I can hear Molly—as I heard the Harijan women in

India—with interest and curiosity. If I view Molly as an emis-
sary from a complex culture, I can more easily see that over
many generations, her family has developed a set of values,
beliefs, and rules that govern each member's behavior around
the difficult issues that can't easily be talked about. I can also
appreciate the slow pace often required by truth-telling and
the necessity at some points to move at glacial speed.

Yet, in my own family, I can lose objectivity as fast as anyone else does in theirs and it takes me effort to regain it.
Humans lean toward dichotomous, polarized thinking under
stress. As we divide into opposing camps, multiple and complex truths are easily lost, with each party overfocused on
what the other is doing wrong and underfocused on our own
options for moving differently. Whether we are talking about
individuals or governments, it is a remarkable achievement
to move against our automatic, patterned responses, which
block the possibility of open conversation and the experience
of a more nuanced and complex view of what we name reality. Changing how we habitually behave in a relationship
may require an initial willingness to pretend, to act, to
silence our automatic responses, to do something different
even when it initially feels nothing like "being oneself." One
can discover in pretending that one has allowed for the
emergence or invention of something "more real."

Playing Dumb

"Do you know how to act dumb?" I once teased Lenore, a
client of mine. In the jargon of family systems theory,
Lenore was an entrenched overfunctioner, who always knew
what was best, not only for herself but for others as well. She
was quick to advise, rescue, take over, and fix. She had little

capacity to stay in her own skin and allow others to struggle with their problems and manage their pain. If someone itched, she scratched. Her partner, Beverly, underfunctioned with as much gusto as Lenore overfunctioned. Throughout their ten-year relationship, each unwittingly reinforced the other's behavior.

During this particular therapy session, I was challenging Lenore to do something different, something "unnatural" at that. "Playing dumb" is hardly a therapeutic prescription for women, but I was wondering whether Lenore could attempt a courageous act of change that would disrupt the relationship pattern for which she sought help.

Could she, for example, experiment with saying, "I don't know," when Beverly asked for help in finding her car keys? Could she let Beverly leave the house with their four-month-old daughter without going through her usual checklist: "Do you have the diapers? Did you pack the formula? Did you remember to bring another sleeper?" When Beverly did leave the diapers behind, or otherwise acted less than competently, could Lenore underreact rather than overreact, allowing Beverly an opportunity to sit with the emotional and practical consequences of her underresponsibility? And if Lenore couldn't do this for a week, would she be willing to try it for, say, two days?

The next time I saw Lenore, she gave the following report on her experiment: "When I saw that Beverly was going to leave the house without Anna's pacifier, I literally had to go to the basement to keep myself from reminding her. Anna can't go for long without it. Thirty minutes later, Beverly came back home to get it. I sat there working on a report and forced myself not to say a word. She ended up being late to meet a client, which was a disaster. When she started to complain about it that evening, I stayed calm and told her I was sorry she'd had a hard day. Again, I had to stop myself from getting preachy. I was amazed at how hard it was for me to stay emotionally separate from her—to just stay out. Anyway, yesterday when Beverly took Anna to the pediatrician, she forgot to pack the diapers. But this time she came back for them before she'd even pulled out of the driveway."

My goal as a therapist was not to provide Lenore with a technique to help shape up her partner. Rather, I wondered what Lenore might learn about herself by modifying her own part in an overfunctioning-underfunctioning polarity that had gone on as long as their relationship had. While Lenore's small experiment with Beverly was hardly significant in itself, it drew meaning in the context of the work that Lenore was doing in therapy.

Many painful events had happened in Lenore's first family, and anxiety had been chronically high. Her parents did not approach problems calmly and factually, or with an eye to a solution, but rather with intense emotional reactivity and symptomatic behavior. Lenore, who had no living siblings, unwittingly supported her parents' incompetence by providing them with limitless care, both functionally and emotionally. When she first entered psychotherapy, she had no experience in being emotionally present in the face of neediness or pain without trying to find answers and solutions. She had sporadically distanced from, or set limits with, her parents, but only *after* she was angry for having done or given too much. Then the intensity in her voice only fueled their anxiety and neediness.

Finally, Lenore had never considered sharing her own problems or vulnerability with either of her parents, nor did she view any other family member as having anything to offer her. But she saw no connection between her inability to reveal her vulnerability and her parents' inability to assume competence.

Only slowly did Lenore understand and modify her automatic and "natural" ways of responding to her parents. In acting any way other than how she always had, Lenore felt that there was initially a strong element of "pretend" or experimentation, as when she let Beverly leave home without all the baby's supplies. What initially felt like "pretending," however, ultimately led her to discover new insights about family patterns and her part in them.

More Pretending

A psychotherapy client says to me: "My friend is dragging me to this meeting about adoptees searching for their birth parents. I pretended to be interested because she needs my support, but I've never been curious about my biological mother or father." In this apathetic spirit, my client attends the meeting and all emotional hell breaks loose for her. So it is that we sometimes learn more about what is "really real" by placing ourselves in a new context. Or, like Molly and Lenore, we *create* a new context by changing our own behavior in an old one.

Consider Jen, who is frantic about the fact that her live-in boyfriend keeps hedging on setting a marriage date. Jen had a disastrous first marriage, but believes now that she's met the "perfect man." The more she pressures him to make a commitment, the more he distances, and vice versa. By the time she seeks my help, the pattern that has been set in motion has a life of its own. All she can do is express dependency and neediness. All he can do is experience a cool distance and a need for space. She's anxiously pursuing and he's putting on his track shoes. Jen is so focused on marriage that almost no energy is going into her work, her friendships, and her life plan.

I advise Jen to consider a bold act of pretending. Can she set aside a period of time—say eight weeks—to stop focusing on her boyfriend and begin to put her energy back into her own life? Can she be the one to seek more separateness, for example, by going out with her own friends a few evenings a week? Can she initiate a conversation in which she expresses her own doubts about marriage? (We all have them.) Can she stay warmly connected to her boyfriend (rather than swinging into a cold, reactive distance), without pursuing him or mentioning marriage?

For a "natural" pursuer, this challenge is difficult. And because such advice smacks of the old "hard-to-get" tactics that women have been taught to play, it may sound phony or manipulative. But there's nothing authentic or true in continuing a pattern where she only pursues and he only distances. Polarized relationships (she stands for togetherness, he for separateness) distort the experience of self and other, and keep us stuck in a narrow view of truth and possibility. Sometimes interrupting the pursuit-distance cycle allows each partner to acknowledge the more difficult and complex—but internally more whole—experience of both wanting and fearing intimacy.

Let's take one final example: A friend of mine, Michelle, was intensely critical of her mother-in-law, Sylvia. Dedicated to expressing her true feelings, she constantly criticized Sylvia to her husband, who invariably came to his mother's defense. This was a typical "in-law triangle," with the negative intensity settling between the wife and her mother-in-law. The two women sparred with each other while the man stayed outside the ring.

From Michelle's perspective, she was dealing candidly with an impossible situation. She told her husband regularly how much she hated his mother. In response to Sylvia's unsolicited advice and critical scrutiny, Michelle became openly sarcastic and coldly withdrawn. Michelle described her own behavior as honest and forthright, but she was unwittingly running interference for the other two. Wherever a wife and mother-in-law are slugging it out, there is a mother and son who aren't addressing the emotional issues between them.

I challenged Michelle to pretend, to experiment with behaviors that at first struck her as unnatural and even phony. I suggested that she lighten up, stop criticizing Sylvia to her husband, and try to relate instead to Sylvia's good qualities, which Michelle had totally lost sight of. I encouraged her to create a less intense emotional climate between herself and her mother-in-law, and to approach her with humor and interest rather than distance and blame. I also suggested that she deal more directly with her own parents to avoid overfocusing on her husband's family.

My point was not to persuade Michelle to do something different for its own sake ("Let's throw red paint on your mother-in-law and see what happens"). Rather, I was challenging her to become an expert on how triangles operate and to change her part in this one.

What began as pretense, as "experimenting," led in time to a more richly textured view of family realities. A year later, Michelle was underreacting to Sylvia while her husband had begun to overreact to his mother. Conflicts were surfacing in Michelle's marriage, as well as between her husband and his mother. These real relationship issues had been totally

obscured by the old triangle, which had sidetracked the negative intensity into the relationship between Michelle and
Sylvia.

Pretending can facilitate truth-telling (or truth-knowing)
when it makes a dent in unproductive, habitual ways of
responding to others. As an old Spanish proverb reminds us:
Habits at first are silken threads, then they become cables.
We can't see what's "true" or possible in a relationship or in a
human being until *after* we change our behavior. Sylvia, for
example, softened her critical attitude (which reflected, in
part, her misguided wish to feel helpful and included) when
Michelle moved toward her, inviting and valuing her perspective rather than bristling at her unsolicited advice.

Goethe once wrote (before inclusive language): "If you treat
man as he appears to be, you make him worse than he is. But
if you treat man as if he already were what he potentially
could be, you make him what he should be." We can never
know the totality or the potential of other human beings (or
what they "should be," for that matter), but who they are
with us always has something to do with how we are with
them.

W. Brugh Joy has paraphrased Goethe's quotation as follows: "If I treat myself as I think I appear to be, I make myself
less than I am. But if I treat myself as if I already were what I
potentially could be, I make myself what I should be." Both
quotations are intriguing meditations on the power of imag-
ining and pretending—and the relationship between the two.

10

Family Secrets: A Disturbance in the Field

During many of my growing-up years in Brooklyn, I kept a lock-and-key diary that I hid in a dresser drawer beneath my sweaters. After each entry, I put the diary back at a particular angle so I could tell if it had been tampered with. I lived in terror that my parents would read it or that my best friend's brother would make good on his threat to find it. Whoever violated my privacy would also discover my most carefully guarded secrets. Ironically, it was my younger son who recently found these same diaries in an attic box and gleefully thumbed through them. Fortunately, enough years had passed that I reacted mostly with amusement when he unabashedly reported his adventure.

Every family has secrets dividing those who "know" from those who "don't know." Secrets between parents and children often reflect healthy boundaries, allowing each generation to have its separate sphere. Other secrets that adults keep from children, and vice versa, are deeply problematic.

Children conceal information from their parents and engage in deception for many reasons. A child may choose to keep a secret to avoid punishment or disapproval, to protect a parent from worry, to carve out a private space, to consolidate relationships with siblings and peers, or to foster autonomy and separateness. Hiding information or feelings from parents can help children feel powerful and independent, and can stave off unwanted attention and intrusion. Children, however, do not always "choose" the secrets they keep or the ways in which they get trapped in someone else's story. Some secrets, such as incest, reflect both the adult's abuse of power and the child's utter terror, confusion, and helplessness.

Parents routinely keep some secrets from their children. Adults need to maintain privacy and naturally want to shield their children and themselves from unnecessary and painful disclosures. Parents make daily decisions about what information to impart to their children and how and when to do so.

But parents differ dramatically in the degree to which they view children as needing protection from "the truth." Bea's mother Ruth, for example, tried to buffer her daughter completely from the inevitable sadness and grief that life brings. By the time Bea was an adult, there was little real communication or exchange of feelings between them. Other parents may do the opposite. They may tell children too much, thus failing to shield them appropriately from adult problems, or they may pressure their children to open up to them. Either extreme reflects an anxious family's efforts to adapt; both extremes are problematic.

How do we distinguish a "family secret" from the countless things that parents choose not to tell their children, and vice versa? The term "family secret" usually refers to the concealment of events and facts (rather than thoughts and feelings) relevant to the person who does not have the information. The term is reserved for subjects that are emotionally loaded in our culture. Family secrets commonly involve matters of alcoholism, drug addiction, imprisonment, suicide, physical and mental diagnoses, untimely losses, migration status, parentage, infertility, adoption, sexual orientation, affairs, employment and financial status, divorce, incest, and violence. If a mother hides what she paid for the new lawn furniture, this act of concealment is unlikely to find its way into the literature on "family secrets," although her failure to disclose the information may have a profound meaning in her family.

The extent to which a piece of information is concealed or mystified is a barometer of family anxiety. In turn, the extent of anxiety reflects the personal meanings that parents bring to a particular subject from their own families and the degree to which a subject is stigmatized within the broader culture.

When I was in the sixth grade, my friend Arlene kept her parents' divorce a secret from every one of her classmates at her mother's request. Her mother not only felt responsible for the failure of her marriage, but she also did not want Arlene to suffer from being the only one in her class from a "broken home." This secrecy would be unusual in the nineties because divorce is now ubiquitous and far less stigmatized in most communities.

Stigma and secrecy are mutually reinforcing and entwined. The more a subject is stigmatized and misunderstood, the more likely it is that stigmatized individuals will resort to secrecy. Yet the keeping of secrets further exaggerates shame and increases our sense of being stigmatized.

But individual acts of insight or courage alone cannot

bring an end to this vicious cycle. Rather, change occurs only when individuals join each other to collectively form a social and political force to be reckoned with. The civil rights movement, the adoption reform movement, and the women's movement all illustrate how a social movement can alter the previously stigmatized meanings that the dominant culture assigns to certain groups. As new meanings develop and become established, more people come forth to reveal their secrets. As a result, individuals begin to feel a positive sense of identity and pride where stigma and secrecy once prevailed. Information among family members (for example, that Mother really is an alcoholic) can then flow more freely, which strengthens relational resources within the family and between the family and the community.

Of course, a secret can be made of any content, and it need not be shaped by stigma and shame. As Vicki's story illustrated, even a secret as neutral and trivial as meeting one's spouse through a personal ad can have a dramatic effect on family relationships, separating "insiders" from "outsiders" and creating hidden alliances and triangles that operate at great cost. Secrets influence relationships, even those secrets that are kept by a single family member who tells no one. The negative power of secrecy derives both from the emotional importance of what is not spoken (the content) and the convoluted alliances, triangles, and distance that secrets can create (the process).

In her book *Secrets in Families and Family Therapy*, Evan Imber-Black offers a dramatic example of the rapid triangular shifts that can occur when secret-keeping has become the relational modus vivendi for a family: Although a mother agreed with her adult son to keep his drug abuse a secret from his father, she revealed it within hours. In turn, the father agreed to keep his knowledge of the information secret from the son and from Imber-Black, their therapist. But then the father came to the next family therapy session alone and disclosed the secret, insisting that the therapist not tell his wife he had done so. In a joint family session, Imber-Black focused on how information flowed in the family, and how their wish to protect each other from harm was connected to the mutually felt experience of constant betrayal.

As the following story about Linda illustrates, the hidden alliances created by secrecy are not always fluid. Rather, triangles can become rigidly fixed—over years, decades, and generations. Secrecy is typically maintained in the name of "protection," and implicit calls to family loyalty hold secrets in place. It is difficult, however, to sort out who is protecting whom and from what—particularly considering the serious consequences of secrecy on individual and family life.

"Your Father Can't Handle Difficult Things"

When Linda came to see me in therapy, she was twenty-two years old and had recently become pregnant with her first child. She was the oldest of four daughters from a Kansas farm family and she was enrolled in a master's program in public health administration. Since her freshman year of college, she had been unable to speak comfortably in front of groups and she sometimes felt panicky even raising her hand in class. She described herself as being afraid that she would blurt out something "stupid or inappropriate."

Despite earlier attempts at therapy, Linda's problem stayed with her. Now an even more distressing symptom led her to seek help once again. Since learning that she was pregnant, she worried constantly about developing a health problem that would require diagnostic X-rays that would damage the fetus. Linda could not understand why she was haunted by this anxious preoccupation since she had no history of medical problems nor, apart from her fear of speaking in public, any remarkable history of worrying.

During Linda's second therapy session, while I was putting together a family genogram (a detailed family tree), Linda revealed a family secret that she initially viewed as being irrelevant to her symptoms. At age ten, Linda had attended the funeral of a neighboring farmer. After the service, the man's daughter told her that Linda had had an older brother who had died from "a heart problem or something" when he was a month old, on Christmas Day. Linda at first thought that the girl was lying, but she later asked her mother, who confirmed this fact and then refused to discuss it further.

During that brief and tense conversation, Linda's mother asked her not to mention the subject to any other family members. There was no reason, she said, for Linda's younger sisters to know or for their father to be reminded of this loss because "your father can't handle difficult things." It was best, she explained, that he remain unaware that Linda even knew. Linda's deep sense of family loyalty led her to put the news behind her rather than dwell on it. I was the first person she had ever told.

Linda's knowledge of her brother's death allowed her to make sense of otherwise inexplicable and mysterious aspects of her past. Her mother, for example, was "inside a dark cloud" during the holiday season, the anniversary of the loss. Linda's father, for his part, expressed profound disappointment that he did not have a son to help him farm. All their daughters were affected by his obvious sorrow and dissatisfaction, but only Linda knew the rest of the story.

One reason that such family secrets wield so much negative power is that a parent can hide crucial facts, but cannot hide the intensity of feelings surrounding these facts. In my family, for example, my mother's cancer diagnosis could be concealed, but the survival anxiety was in the air. When children sense a disturbance in the field, but do not feel free to ask questions, they flounder in unconscious fantasies that cannot be put to rest. As the family therapist Peggy Papp notes: "When children sense information is being withheld, they become confused and anxious, lose their sense of trust, and often end up blaming themselves. In searching for a way to explain the inexplicable, they create private beliefs, myths, and fantasies. These often get acted out through symptomatic behavior and become a metaphor for the concealment in the system. The tensions and conflicts produced by secrets remain irresolvable as long as the information necessary for their resolution remains inaccessible."

In Linda's case, she knew the secret. But the forbidden subject was still off limits, so Linda didn't ask questions about all the things she did *not* know: What exactly had her brother died from? What caused the problem? Why couldn't it be fixed? Where was her brother buried? What was his name? Why was his death so terrible that no one was allowed to talk about it? If Linda suddenly died, would the family never again speak her name? Does death mean that one is erased forever from family history and memory? And how did the loss of the firstborn child affect Linda's entrance into the family?

When a subject is taboo for ongoing discussion, children stifle their feelings, as well as their natural curiosity to make sense of their world. Sensing her mother's anxiety, Linda repressed her questions and put all thoughts of her brother out of consciousness. At the time of her first pregnancy, however, that underground emotionality surfaced as symptoms and perhaps as metaphor. X-rays not only harm (as expressed in Linda's worry about the survival and well-being of her own firstborn) but they also expose what is hidden from sight. Similarly, Linda's longstanding fear of publicly blurting out something stupid or inappropriate might also have reflected the burden of secret-keeping and her unconscious wish to talk openly about the truth.

Once Linda was able to examine the forbidden subject in the broad light of day, she felt lighter, less burdened, and more calm. She then told her husband about the secret she had discussed in therapy. He was glad to have information that helped explain her seemingly inexplicable fear that some unknown danger threatened their firstborn. Feeling supported and eager to control her anxiety, Linda gathered the courage to open up the secret in her family.

Linda spoke first to her mother, Fern. She picked a calm time and told her mother how fearful she felt about being pregnant. She asked Fern to help her get a grip on her anxiety by providing a bit of information about her brother's death. Linda began by asking a few factual questions ("What was his name? Did you have a normal pregnancy? Who first noticed there was a problem?"), rather than inquiring about difficult feelings or expecting to cover a broad territory all at once. Linda also told her mother that it was only when she became pregnant herself that she understood how devastating it would be to lose a child. She had anticipated a cold response from Fern. Instead, they cried together.

In a later conversation, Linda let her mother know that she planned to talk about the loss with other family members, including her dad, John. At this point, Fern's anxiety skyrocketed and she angrily accused Linda of being selfish, disloyal, and disrespectful. But Linda was able to maintain a firm stance without distancing or becoming defensive. She told her mother, "You know, Mom, I suppose I *am* being selfish, because I need to do this for myself. I'm sorry that I'm hurting you because that's not my intention."

Linda explained to Fern that keeping the secret was too big a burden for her because it kept her distant from the other family members. She also told her mother that she loved her family and wanted to be able to talk with them about important things. Linda didn't try to change or convince her mother—only to be as clear as possible about where she stood and what she needed to do for herself. Getting *out* of the secret-keeping business in families is as important a skill as keeping a confidence when appropriate.

In excavating a family secret, one revelation leads to another. Linda began to learn about other losses in the previous generation that had never been grieved or openly talked about. She learned from her father that her brother had died of a viral illness rather than some kind of heart problem. Her parents had felt particularly devastated because of their own failure to call a doctor in time. As a result, they had never bothered to clarify false rumors about the cause of their infant son's death.

As Linda replaced fantasy with fact she was able to separate out her own pregnancy from her mother's painful experience. Her fear of speaking out in groups diminished and her preoccupation with X-rays all but disappeared. Linda's parents, however, initially became *more* anxious as the fragile equilibrium in their distant marriage was disturbed by their daughter's challenge to secrecy and silence.

For Fern and John, having to face their grief about their son's death once again was not the only difficult aspect of the change initiated by Linda. Linda's move toward her dad also defied a long-established, multigenerational legacy of father-daughter distance. In her effort to share her own fears with him, and to ask him about the losses in his life, Linda challenged the myth that fathers must be protected (or more accurately, excluded) from family emotional life. When Linda told Fern, "I can't keep such a big secret from Dad," she was refusing to collude with John's outsider status. In so doing, she made waves that rippled throughout the entire system and ultimately affected all their family relationships.

Insiders and Outsiders

With family secrets, there are countless ways that the boundaries are drawn and redrawn between insiders and outsiders. In Linda's family, for example, John thought that he and his wife were keeping a secret from the children. But, in fact, from the time Linda was ten years old, his wife and daughter had kept a secret from him.

Secrets have different "locations" in family life. A mother may have a secret, such as her addiction to Valium, that she tells no one. Or she may tell her adolescent daughter and swear her to secrecy. All the family members may know about her addiction but may behave with each other as if no one knows. Or the children may be warned not to mention their mother's secret to anyone outside the immediate family. Another kind of secret might involve a child and one parent and an outside agent, as when a child's problem is discussed by one parent and a teacher or therapist, but the other parent is not told.

In her book *Deborah, Golda, and Me*, Letty Cottin Pogrebin observes that most of her family's secrets were guarded by women, who revealed information bit by bit like time-release pain capsules. She speculates that shame was a major factor that might account for this guardedness, perhaps because women are socialized to be more conscious of appearances than men and to rely more on "how it would look" or "what people might think" in the absence of more concrete measures of worth. Pogrebin also wonders whether keeping certain behaviors under wraps allowed the women to look presentable yet do what they wanted to do anyway.

In recalling the secrets in her own family, including who was in cahoots with whom, Pogrebin also draws a connection between secrecy and power: "While men control the history of nations and civilizations, women use family history as their negotiable instruments. And if knowledge is power, clandestine knowledge is power squared; it can be withheld, exchanged and leveraged. For women, who traditionally were excluded from prestige-building occupations or the exercise of worldly influence, guarding secrets may have been the only power they know."

I agree with Pogrebin's premise. While women and men may not consciously intend to exclude each other, there is surely a connection between women's outside position in the public sphere and men's outside position in the private sphere of family emotional life.

When Fern told her ten-year-old daughter, "Don't tell Dad," her stated intention was to protect her husband from unnecessary upset. But when Linda, twenty-two years old and pregnant, did tell her dad, it became clear that her mother had most needed to protect herself from grief and rage stemming both from the loss of her son and her husband's emotional withdrawal from her. Perhaps she also wanted to protect her emotionally central position with her children. Fern taught all her daughters that their father couldn't be expected to deal with difficult things and that he mustn't be bothered. Whatever her intentions, she reinforced rather than challenged John's outside position in the family.

Yet family secrets, more often than not, are profoundly disempowering, even for the secret-keepers. Secrets erode connection, block authentic engagement and trust, and strip the family of spontaneity and vitality. Secrets not only rob individuals of relational resources within their families, but they also rob the family itself of external supports. Keeping a secret from the outside world ("Don't tell anyone Dad lost his job") lowers family self-esteem and may lock the family into an atmosphere of shame, silence, and social isolation.

Secrets support pathological family processes, bonding insiders together with false bonds and estranging outsiders. Secret-keepers may become physically but not emotionally present, "missing in action," as a friend puts it. As outsiders remain blocked from knowing what is true, they may become increasingly unable to recall the past, gather facts in the present, and anticipate and plan for the future. And what begins as one family secret often spreads to ever-widening circles of lying, silence, suppression, and denial.

The negative effects of secrecy on children may stay underground for years, even decades, until the child reaches a key anniversary age or a particular stage in the family life cycle. Linda, for example, moved forward with her life, despite her fear of speaking publicly, until she conceived her first child. At this time, her anxiety became almost incapacitating.

Some children react to secrecy on the spot, as I did in response to the silence surrounding my mother's first cancer diagnosis. A child or adolescent's symptomatic or acting out behavior may be a random, anxious response to secrecy. Or it may speak metaphorically to what is being concealed and may serve to blow the whistle on the family.

Secrets and Symptoms

Many years back, a wealthy, socially prominent couple from Kansas City requested my professional help. They were concerned about their adolescent daughter, Catherine, whose downhill slide both embarrassed and alarmed them. Catherine had refused individual psychotherapy but agreed to see me with her parents.

At the start of our first meeting, Catherine's father bluntly stated his view of the problem, while his wife nodded in assent. Catherine was "looking like riffraff, behaving like riffraff, and hanging out with riffraff." Her recent appearance, something between punk and porn, humiliated her parents, who were both highly visible in the business community and especially concerned with image and status. Also, Catherine had begun staying out all night and engaging in promiscuous adventures, which she flaunted rather than concealed from them. Her father responded by lecturing Catherine on matters of morality, while her mother expressed panic about her daughter's safety and the risk of AIDS. Catherine, for her part, dug in her heels, insisting that she would do as she pleased with her life.

My initial attempts to help the parents work as a team to formulate clear rules and discipline were not helpful. Suspecting the concealment of crucial information, I asked that

Catherine's older brother be invited to join the sessions. In a meeting that included only the two children, a family secret did indeed emerge. Catherine's brother let it be known that their mother was going to elaborate lengths to avoid acknowledging that her husband was having an affair with his business partner. He explained, "The two lovebirds are screwing all over the country and everyone knows it but Mom."

Catherine had also suspected her father's affair from its inception a year earlier, having overheard bits and pieces of flirtatious telephone conversations. It was not her conscious plan to "blow the whistle" on her family through her own less-than-respectable behavior, but she did just that. And while Catherine was contemptuous of her father's hypocrisy and deception, she was angrier still at her mother's unwillingness to face reality and stand up for herself.

At sixteen, Catherine understandably had little perspective on the profound economic, emotional, and social vulnerability of women in marriage. As she looked into her mother's eyes and worried about her own future, she saw only a woman who was "phony," "cowardly," and "superficial," and who would not defend or define herself. Catherine was furious that her mother seemed unwilling either to protest the affair or even to react to it. As a result, she ended up doing the job for both of them.

Symptoms can serve both to *protest* and to *protect* the status quo in family life. Catherine's problematic behavior brought her family into treatment, making it impossible for business to continue as usual. She did, indeed, blow the whistle on her family's deceptive image of propriety. At the same time, she protected her parents from confronting her father's secret affair, and the profound marital distance surrounding it. Like a lightning rod, Catherine attracted to herself all the negative attention. She provided both of her parents with an ongoing focus of concern, so that by the time the family entered therapy, Catherine was all her parents talked about—and perhaps their only "safe" topic of conversation.

Shortly after the secret came out in the open and the spotlight focused on her parents, Catherine began to settle down. At her own initiative, she had an HIV test, which proved negative, and she announced in a therapy session that she was "taking a vacation from sex" to catch up with her schoolwork. Catherine's mother was no longer able to stick her head in the sand, although she initially felt totally at a loss about how to respond to her husband's affair. When the facts were out on the table, she first reported feeling dead inside and unable to react. However, as she waited for the results of *her* HIV test, rage and fear swept through her like a tornado.

My own attention was now focused on helping the parents address the affair and turn their primary concern toward their own marital problems, which had been obscured by their concentration on Catherine. I dismissed Catherine and her brother from the therapy sessions, encouraging them to get on with their own lives, as their parents needed to deal with adult problems that were private. Only much later did I work briefly with Catherine and her parents to help restore communication and establish mutual regard.

While I have focused on the negative effects of secrecy in families, the subject is far too complex to allow for glib generalizations or sweeping conclusions ("All secrets in families are bad and should be immediately revealed"). The challenge for parents is not to rush in to "tell all," or for therapists to ferret out all that is hidden. As we have seen, revelations and confrontations may do more harm than good when family members bounce into each other's lives, often in a context of distance or tension, and try to do too much too fast. Telling a secret may not be productive if it occurs in an anxious emotional field, before at least one adult is motivated and thoughtful enough to get a grip on their own intensity.

There is little agreement on what constitutes a "family secret" or on definitions of what is "normal" or "functional" secret-keeping in families. Some family therapists believe that all secrets are toxic. Others pay attention to the strategic and adaptational value of secrets, which functions differently depending on their location in a particular family, ethnic group, generation, community, class, and culture. From my perspective, the challenge of revealing secrets is one of process and direction, of creating an emotional climate in which sensitive information can be shared and the conversation can continue long after the secret is revealed.

It is one thing, for example, to tell a preschool-age child that she is adopted. It is another to create a calm emotional climate where the child can feel safe to ask questions and share a range of honest emotions, including grief over her loss of significant people, separation from her birth mother, and the possibility she may never meet her birth parents. As children mature, they raise new questions, or the same question changes in meaning over time. The question "Who is my mother?" means one thing to a kindergarten child, and another to an adolescent girl wanting genealogical information to help clarify her identity and make sense of her world.

Whatever the subject, at least one family member will pay a price when an important matter can't be noticed, talked about, or even remembered. In the shadow of secrecy, children are especially vulnerable to acting out or developing symptoms. They are the most dependent family members and, as such, are fiercely loyal to unspoken family rules and traditions. No matter how outrageously children and adolescents behave, they *"know"* at a deep, automatic level what not to ask about. When they sense undercurrents of hostility, fear, or distance in the family, they are most likely to create self-blaming fantasies to fill in the missing pieces or to explain the tension. Children also put on blinders that obscure more than the original secret from view.

No Thinking Permitted Here

Peggy Papp worked as a family therapist with Billy, an eleven-year-old boy with a "learning deficit" in history who was unable to remember dates or places. His symptom was a puzzling one, for he did well in all his other school subjects. In therapy Papp discovered that Billy had been kept from learning his own history, which was filled with mystery and chaos. Billy's mother wanted to protect him from any knowledge of his father's alcoholism and job losses. Billy, for his part, wanted to protect his mother by not asking her upsetting questions, like why the family kept moving from one place to another and why he and his mother suddenly left his father.

For Billy, the past was dangerous territory that could not be explored or even thought about. When Papp was able to help Billy integrate the facts of his past with his current life, he was able to recall historical dates and places, and his "learning block" disappeared. The taboos that had prohibited Billy from gaining knowledge of his family history had generalized to a prohibition of learning the history of the world around him. In a similar light, Papp reports the work of another therapist who treated a girl with a "selective math disability," related to the fact that she had never been told about her adoption. Once she was permitted in therapy to add up the facts of her own life and to compute the arithmetic related to her birth (she was fifteen months old when her adoptive parents married), her "math disability" disappeared.

Any large family secret, or mystification of what is real, can ultimately lead to a more generalized prohibition against knowing, seeing, talking, feeling, and asking. This occurs even when the broader culture *prescribes* secrecy and mystification in family life, as with the ubiquitous practice of mislabeling female genitals ("Boys have a penis, and girls have a hole where the baby comes out"). False and mystifying communications create broader taboos against a child's clear articulation of inner experience and outer reality.

One woman I saw in psychotherapy was unable to think clearly about geography, directions, and maps—a confusion related to the prohibition against "figuring out" her genitals. In therapy, it emerged that her inability to comprehend the geography of her genitals, or her world, was a promise to "not look." Looking meant that she would see something (her vulva, especially her clitoris) that wasn't supposed to be there. "What I had that felt good didn't have a name," she explained. "It wasn't supposed to exist. Only boys had something on the outside. So I couldn't have my clitoris and still be a girl." As she put it, "Everyone knows that men have a penis, and everyone can say the word—even at parties. But the only word that people will say to describe what women have is 'vagina.'"

Is the clitoris a societywide family secret? The idea sounds silly enough to demand that we consider it. The fact that a secret is normalized or culturally sanctioned does not make it less of an assault on female reality. It only makes it harder to look squarely at its implications. When women publicly examine "the trivial" or "unimportant" (like the cultural prescription to keep our age a secret, to joke or even lie about it), we may begin to move toward the center of what keeps us sleepy and disempowered.

Family secrets appear to be private business, derived from the deepest interior of family life; but patriarchal injunctions promote silence and denial even about life-and-death matters, such as the horror and extent of male violence in women's lives. The cultural context determines not only which secrets can be told, but also which secrets can be remembered and which secrets can be heard. Today, for example, my colleagues and I see a startlingly large number of women who have been victims of incest or sexually abused. Why were we not hearing all these stories fifteen years ago? Did our cultural climate then deny our clients their capacity to remember? Were women remembering yet not telling their therapists? Or were they telling their therapists and not being heard? However one understands it, something in the cultural emotional climate has shifted to allow for the honest memory and frank disclosure of even the most horrific of family secrets.

Significantly, discussions about violence and sexual abuse are taking place *among* women, as stories move more freely between the therapist's office and the public sphere. As women make the transition from the private to the public, they can begin to understand their personal experience within a wider context of gender and power. As more women remember, the ability to do so is renewed within us all, which makes remembering more likely for any one of us. The presence of powerful social and political movements—the civil rights movement, the feminist movement, the human rights movement, to name a few—ensures that once we remember and speak, we will not forget and fall silent. Nor will our stories be erased from history and the future.

11

An Affair Is a Big Secret

Jane had been living with her lover, Andrew, for five years when she found herself attracted to Bill, a man she worked with closely in a small veterinary clinic. Their flirtation, playful at first, intensified over time. For several months, they did not act on, or mention, the obvious sexual energy between them. But Bill was on Jane's mind and under her skin. At home, she talked to him in her head and thought about him while making love with Andrew. The nature of their work and the setup of the office kept Jane and Bill in close physical proximity, even had she wished otherwise.

Jane never questioned her primary commitment to Andrew. Not for a moment did she consider leaving him for Bill. She was, however, surprised by the strength of this attraction, and particularly by its emotional hold on her. She was confused about its meaning, not knowing, as she later put it, whether her feelings were "real" or whether she was getting into "some crazy, addictive, crushlike thing." As Jane felt increasingly anxious and driven by the attraction, she concluded that getting to know Bill better, rather than forcing distance, was the only route to gaining greater clarity about her feelings.

In keeping with a mutual agreement to tell each other about sexual temptations, Jane had, until now, been open with Andrew whenever she had felt attracted to someone else. This time was different. Jane feared that he would be inconsolable if he knew how compelling the attraction to Bill was, and she predicted that the emotional atmosphere at home would become so highly charged that she would be pressured to cut off from him entirely. She imagined Andrew anxiously grilling her every day after work, even insisting that she leave the job she loved. Jane wanted the time and space to move toward Bill and to sort out her feelings, time and space that would not be available if she brought the situation out into the open.

Jane also suspected that ending her relationship with Bill at this point would ensure that she'd stay stuck on him, if only in fantasy. She believed their ongoing contact would "normalize things" and "add more reality to the relationship," ultimately helping her to find her way out of the emotional woods. Also, Andrew wasn't asking questions about Jane's relationships at work, suggesting that perhaps he didn't really want to know about any possible rivals.

When Jane slept with Bill for the first time, vowing it would never happen again, she began to feel overwhelmingly anxious at home. In a panicky moment, she revealed everything to Helene, a long-time best friend who was also like a sister to Andrew. Sharing her secret helped alleviate Jane's anxiety only temporarily, because Helene became increasingly uncomfortable in her role as confidante. "I can't keep hearing about this," she finally told Jane during a late-night phone call. "I feel like it's putting a big wedge between me and Andrew, and I'm worried about the whole thing." Jane became terrified that Helene would violate her confidence.

Then Jane became anxiously preoccupied with the idea that she might have contracted the AIDS virus from Bill and passed it on to Andrew. She began having difficulty sleeping through the night and often awoke in the early morning with fear radiating through her bones. Jane had slept with Bill a total of three times and had practiced safe sex each time. Nonetheless, her anxiety and guilt increased, focusing on the chilling thought that she had brought the deadly virus home.

In response to her escalating anxiety, Jane stopped sleeping with Bill and made a concerted effort to renew her closeness to Andrew. When Bill became romantically involved with another woman, Jane felt wounded but ultimately relieved. In the months that followed, Bill became increasingly committed to his new lover and Jane's attachment to him lessened. She still revealed nothing of the affair to Andrew, though, because she was afraid to do so so soon after its occurrence. "Later . . . " she promised herself. And at other times, "What's the point of bringing it up? It's over."

Several months later, about a year after her relationship with Bill first heated up, Jane finally told Andrew about the affair. Helene had been pushing her to get the truth out into the open, because the secret was at Andrew's expense in their close threesome. Jane did not reveal the details easily, or in one sitting, but she did begin the process of laying the facts out on the table. Andrew felt enraged and devastasted, but their relationship survived and deepened over time as they ultimately learned to request more from each other in the way of intimacy and self-disclosure.

* * *

An affair is a big secret because increasingly, and in ever-widening circles, it causes the persons involved to operate in a "pretend" way in their primary relationship. The longer Jane continued her emotional and sexual involvement with Bill, the more censored and less centered she felt with Andrew, so that eventually she was physically but not emotionally present in her primary relationship. She often *appeared* to be attentive, because her efforts to be solicitous to her partner increased in direct proportion to her growing anxiety and guilt about the betrayal. But her solicitousness was more deliberate than spontaneous, more tacked on than deeply felt.

In his book *Private Lies*, the family therapist Frank Pittman notes that it is the secrecy more than the sexiness in an affair that creates distance and disorientation in a marriage or primary partnership. The secrecy also helps make the lover a more emotionally compelling partner than the spouse. Typically, the lover knows all about the spouse, while the spouse knows nothing—for certain. The sharing of facts and feelings can be relatively free and uncensored with the lover, while the opposite is true with the spouse. No matter what the potential for intimacy in a marriage, it is impossible to feel close to a person one is hiding from, confusing, throwing off track, deceiving.

Thus, the very way the three players are positioned in this triangle keeps the spouse in an outside and increasingly distant position. Pittman's advice to men who have fallen in love with the "other woman" is: "Bear in mind that a man feels closest to whichever woman shares his secrets. And he feels uncomfortable around anyone to whom he's lying. If you've been deceiving your wife while sharing your innermost thoughts and feelings with your affair partner, of course you will feel in love with her and out of love with your wife.

This is why having an affair—although it is not a loving thing to do—does not necessarily mean you don't love your wife. See what happens when you tell your wife the truth and start lying to the other woman." Pittman concludes that the issue is less whom one lies with, than whom one lies *to*.

The Unconscious Seeks Truth

What made it impossible for Jane to continue her double life? Some of us continue in one or more affairs over several years, even decades, never coming clean with our partners. Infidelity may be congruent with our family and cultural legacy, or sanctioned by our social group and close friends. Or, we *believe* one way and *behave* another, without allowing ourselves to acknowledge the incongruity between our beliefs and actions. We compartmentalize our experience, keeping contradictory beliefs and behaviors separate, so that they don't rub up against each other and cause us trouble. And, of course, all of us have a refined ability to rationalize, to fool not only others but also ourselves.

Jane, however, was not wired this way. She was committed to monogamy and, even more strongly, to honesty. When she found herself first having an emotional affair with Bill, and later a sexual relationship, she did not engage in multiple self-deceptions to comfort herself. She did not tell herself, "If Andrew doesn't know, it won't affect him," or, "My attraction to Bill livens things up in bed with Andrew, so it's not such a bad thing." Jane knew she owed Andrew the truth. She believed everyone has a right to live life based on facts rather than deception.

At the same time, Jane felt in her guts that she needed to allow her relationship with Bill to develop, unimpeded by

Andrew's emotionality. "I needed to do what I needed to do," she later explained, "so I just couldn't tell." Still, being deceptive—even toward an end Jane viewed as necessary or irresistible—violated the dictates of her conscience. The contradiction between her values and her behavior eventually took an emotional toll.

Jane did not exactly think her way out of this moral dilemma—that is, her decision to back off from Bill was not made from the neck up. One might say that Jane's unconscious, speaking through her body, ultimately pushed her to set limits with Bill and later to tell Andrew about him. When our behavior violates our core values and beliefs, our unconscious and our body seek truth. If we ignore a signal—in Jane's case, anxiety—we may receive a bigger one, and then a more urgent one still, until we are forced to pay attention.

As Jane failed to put limits on the intensity with Bill, or to talk to Andrew about him, she experienced increasingly higher levels of anxiety. When she could no longer contain her anxiety, she established a potentially unstable triangle by confiding in a friend who was also best friends with Andrew. She subconsciously chose a confidante who would kick her anxiety higher; she now worried constantly about how long Helene would keep the secret at Andrew's expense.

Jane persisted in trying to ride out the anxiety without letting go of Bill, or telling Andrew, but it didn't work. Her sleep was disrupted by an anxious, obsessive preoccupation about bringing death home in the form of AIDS. At this point, Jane stopped having sex with Bill and moved toward Andrew. If Jane had continued her relationship with Bill, she might have gotten herself "caught," as so frequently happens when anxiety about betrayal mounts. Or she might have developed a more severe emotional or physical symptom. A friend quotes her old country doctor as saying, "If we do something wrong and pretend to ourselves that we don't know what we are doing, we will get very sick—physically, or in our head, or both."

Of course, we all know people who do not seem to feel guilty enough in response to lying and deceiving others. Some of these people occupy top governmental positions— or share our beds. At one time or another, we ourselves may fall into this category. Sometimes, however, guilt is there, unfelt and unacknowledged until triggered by time or circumstance:

A business executive once sought my help for severe depression after the death of his fifteen-year-old son. He had been having an affair with his assistant over a period of several years, and experienced no apparent guilt or remorse for lying endlessly to his wife. But one evening while he was enjoying a clandestine romantic dinner with his lover, his son was struck and killed by a truck while jogging.

On learning of his son's death, this man felt such intense anxiety that he ended the affair the next day. Then he told his wife everything en route to the funeral. He did not examine his motivation for telling, nor did he consider the matter of his timing. His "honesty" was a reflexive attempt to lower an unmanageable degree of emotionality that threatened to overwhelm him.

When I saw him during his period of crisis, his mourning for his son was complicated by his fantasy that his behavior had contributed to his son's death. He had arranged for his assistant to be transferred, and the thought of ever having another affair was beyond his imagination. A year later, however, he had formed a new sexual relationship which he kept secret from his wife. His initial self-disclosure had been motivated by an acute state of panic, not by anxiety that signals a violation of well-integrated values and beliefs. Most importantly, he and his wife had not looked honestly at their own relationship following the disclosure of the first affair. Instead, they had reacted to their traumatic loss by moving even farther apart into a position of entrenched distance.

Finding Out . . . Then What?

Why a secret comes out into the open is less important than what happens after it is discovered or revealed. The discovery of an affair can wreak havoc on a marriage, or it can strengthen it, depending on the commitment of both partners to honesty and to each other.

Andrew initially felt devastated by Jane's involvement with Bill. He and Jane alternated between explosive interchanges, marathon late-night talks, and passionate lovemaking. These heightened levels of both positive and negative intensity surprised them both by enlivening their relationship at a time of crisis. Yet emotional intensity, either positive or negative, is often an anxiety-driven response, more likely to impede than foster clear thinking about the relationship. Despite being a necessary first step in processing the pain of sexual betrayal, it is no more than that.

How does a couple process infidelity and rebuild trust? For starters, Jane and Andrew recognized how very distant their relationship had become prior to the affair. They both had become lazy about paying attention to each other. Andrew, for example, was not registering important information about his partner, including obvious signals during the time of the affair that something was different or "not right." When we aren't receiving and processing information from the other person, we become dishonest with ourselves.

We are all responsible, in part, for how our relationships go; we may collude with or even invite dishonesty. But Andrew neither caused Jane's affair nor could he have prevented it. Most importantly, Andrew and Jane used the revelation of the affair as a springboard to deeper levels of truth-telling and self-disclosure. The affair served as a vivid reminder that sexual temptations are a reality of life, especially, but not exclusively, when a primary relationship is distant. Denying that one's partner, or oneself, is vulnerable to powerful outside attractions is a form of sleepwalking. Jane and Andrew both decided they would keep the subject of sexual and romantic attractions in their consciousness and conversation, while trying not to overfocus anxiously on each other. They recognized that trusting each other—when "trusting" meant taking each other for granted and not paying attention—was not useful.

The dishonesty and secrecy of Jane's affair made it intolerable to Andrew, and he wanted to know the facts, no matter how painful. How could they establish an emotional climate in which honesty about sexuality was increasingly possible? Toward this end, they renewed their promise to each other to openly share any outside attraction before acting on it. This would include revealing strong emotional and romantic attractions, not just genital ones. The one listening would try to respond with honest feelings, without punishing the other for honesty by becoming overly reactive or controlling. Both would feel free to ask each other about outside attractions, and to remind each other that honesty, not monogamy, was their most important shared value.

In her book *The Monogamy Myth*, Peggy Vaughan underlines the fact that we cannot assume monogamy without discussing it, nor can we assure it by extracting promises or issuing threats. Only honesty can create the groundwork for monogamy. Attractions kept secret from a partner are far more likely to intensify and be acted on.

In keeping with their goal of increasing intimacy, Andrew eventually asked Jane for more detailed information about her sexual and emotional experiences with Bill. Although it was painful to hear the details, Andrew knew he would do better with the facts than with fantasies and fears. As Andrew gradually asked the questions that he was ready to hear answers to, Jane refined and expanded on the truths she shared. In turn, Andrew told more about his own sexual history and fantasies. He had a few transgressions of his own to share.

Andrew talked to a few good friends and supportive family members about Jane's affair, enlisting their much-needed empathy and support without inviting them to come to Jane's defense or to side against her. He learned as much as possible about how others manage the crisis of infidelity, whichever side of it they are on, and about the more general issue of sexual attractions outside committed relationships. Jane did the same. How did her sisters experience and deal with sexual temptations outside their marriages? What beliefs and values did others have about telling or asking their partners about their sexual feelings and fantasies? What did her good friends expect from themselves and their partners in the way of sexual truth-telling? Where did people draw the line between privacy and secrecy?

As Jane and Andrew engaged other people in deeper levels of conversation, both were surprised by the remarkably diverse beliefs about sexual honesty they encountered. These differing perspectives helped each of them to refine and clarify their values on the subject. Being open with others was a crucial part of the process of being more open with each other.

* * *

Individuals hold very different views about what constitutes honest and appropriate self-disclosure between sexual partners. We each have our own "philosophy" on the subject, even if we don't articulate it to ourselves or our partner. What one woman deems essential information about her spouse or lover another woman may consider irrelevant, inappropriate, or invasive.

Consider, for example, two very different perspectives voiced by Jane's sisters, women who otherwise shared similar values and worldviews. On matters of honesty and fidelity, Bess is concerned only about what her husband does. Mary Anne, in contrast, cares primarily about whether her husband is *emotionally* present in bed.

In Bess's words: "My only rule is that George keeps his hands off other women. It's like that old saying, 'It doesn't matter where his appetite comes from as long as he dines at home.' I don't want to know who he's thinking about when we're having sex and I would never ask him. Fantasies are private and I can't see anything useful in sharing them. George can think about the Pope if he wants to, as long as he's in *my* bed and no one else's."

In Mary Anne's words: "I would feel most betrayed if Sid had an affair of the heart—even one he didn't act on. Last year Sid was infatuated with a woman at work and for months he was thinking of her every time we made love. It was incredibly painful for me *not* to have this information and to learn about it much later. It was also dishonest of Sid to keep this secret from me. Now we have an agreement to talk when this happens. We don't share every passing fantasy about another person or grill each other after sex. But when a fantasy gets so heavy or persistent that one of us isn't really *present* with the other in bed, we tell. When we're open about it, we get through the problem and become close again."

Mary Anne demands more in the way of intimacy from her husband than Bess does. This difference between them is not a matter of "right" or "wrong," "better" or "worse," because there is no correct amount of closeness or distance for all couples, or even for a particular couple over time. It is useful, however, to be clear about our own beliefs and expectations about sexual honesty and to act accordingly. We are never guaranteed that the other person will tell us the truth, but if we want *really* to know, we need *really* to ask, over time and from the heart.

The Monogamy Paradox

Jane and Andrew responded to the crisis of betrayal by deepening their connection to each other. A more typical response, however, is to try to control a partner or swear him or her to monogamy. Naturally, we may *want* our partner to swear fidelity, but none of us can make an absolute promise about what we will or won't do over the course of a lifetime. To do so is again a form of pretending. When people marry, they take an oath in front of God and everyone to forsake all others; yet statistics suggest a very high incidence of both divorce and extramarital sex. There are well over a dozen species of mammals (including wolves and gibbons) more monogamous than our own. We tend to desire both the security of a lifetime partner and the excitement and liveliness of sexual and emotional variation.

Societal untruths about monogamy (like that one that it

is the only normal and normative way to live for everbody) invite us to be less than honest with ourselves and our partners. Another cultural myth inviting dishonesty is that the "real reason" behind an affair is a faulty spouse or bad marriage. True enough, marital distance and discontent is often managed by overinvolvement with a third party, be it a lover, child, therapist, or whomever. But affairs, like other triangles, are often a reflexive response to anxiety from any hidden source.

Jane, for example, began sleeping with Bill as she approached the age of her dad when he died in a work-related accident. People commonly begin affairs on the heels of an important loss or, as in Jane's case, at the anniversary of an earlier one. Lying about an affair may signal that a more anxious emotional issue is unacknowledged or unaddressed.

The myth that we are a perfectly monogamous species, and that affairs are terrible aberrations that never happen among good people in loving relationships, encourages self-deception and denial ("My partner is never attracted to other women"), isolation and shame ("I wouldn't want anyone to know that my husband betrayed me"), and exaggerated feelings of personal responsibility and failure ("What was wrong with me that he needed to go outside the relationship?"). As a result, many people are hesitant to talk openly and frankly about the reality of affairs, both before and after they happen.

While Jane and Andrew responded to the crisis of betrayal by working toward deeper levels of honesty, not all couples respond similarly. The following sequence of events is more typical:

Rosa called for a brief consultation after learning of her husband's infidelity. She told me that several months earlier she had become suspicious about a "funny distance" in her marriage. At the time, she grasped her husband by the shoulders, looked him in the eye, and said firmly, "John, I have a very strong feeling that you are having an affair. If you are, I want you to know that I'm leaving you. I really need to know the truth about this."

John said, "Nothing is going on," so when Rosa later discovered a different truth, she was outraged. "It's unbelievable," she told her friends, "that John lied in the face of such a direct confrontation." Rosa did not ask John questions about this relationship but insisted that he end it, which he did. Then she asked him to swear, over and over, that he would never again be unfaithful. John renewed his vow to Rosa and she reiterated her bottom line: "If I ever find out that you're screwing someone, we're finished, no questions asked!" To me, she said, "I can't get over feeling devastated. I wonder, and I wonder, how I'll trust him again."

Of course Rosa wondered. Threats and promises do nothing to guarantee fidelity or bolster trust. Nor can we ensure that a partner will remain monogamous forever. What we can do, though, is work toward establishing increasingly greater levels of honesty and open communication in a relationship, which is the only foundation on which trust can be built. Rosa did the opposite. The rigidity and finality of her ultimatum ("If I ever find out . . . we're finished!") only served to invite deception, shut down the lines of communication, and make future affairs more likely.

Paradoxically, monogamy becomes more attainable when we honestly recognize that we can't guarantee it. Then we can talk openly about the fact that strong attractions, and affairs, occur in the best of marriages. Future temptations may well arise for both Rosa and John, depending on opportunity and circumstance. Rather than saying, "If it happens again, I can't take it," Rosa might say—as Jane did—"Of course, temptations will be there again . . . perhaps for me as well. I want us to be able to talk about it. And I want to do my part in making such conversation possible."

Rosa could not sanction extramarital affairs because she required monogamy to feel comfortable in her marriage. When I first saw her in therapy, however, she could find no middle ground between accepting infidelity or immediately bolting. Through our work, Rosa took a new position with John. She asked him to talk openly about attractions before they were acted on, and to tell her the facts directly if he did have sex with another woman. She told him, "Of course, it would be devastating to hear the truth from you. But I would stay in the marriage long enough to struggle with the issue and to try to get some clarity about it, so we could make a thoughtful decision about where we would go from there. If I discovered you were having an affair and lying to me about it, our marriage would be in far greater jeopardy."

As Peggy Vaughan emphasizes, there is a huge difference between issuing threats about what we would do if our partner is not faithful, and asking for a commitment to honesty—not only about present and future sexual attractions but also about all emotional issues affecting our relationship. Trust evolves only from a true knowledge of our partner and ourselves and a mutual commitment to increasing levels of sharing and self-disclosure. Monogamy can neither be demanded nor taken on faith.

Not all "honest sharing" is motivated by the wish for greater intimacy and deeper levels of self-disclosure with a partner. A friend of mine was married to a man who, early in their marriage, described his lusty fantasies for other women in vivid detail. His wife initially felt jealous, then alienated and put off. When she told him so, he did some soul-searching and recognized that these provocative communications reflected his insecurities and created distance.

Several years later, he approached his wife about his intensifying feelings of sexual attraction to his business partner. He was, as he put it, becoming intoxicated. He was scared to open up this conversation with his wife, but felt it was a matter of conscience to do so. His self-disclosure was fueled by his commitment to keep his marriage primary and to detoxify and defuse the power that attractions have when kept secret. He also wanted to create the conditions in which he would be least likely to act on his desire. Telling his wife ensured that she would continue to ask questions and express her pain. It ensured that he would consider her, even during those moments when he might prefer not to.

His wife, to her credit, recognized that her husband's honesty reflected his wish to protect their marriage and keep himself in line. Thus, she did her best not to distance herself from him, or try to control him, or otherwise punish him for his truth-telling. While her gut reaction to his disclosure was a fight-or-flight one, she managed to move toward him with love, while sharing her own feelings of threat and hurt.

To Tell or Not to Tell

The cost of confessing a sexual betrayal is obvious and immediately felt. In telling, we deal with our partner's pain and rage, with our own conscience or lack of it, with a lengthy process of reviewing and rebuilding intimacy. If the affair is ongoing, we can no longer have our cake and eat it too; either we end the affair, or deal with the consequences of refusing to do so, or else resume lying again.

In telling—in extending the possibilities of truth between two people—we also open the door for greater integrity, complexity, depth, and closeness in a relationship. Concealing an affair, even when it is long past, brief, and unsuspected, creates a subtle distance, disorientation, and emotional flatness in a relationship. Apart from issues of morality and conscience, concealing or confessing an affair has a great deal to do with the amount of distance we want or will tolerate in a primary relationship. And when we say, "I can't tell, because it will cause him too much pain," what we really mean is, "I don't want to deal with his pain and anger"—which is a different matter.

Whether we tell, or are told, also depends on the spoken or unspoken "contract" that evolves between spouses or intimate partners. We may communicate, as Rosa did, that we had better not find out about an affair because we couldn't take it. We may say this explicitly or we may convey it through our failure to ask questions that will allow us to know our spouse better as a sexual human being.

There is nothing wrong with communicating to our partner that we do not want the entire truth at a particular time about sexual fidelity, or any other issue. Being honest about our vulnerability, and our wish to be spared the whole story, may be a self-loving and self-protective act. Whatever the subject, we can be direct with others about what information we want and are ready to handle. Obviously we do not share information that may evoke violence or precipitate abuse.

But we should be clear with ourselves that extended silence ultimately invites secrecy (which requires lying and deception to maintain it), not only about affairs but about other emotionally painful issues that affect a relationship. It is simplest, of course, to ask our partner to conceal from us what brings pain, to spare us from the truth. But if we go along with such a contract, we narrow the possibilities of truth-telling and connection between two people.

12

The Body Seeks Truth

Some folks have bodies that won't let them lie. Or perhaps, more correctly, some folks *are* bodies that won't lie. A friend reminds me that we are our bodies. We don't just reside in them, like borrowed or rented space.

This friend is an honest body. He had a one-night stand and then confessed it to his wife the following evening, not from choice but from necessity. He cried rather than slept after it happened. He went through the motions at work the next day, feeling exhausted and nauseated. "I felt like I had the mental flu," he told me, when I asked him about the timing of his disclosure. "So I just collapsed into bed and waited for my wife to ask, 'What's wrong?'"

He didn't reflect on the timing of a revelation determined only by the extent of his own distress. His timing, in fact, was lousy, because his mother-in-law was visiting from Philadelphia and was inescapably drawn into private business. But reflecting on his actions, or even waiting to reveal them, wasn't an option. He couldn't have bluffed his way through his symptoms without engaging in further deception.

His wife, also a friend of mine, was distraught. I could empathize well enough with her shock, anger, and pain. But I also found myself thinking, "I'd vote for this man for president. I, for one, would sleep better at night if we had a president with an honest body. A president who *was* an honest body."

I don't know what combination of personal integrity and biological wiring brings on a mental flu, or why, for that matter, my friend's guts didn't kick up in protest *before* the act. I do know that his body (feeling nauseated and exhausted), not just his head, kicked him into truth-telling, just as his body (feeling aroused) contributed to his transgression.

In different contexts, this same friend can be a "natural liar." Once, I enlisted his help in an elaborate plot designed to throw my husband off track when a family surprise was being planned for him. My friend schemed, concealed, connived, and kept secrets with the rest of us. Despite my worry that his voice would crack, his face would turn red, or his body would otherwise leak the truth—he lied like a trooper.

But not when he had slipped into another woman's bed.

Most of us can count on our bodies, like the dreams of our unconscious, to at least *try* to keep us honest. If we engage in deceptions that violate our values, we may not immediately get a dose of mental flu, or even a jolt. But like Jane, who was sexually involved with her partner at work, we may get a little signal that changes into a bigger one over time if we fail to pay attention. Similarly, our bodies may react to the deceptions of others, as when a child becomes anxious, depressed, or otherwise symptomatic in response to a family secret.

Clark Moustakas's description of his experience with encounter groups illustrates how our bodies can grab us by the collars when our behavior is incongruent with our true values and beliefs. Moustakas, you may recall, was encouraged by his colleagues to try a more aggressive style of leadership. But when he experimented with pounding away at the defenses of others, his body gave him a pounding of its own. Ultimately, he couldn't ignore the physical signals which revealed that, at least for him, something was wrong with this confrontational style of leadership.

Our bodies react to our own deceit, even to a single incident of lying, particularly if we feel conflicted and guilty about it. These clues provide important nonverbal information to others in relationships. The last time I told an outright lie, I reflexively turned my face away while speaking, knowing that my expression might "give me away." Similarly, I rely on my reading of other people's bodies to detect deception, as we all do: I register what is popularly called "body language." I note obvious incongruities (my client says she's not angry but looks angry). I pick up subtle ones (my husband says he is paying attention, but I sense he's distracted). When a person's words tell me one thing ("I'm feeling close to you") and my automatic "knowing" intuits something different (I sense distance, a "not-thereness"), I put more trust in what my body registers than in the words I hear.

It's not surprising that our bodies register the lies and incongruities of others. Nor is it surprising that we respond with detectable physiological changes when we are dishonest and we know it. What is more remarkable is how the deceptions that we are denying or, indeed, living, sound a wake-up call to which the body responds. Turning points in my own life have occurred when my body has acted up to prod me away from a false path. A couple of instances stand out vividly.

The Body Protests

Early in my career I formed part of a multidisciplinary team in a psychiatric hospital. I was unhappy and believed I shouldn't be there. I had been told, however, that my skills as a psychologist were needed on this particular team and that I did not have the option of leaving. So I convinced myself that I must stay and that staying was the responsible thing to do. I redoubled my efforts to be heard, but I felt ineffective in that particular context.

During staff meetings, I became increasingly tense but decided this was life. After all, no one has a perfect job. I differed theoretically and personally from the psychiatrist in charge, but I reminded myself that differences present a challenge as well as being a fact of existence. Then I began to nod off during staff meetings. My struggle to stay attentive and involved became so intense that I was constantly battling sleepiness. Paradoxically, sleepiness was itself a "wake-up call," and I finally got the message. In the midst of this turmoil, I had a health scare, which proved to be a false alarm but provided me with the final incentive to find a way out. I became inventive and created a new career option where I had believed none existed.

At an earlier turning point in my life, my body gave me a more dramatic signal that I was about to make an important wrong turn. I was a graduate student in clinical psychology, living in an apartment on New York's Upper West Side. Eager for love and marriage, I became seriously involved with a fellow graduate student who met the checklist of qualifications I was looking for. He was bright, funny, ambitious, kind, fair—an all-around wonderful person. We shared similar interests, from playing the guitar to our love for psychology. But I didn't love him passionately or even romantically. And at the time I couldn't get clear about how much this mattered.

He was a terrific buddy and I felt comfortable in bed with him. I don't know whether my lack of passion was a matter of chemistry or one of circumstance. He and I had shared a "previous life" together on East 9th Street in Brooklyn. During my early teens, he had been pals with my friend Marla's older brother and we all had hung out together at Marla's house. Now, I couldn't separate out the old stuff from the man and woman we had become. But I thought I should because I didn't see anyone better out there.

I have never been an indecisive person, particularly not in matters of the heart. For the first time in my life, I understood how excruciating it is to feel suspended in a state of ambivalence and confusion. Should I break up with this man or marry him? I wanted to avoid doing either for the wrong reasons. I had met a number of attractive men at Columbia University who stirred more passionate and romantic feelings. But after dating them briefly or knowing them more intimately, none was, as I put it back then, "a really good catch."

I did everything I could think of to clarify the matter. I talked to countless people and solicited their advice and perspectives. I weighed the pros and cons. I tried to envision the future and to imagine worst-case scenarios. I also tried to be silent and meditative, to listen to the wisdom of my own soul. But I kept swinging first one way, then the other.

Eventually, there came a point where I could no longer tolerate the situation. After carefully considering everything I could think of, I decided to make marriage my goal. I resolved to stop looking around and to make a full emotional commitment. And I believed, by all objective criteria, I was doing the right thing. All logic, all rational thought, urged me to hold on to this man and "work on it." That night, I fell asleep feeling relieved.

But when I awoke the next morning, I was so depressed I could hardly rise from the bed. I had never felt so depressed, nor depressed in that particular way. It was paralyzing, but it didn't last through the day; it lasted just long enough for me to get the message.

My body was warning me about my self-deception and pretending. It was proving false what I was trying at the time to convince myself was true: "Passion eventually goes out of relationships, anyway"; "All relationships require compromise"; "My chances of finding someone better are slim"; "There is no perfect marriage." But I was deceiving myself. Without a crystal ball, I could never know which choice would ultimately prove "best" for me. But the absence of romance, or passion, or chemistry, or whatever, was too big a compromise to make.

Lying in bed that morning, heavy and immobilized, I knew I would never marry my friend. Yet for whatever reasons, I didn't have the strength, integrity, or will to end it then and there, or even to speak frankly with him. Instead, I behaved ambivalently, indeed, obnoxiously enough to bring about the inevitable. Shortly thereafter, he met and married a terrific woman who loved him without reservation.

The body, guided by the unconscious, can be a primary

source of personal truth and self-knowledge. We rely on this source of wisdom because the capacity for self-deception is extraordinarily well developed in our species. Women, in particular, are socialized as a class to pretend, to settle, and to call our compromises "life." Our bodies are harder to fool.

Interpreting Gut Feelings

"The body seeks truth," I tell a friend.

"The body misleads," she responds.

We know we're both correct, so we begin to refine our ideas further. We conclude that the body, seeking truth, sends a signal. But decoding it, interpreting its meaning, and knowing how to proceed from there is another matter entirely.

My friend, also a psychologist and psychotherapist, challenges me on the interpretation of my experience. We talk first about the example of my unhappy work situation and how it lulled me into sleepiness. She tells me about her experience, several years earlier, of becoming sleepy whenever a particular client talked about sexual abuse. Later, my friend uncovered repressed memories of sexual abuse in her own life that were similar to her client's: that is, for both women the abuse occurred while they were being bathed by their fathers. Sleepiness—like recurrent headaches, or other symptoms—is a signal to examine unconscious conflict, my friend says, not to leave the field.

The same friend challenges my interpretation about the immobilizing depression I felt after deciding I would compromise and marry without passion. "Who knows?" she asks. "Maybe it meant that you had conflicts about intimacy. Maybe you had an unconscious fear of commitment. Maybe your depression was a signal that you needed therapy to explore what was blocking you from a richer, more passionate response."

I'm not one to bolt from either love or work. I tell her simply, "I knew." That is, I knew in both instances what I needed to do.

Our conversation turns to a colleague, Sybil, who lives in California. Sybil, who is thirty-two years old, has metastasized breast cancer. My friend says that Sybil lives a compromised life, always withholding her honest responses, desires, and evaluations. She wonders if Sybil has chosen illness or death as a way out of an unbearable family situation that she can neither tolerate nor leave. My friend says, "I work frequently with breast cancer patients. They cannot begin to heal themselves until they uncover the meaning of the disease in their lives."

I have a powerful negative response to my friend's interpretation of Sybil's illness. It's not that I doubt a connection between our emotional and physical well-being. When we live unauthentic lives, our bodies may indeed give us a signal, in the form of illness or physical distress, that something is wrong. When our relationships or selves are severely compromised, our immune systems may also be compromised. Surely our bodies can only be strengthened when we live examined lives that include a large share of love, wisdom, truth, courage, and risk.

But I'm also convinced that Sybil, whom I met only briefly, did not cause her cancer. I don't believe that acquiring a life-threatening disease means that one hasn't lived authentically or truly enough. Following one's true path is undoubtedly a good and healthful idea, but it is no guarantee against getting cancer or preventing its return. I remind my friend that countless numbers of dishonest, fraudulent folks will continue to ripen to a mean-spirited old age while alarmingly large numbers of joyful, loving women will continue to die prematurely of breast cancer. From my perspective, it is profit madness—the poisoning of our soil, water, food, and sky—not personality deficit that is leading to a startling increase of cancer among the young people we know. It is our environment, not our psyches, I tell her, that demands a cleanup.

Despite our differences, my friend and I agree on one main point. The body may signal us, but it will not tell us how to interpret the signal. There is no instruction manual, no map. We both tentatively conclude that the body does not mislead. Rather, to be more accurate, *we misread*. We overanalyze, on the one hand, or on the other, we fail to pay attention at all.

Being in touch with our bodies, or more accurately, being our bodies, is how we know what is true. From moment to moment, we read our bodies so automatically that, like a cat, we don't think about it. We know, through our bodies, when we feel like sitting, or standing up, or leaving a restaurant. We know, through our bodies, whether we want to lie in someone's arms or just go to sleep. We know, through our bodies, whether a particular interaction leaves us feeling energized, uplifted, and inspired, or the opposite.

Our most direct route to self-awareness, to personal truth, is through the gut. We say, "I'm bored," or, "I want to be left alone." We say, "I love her," or, "I just don't trust her." We say, "I'm terrified." All this comes to us through the body.

Yet we do misread and lose touch with what we are feeling, especially when it threatens to overwhelm us or make

waves in our lives. We may misname our most basic emotions. "No, I'm not angry," we say, as we transform an unacceptable emotion into tears and hurt. Or perhaps we do it
the other way around. But even when we call it straight
("Yes, I'm furious"), emotions are only starting points. We
still must think about feelings, decode them, and decide on
the next step. The quest for truth has at its center the struggle to identify the body's deepest truths and to distinguish
these from automatic conditioned responses that begin in the
body and then mislead.

Take Anger, for Example

Anger is in the body, a signal worth attention and respect.
Perhaps we are doing more or giving more than we can comfortably do or give. We may be failing to clarify what we
expect from or will tolerate in a relationship. Or our behavior is incongruent with our stated beliefs: that is, we say we
can't live with something, but then we continue to put up
with it. Anger exists for a reason; it can inspire us to define
our own truths and to take a new and courageous action on
our own behalf.

But the opposite occurs as well, and just as frequently.
Anger creates tunnel vision that leads to a narrow, rigid view
of what is true and whose truth counts. Anger, like any
strong emotion, tells us that something is not right, but it
doesn't tell us *what* the real issues are, or even *with whom* the
real issues are, or how best to proceed. When we feel angry
and intense, we may be convinced that there is only one
truth, our own, and our job is to convince the other person
to see things our way.

Anger can sharpen our passion and clarity, but it can also

blur it. When we angrily confront another person, convinced that truth is on our side, we often move the situation from bad to worse. When anxiety is high, people divide into opposing camps and lose the capacity to see both—or better yet, four or five—sides of an issue. The capacity for empathy and for creative problem solving that considers the needs of all is diminished. The emotional climate may become increasingly intense, ensuring that people will have to struggle harder to uncover and share their own truths, to hear each other, or simply to stay in the same room.

Venting anger rarely solves the problem from which our anger springs, nor does it necessarily clear a wider path for truth-telling. When it comes to anger, or any form of emotional intensity, we will have difficulty distinguishing anxiety-driven emotionality from true feeling, and deciding what to do next.

Decoding anger, or even feeling it to begin with, requires a sense of entitlement and possibility. The challenge is not only to "get in touch with our bodies," but also to create a context that makes this awareness possible and that validates our response. For most of us, private experience has no name when there is no ear to hear it, no cultural legitimacy for what we feel in the gut.

One girl in my high school in Brooklyn often made a fuss about apparently trivial things that didn't seem to matter. Judy just couldn't leave well enough alone. "Why is God male?" "Why does she give up her name and go by Mrs. John Smith?" "Why should she hide her age, calling herself a girl?" We thought Judy was overreacting, always making something out of nothing. I don't think Judy was seeking political analysis back then; just validation for her own gut reactions. Looking back, I imagine that she felt sexism in her bones the same way an African-American man felt racism when he was called "colored boy," or told to sit in the back of the bus. But there was no word "sexism" back then, and the rest of us were in a coma. To be awake in a world of sleep-walkers is possible but never easy. So, like a child, or like a woman, Judy was seen but not heard.

Now, three decades later, my body can detect sexism like radar. I register it somewhere in my chest, before I have words to explain what is wrong or to justify my irritation. Today, the feminist analysis that begins in my gut is cheered and read by other women. I am privileged to be part of an extraordinary movement of women, raising questions like Judy's, rethinking and re-viewing everything, taking nothing as a "given." Some women still say, "Me? I'm not angry," or, "How trivial," but most of us say differently. I wonder what happened to Judy, who had no one to affirm or support her, or even to listen.

Anxiety and Fear

Anxiety—like anger—requires interpretation. Like other messages from the body, the true meaning of anxiety may be obscured. Yes, we're anxious. But what is the danger? Is it past or present, real or imagined? Should we stop to consider it or try to ignore it? Are we feeling anxious because we are boldly charting new territory, or because we are about to do something stupid? Who is being served or protected by our fear?

Anxiety drives other emotions. When anxiety is high, we are most likely to fly into a rage or fall mindlessly in love. Or we may feel just plain scared. Anxiety, like anger, may propel us into action, but just as often it operates like a stop sign or a flashing red light that says, "Danger! Do not enter here!"

I've learned through experience (the name we give to our mistakes) to recognize and pay heed to a particular type of anxiety or tension as if it were a stop sign. My body is warning me to come to a halt because I'm off track. Perhaps I should not mail a letter or make a phone call, or rush into a particular conversation. Anxiety makes me think twice.

When I'm anxious, I become intense. I may feel an urgent need to confront a friend with "the truth," or, more specifically, to tell her what she is doing wrong. But when I feel this way, I've learned to wait, to see whether the need endures over the course of a day or two. Usually, the intensity dissipates because it's been driven by my own stress. Waiting also allows for a clearer intuitive response about how to put things and whether to even bother.

I've learned that I'm obnoxious when I offer unsolicited "truths" to friends at the time I feel most driven to confront them. I also distinguish between different sorts of emotional intensity. There's a difference, in my body, between an anxious, uncentered sort of intensity, and the passion—the fire in the soul—that lends energy and zest to friendship and work.

Sometimes I feel anxious and I decide to ignore it. If anxiety were *only* a warning sign, I might never show up for my mammogram, get behind the podium, or speak out when my heart is pounding. There are many occasions when I feel anxious or frightened and I just decide that I won't let it hinder me from doing what I need to do.

During a year when I was terrified to fly, or more accurately, terrified to crash, I crisscrossed the country on countless airplanes. Waves of anxiety washed over me as I imagined my plane, engulfed in flames, plummeting to the ground. These fearful imaginings began days before every departure, but I flew so much that my fear eventually went away. Another therapist with the same story says: "When people tell you they don't fly because they are afraid of flying, you need not believe them. They don't fly because they don't buy airline tickets."

We need to respect our anxiety and pay attention to what our bodies are trying to tell us through it. But we don't have to succumb to fear. Fear is women's worst enemy. And it is not by accident that we are taught to fear. Fear serves to paralyze women, holds us in place, saps our energy and attention from important work, and limits our creativity and imagination. Fear keeps us close to home. It silences us. And if we wait until we are unafraid, or fixed, or analyzed, we may have waited too long.

In Audre Lorde's book *The Cancer Journals*, she speaks eloquently on this point. "I realize that if I wait until I am no longer afraid to act, write, speak, be, I'll be sending messages on a Ouija board, cryptic complaints from the other side. When I dare to be powerful, to use my strength in the service of my vision, then it becomes less important whether or not I am afraid." She warns us not to allow our fear to fossilize into silence because imposed silence in any area of women's lives is a tool for separation and powerlessness.

Audre Lorde makes no claim to have banished fear entirely. In describing her response to the crisis of breast cancer, she tells us that fear remains an uninvited companion, but one that she refuses to surrender to, or to dissipate her energies fighting. Breast cancer heightened Lorde's clarity about the necessity for women to break our silences, to scrutinize and speak our truths. She exhorts us to work and speak when we are afraid, just as we work and speak when we are tired. "For we have been socialized to respect fear more than our own needs for language and definition, and while we wait in silence for that final luxury of fearlessness, the weight of that silence will choke us."

Our silence, Lorde reminds us, does not protect us. Women can be silent our whole lives for safety and we will still die. Our invisibility on matters both personal and political may help us to feel less vulnerable, but not, in the long run, less frightened. "We can sit in our corners mute forever while our sisters and our selves are wasted, while our children are distorted and destroyed, while our earth is poisoned, we can sit in our safe corners mute as bottles, and we still will be no less afraid."

The body's first response to anxiety is not courage. Rather, when we are anxious, we seek comfort, which means doing what is reflexive and familiar. "Doing what comes naturally" can lull us into a psychic slumber, a life on automatic pilot where our commitment is to security and safety rather than truth and honor.

Dr. Sonia Johnson is a nationally prominent speaker, feminist author, and excommunicated Mormon who once ran for president of the United States. In her passionate quest to discover her own truths, she has never been stopped by the immensity of her fear. To the contrary, she has interpreted her experience of greatest terror as proof that she was mucking about in the deepest strata of patriarchal taboos. In working to strip herself of layer after layer of indoctrination, she became most distrustful of what initially felt deceptively natural, comfortable, safe, and right. Early in her feminist life, she learned that the first emotions she identified in herself at any given moment were not her genuine feelings. And in her quest to discriminate between her conditioning and her true feelings, she has over and over stepped into alien, lonely, and uncharted territory, no matter how great her terror.

I respect Sonia's courage for jumping off the high dive and creating a radically new vision of female reality. Her unraveling of all that patriarchy has taught as "true" and "real" has taken her on a couragous personal quest, which she generously shares in her books. In the process of inventing and discovering what is most authentic and alive within herself, she has discarded both relationships and sex, at least as the rest of us define these. Today, Sonia could no sooner return to her old beliefs than she could fit herself into the outgrown clothes of her youth.

Sonia's glorious leaps out of her patriarchally conditioned mind make almost everyone nervous. Even some of my more radical feminist friends have concluded that she has gone off the deep end. Sonia might happily agree, since she observed early on that truth is reversed in patriarchy, and thus to go out of our minds is to become most truly sane. Visiting her in the mountains of New Mexico, I found her to be anything but crazy. Rather, I felt admiration and love in response to her uncompromising commitment to free herself from patriarchial injunctions.

Yet I have no less respect for women who move slowly and cautiously on their own path toward greater truth-telling and self-discovery. Perhaps that's because I'm one of the slower ones. I believe that the direction of our lives is more important than the speed at which we travel them. Laying the groundwork for truth-telling can be a slow process for those of us who try to preserve both our connections and our integrity. Our bodies may not only protest deception but also warn us about the hazards of precipitous honesty.

Respecting Resistance

Maria sought my help at a time when she was struggling with a profound dilemma in truth-telling. She hadn't told her parents that she was living with an African-American man in a love relationship that spanned almost two years. Her partner, Cyrill, lost patience. At first, he encouraged Maria to tell her parents. Then he pushed her to do so. Now he was delivering an ultimatum: "Tell them the truth or I'm history." It was at this crisis point that Maria came to see me.

When Cyrill criticized Maria for keeping his existence and their relationship a secret from her family, Maria concurred and said nothing in her own defense. She told me that she hated herself for being a coward, yet she couldn't bring herself to tell her parents the truth because she feared their rejection. Cyrill argued that if Maria's parents rejected her, they weren't worth worrying about and that acceptance had no meaning when it was founded on deception.

Maria's silence violated her own values. Yet she felt paralyzed to act. A month earlier she had gone back home with the intention of telling her parents about Cyrill. She became so nauseated that she couldn't proceed with her plan. More than once, her body acted in protest—not of deception but of honest self-disclosure. Once she developed back spasms while having an imaginary conversation with her mother in which she told her about her love for Cyrill and their plans to eventually marry.

Maria thought that she should plow through her resistance. She compared herself unfavorably to Cyrill, who was not in hiding, even though his parents were vehemently opposed to their son dating or marrying outside his race and culture. Yet Maria felt frozen in place. Then, as we constructed a genogram of Maria's family and examined how differences were managed over the generations, her gut resistance began to make sense.

Families have differently patterned ways of managing anxiety and emotional intensity. Over four generations, Maria's family had developed a predominant way of navigating relationships under stress: emotional cut-off. Many family members did not stay connected in the face of differences. Instead, when people got mad, they might not speak to each other for, say, a couple of hundred years.

The stated "reasons" behind cut-offs ran the gamut from the sacred to the absurd. Maria's Irish grandparents, for example, never allowed her mother back into their home after she married out of the Catholic faith and converted to her husband's religion. Her father's siblings stopped speaking when they could not agree about the settlement of their deceased mother's limited estate. Maria's maternal uncles severed their ties following a feud about the sale of Amway products. A number of first cousins had never met because their parents weren't on speaking terms. Also, forgiveness was not culturally valued in their family. If someone did something bad to you, you weren't supposed to forget it. One prominent family therapist, herself Irish, jokingly call this the "Irish grudge syndrome."

Cyrill's family, like most, also had a difficult time managing differences. But while family members flared up in anger, there were no emotional cut-offs. In the end, blood proved thicker than water. Family was family, no matter how much you disapproved of, or gossiped about, your crazy relatives. As far as Cyrill knew, no family member had ever been extruded from the family because of a conflict or difference.

Both Maria and Cyrill faced a racist society. And both would have to deal with friends' and co-workers' reactions to their relationship. But they did not face the same family. How might Maria approach the challenge of truth-telling, considering the family legacy of cut-off? This was her challenge. As I saw it, her body was warning her to slow down and proceed with care.

And so she did. At glacial speed, Maria finally started to move. She began laying the foundation for truth-telling by first increasing the amount of contact she had with each of her parents. Before telling them about Cyrill, she initiated any number of conversations with family members about how differences were handled in the family. She inquired about relatives who had been excluded or "denied membership" because they believed or behaved differently. She told her parents how painful it would be for her if a family member didn't recognize her existence.

Most importantly, Maria entered into all these conversations with a loving heart and from an emotional space that was free from judgment or blame. Although she hoped for acceptance, she became increasingly less focused on needing her folks to change or respond in a particular way. When she did finally tell her parents about Cyrill, about two months after our initial meeting, she felt good because she was navigating her part of the process in a solid way. She didn't receive the acceptance she had hoped for, but neither was she cast out by her family.

In my work with Maria, I didn't want her to succumb to anxiety. I did, however, wish for her to respect it. The body, which is closely linked to the unconscious, has a particular wisdom about matters of timing. If we are absorbing too much anxiety, we may need to slow down or make a different plan.

The Body Stores Truth

The body not only seeks truth (again, to be distinguished from momentary honesty) but also, for want of a better word, it *stores* truth. When we're ready, our body may provide us with clues about painful truths that our conscious mind has repressed. Many of us receive the precious gift of memory through the body first.

Consider the matter of early sexual abuse and how we begin to remember: One close friend experienced "a tornado" moving up through her chest—an intense experience that took her by surprise as she casually thumbed through a book on incest. This physical reaction was her first awareness of a sexual trauma that occurred on a train when she was four. Another friend, in the course of psychoanalysis, began to experience a "suffocating feeling" in her throat, accompanied by difficulty swallowing. Along with her dreams (another primary source of truth and wisdom), her body was beginning to give her knowledge of a childhood experience of being orally sodomized by an uncle.

The body does not "forget." It is not uncommon for people to begin to uncover traumatic memories during movement, breathing exercises, deep massage, or various kinds of therapeutic body work. The profoundly wise body/unconscious "knows" what truths we can handle when and in what doses. The return of memory—along with the emotions surrounding early trauma—marks the beginning of transformation and healing. As we begin to recall an incident of sexual abuse, for example, our past and present lives make better sense and we view our world and ourselves with a new clarity. The gift of memory usually does not come to us first by "thinking things through," although thinking is essential in figuring out how to process new information and what to do next.

Of course, our mind/body/unconscious are not truly separate entities. Granted, we may *experience* the distinction, as in the examples I have described where the rational mind says, "Go!" and the body says, "No!" We may even describe different "ways of knowing" as if we were a composite of different selves that inhabited separate spheres.

For example, I ask an acquaintance about how she uncovers her deepest truths and she tells me about her intuitive self, her intellectual self, her spiritual self, and her body wisdom. She refers also to her "inner wise woman" and to "the child within," as well as to her "masculine" and "feminine" sides. These distinctions may be useful to her but they are not real. The categories we create reflect our limited understanding of the infinite and mysterious complexity of how we ourselves "know" and think/feel/intuit our own truths.

Love and Connection

Regretfully (or happily), there are no "how-to" guidelines for deciphering the body's signals. Obviously, we can "read" our bodies more accurately during a calm, meditative moment than during an anxious, frenetic time. And we will be in tune with our bodies only if we truly love and honor them. We can't be in good communication with the enemy.

Alienation from our bodies leads us to ignore signals as basic as those regarding hunger and touch. Few of us, for example, eat when we are hungry, stop when we are no longer hungry, or even recognize what our bodies are signaling to us. Instead, countless women are trapped in cycles of dieting and self-contempt that may last a lifetime. Our sexuality is similarly encumbered with emotional baggage. Many of us have difficulty staying "in the moment" and feeling whatever we are (or are not) feeling. Instead, we may prod our bodies to feel aroused or to achieve orgasm. Our attention may shift to how we look, what our partner is thinking, whether we are taking too long to get excited, to come, or whatever.

Over the past year or so, I have experimented with the challenge of listening to and regarding my body and refusing to push myself to do what I do not feel in the moment. I have not so much "succeeded" in these experiments as I have arrived at a deep appreciation for the layer upon layer of female conditioning that removes women from a truly loving, respectful connection with our bodies/selves and thus from a deeper knowledge of our power and personal truths.

As women, we are taught to hate our bodies and to disconnect from them. On my desk, for example, sits a full-page ad from two full-service hospitals. It features a glamorous young blonde in pink lingerie holding a single rose. *Life Looks Better When You Do*, reads the caption of the advertisement inviting women to begin the "natural" process of "Becoming" through plastic surgery. The "You're Becoming" program offers breast proportioning, nose improvement, face, brow, or neck lift, eyelid surgery, chin reshaping, ear modification, suction lipectomy for the reduction of localized body fat, and other corrective procedures to help women gain the "beauty, confidence and health" (yes, health) we wish to project to others.

There's no particular reason to single out the plastic surgery industry—or the cosmetic industry, the diet industry, the fashion industry, the pornography industry—as *the* problem. What we learn about "being a woman," being "like other women," and "satisfying male demand" involves massive deception, concealment, and self-betrayal that ultimately breeds shame, alienation, and disconnection from our bodies/selves, and even from our place in the life cycle. How extraordinary, for example, that we are told to withhold, to joke about, or even to lie about our age. How remarkable that any one of us would actually agree to mystify and conceal the number of years we have been alive, thus perpetuating the notion that there is something shameful or lesser in growing older, which is, after all, everyone's goal.

It is not only possible but natural for each of us to love our bodies, to find ourselves beautiful—no matter how different, disabled, old, or battle-scarred we may be. I love Audre Lorde's description of her decision to avoid prosthesis after her mastectomy, to go proudly into the world as a beautiful, one-breasted black warrior, to find the strength that came from her own perception of her body, and the courage to challenge what we learn is "normal," meaning the "right" color, shape, size, or number of breasts. I'm further inspired by a vision she shared more than a decade ago of an army of one-breasted women descending upon Congress and demanding that the use of carcinogenic, fat-stored hormones in beef feed be outlawed.

It is not any one thing we do: wearing clothes and shoes that constrict movement or comfort; covering our gray hair, wrinkles, and smells; kissing or embracing without connection or desire; eating when we aren't hungry. None of these things on any particular day is "a big deal." But the larger picture, the infinite ways we are taught that we do not belong to ourselves, may amount to a total erosion of connection with and love for our bodies and what they stand for.

We are all products of a culture, but we are also shapers of culture. Here is the oldest and deepest feminist challenge: to create the contexts in which we can define more authentically our own desires and aesthetics, and to be more connected to our bodies and how we wish to use them.

13

Will the Real Me Please Stand?

Pat Parker, a poet of humor and passion, once told a friend that she was waiting for the revolution that would allow her to take all her parts with her wherever she went—"not have to say to one of them, 'No, you stay home tonight, you won't be welcome, because I'm going to an all-white party where I can be gay but not black. Or I'm going to a black poetry reading and half the poets are anti-homosexual.'"

Parker, who died in 1989, did not spend her life sitting back waiting for such a revolution. Like countless women, she was creating it. "If I'm advertised as a black poet, I'll read dyke poems," she once said. Most of us are not so bold, but all of us can probably identify with Parker's words about leaving parts of ourselves at home.

It's not that women are openly exhorted to hide or silence important aspects of the self. Quite the contrary. Experts everywhere encourage us to express our "true selves," despite whatever anger or disapproval this might evoke from others. Such advice, which I myself have sometimes advocated, is both accurate and absurd.

It is accurate because living more authentically and truly is unarguably a good idea. The dictate "Be yourself!" is an agreeable cultural cliché—and as a friend of mine quips, no one else is as qualified for the job. Surely, there are times when we must gather the courage to clarify and stand behind our beliefs and values, even when doing so leaves us feeling separate and alone. And, undoubtedly, we all might benefit from accommodating less to others and becoming more attentive to our own inner voice.

But the advice to be one's true self, and to value one's true self apart from context and how others respond to us, is as absurd as it is advisable. For starters, we are relational beings who need approval and appreciation from significant people in our lives. Our wish to be valued, and to belong, is not excessive dependency but a basic, enduring human need.

Also, we don't have one "true self" that we can decide to reveal on the one hand or hide on the other. Rather, the particulars of our situations define, limit, and expand what we assume to be "real" and "true" about ourselves. Nor is there ever a point in human life when the self is "finished" or "set." Situations are always redefining who we are. It's not just a matter of what we present to others but also what we *become* within different contexts.

Take the workplace, for example. The story of Angela and Jan in Chapter 6 reminds us that people don't just bring their true selves to the job. Jobs also "create" people. You may recall that Angela behaved "like a woman" (affiliative, "people-oriented," and devoid of ambition) in a low-opportunity work setting. But she behaved more "like a man" when she was offered economic opportunity and status.

Similarly, men in dead-end jobs begin to resemble the

female stereotype. The sociologist Rosabeth Moss Kanter has pointed out that men in jobs with little or no opportunity for advancement "limit their aspirations, seek satisfaction in activities outside work, dream of escape, interrupt their careers, emphasize leisure and consumption, and create sociable peer groups in which interpersonal relationships take precedence over other aspects of work." In her book *Men and Women of the Corporation* Kanter demonstrates how the differing fate of men and women in the workplace is largely a matter of the structure of work systems themselves, rather than a function of psychological, biological, or socialization differences between the sexes. Many gender differences that we take to be "true" or "fixed" disappear, or even reverse themselves, when the context changes.

We can never unravel the tightly interwoven fabric of situation and self, because "self" does not exist in isolation. For example, the "feminine" traits, qualities, and behaviors identified as the "special" strengths and weaknesses of our sex are identical to those that characterize subordinate, oppressed, or disempowered groups. What, then, are we observing or measuring when we define a trait or behavior as "masculine" or "feminine"? Only after we begin to change our situations, or someone else changes them for us, can we appreciate how remarkably contextual is our "true self"—male or female.

A Seminar on the River

In a moment of either ignorance or courage, I accepted an invitation to join a group of colleagues conducting a seminar for business executives on the subject of how to understand human behavior. I had participated in these executive seminars before, as both a lecturer and a small group leader, so the work was not new to me. This particular seminar, however, would not be held at the familiar conference center on Menninger grounds. With the cooperation of Colorado's Outward Bound program, the week-long executive seminar would take us down the Yampa and Green rivers in Utah and Colorado. A core Menninger staff group had been conducting river seminars for some time and several had become veteran whitewater rafters. But this was a first for me.

On land or on water, women executives are a numerically scarce commodity. This posed a dilemma for our seminar staff, who had to determine the composition of the small discussion groups that would meet twice a day as a key part of the experience. As only a small fraction of our participant group was female, we had limited options for group assignments. We could sprinkle one or two women in each group; we could create two mixed-gender groups and twice as many men's groups; or we could put all the women together in one small group. I argued for the third alternative, and—as the only woman on the professional staff of this trip—volunteered to lead that group.

The first option (sprinkling a woman or two in each group) was objectionable to me because I was concerned about the negative impact of tokenism, a word used to refer to the intentional placement of a minority person in a visible position of power in a group or organization, so as to convey the appearance of inclusiveness when there is no real commitment to this goal. Tokenism, however, also refers to the *fact of numerical scarcity*, irrespective of how it came about or why it is maintained. The negative effects of tokenism need not reflect the questionable intentions of the leadership, but rather the skewed proportions of the group. In a skewed group where there is a large preponderance of one type of member over another, the "rare" individuals are tokens.

The handful of women participating in the river seminar were tokens in their work setting. Like them, I was a token in the Menninger staff group. By placing the women participants together in the small group, I argued, we could provide them with one context in which they would not continue to suffer that predictable fate within the group.

What is such a fate? Rosabeth Moss Kanter's careful research on tokenism is in keeping with my own observations of the behavior of the numerically scarce. Kanter reports that tokens often feel they have to "do better" while maintaining a low profile and playing down their successes. The fear of visibility often displayed by the numerically scarce is yet another way to understand the "fear of success syndrome" that has been observed in women and other marginalized groups. Numerically scarce individuals usually end up conforming to stereotypes—or bending over backward to fight stereotypes. In either case, the amount of "watchful effort" required often precludes the option of relaxing and being oneself.

Tokens typically show excessive loyalty to the dominant group culture and do not generate alliances with other tokens that might influence the group. The numerically scarce are unable to establish effective support systems among themselves and will meet resistance from their own kind when they attempt to do so. ("I just don't feel the need to meet together as women"; "What will people think if they see black people sitting together at lunch once a week?")

In the end, Kanter notes, tokens *underline* rather than *undermine* the dominant group culture. For example, exaggerated macho conversation is more likely to be displayed and tolerated in a skewed group than in one where women are either entirely absent or well represented. The flip side of such behavior is that those in the dominant group end up carefully "watching" what they say in front of tokens. Both macho talk and "gentlemanly" behavior highlight masculinity and isolate the women.

Tokens themselves unwittingly protect, rather than protest, the status quo. When women, for example, are included in token numbers in group life—medical school, say, or the military—they are viewed not as individuals but as representatives of their kind. The pressures to be "as tough as the boys" and to avoid doing anything "out of line" make it difficult to support or identify with other women. Also, the gratification of being viewed as "special" and the distinction of occupying a position previously denied to members of one's own group further increase the pressure to conform.

Kanter reports that as ratios shift (just over 2 to 1), tokens become a minority and have the possibility to behave differently: "Minority members can find potential allies in one another, can form coalitions, and can affect the culture of the group." Balanced groups (at a ratio of about 3 to 2 or better) put the least negative constraints on group members and offer the greatest possibility for people to behave naturally and be viewed objectively. As groups become balanced, people can begin to relate to one another as individuals rather than as "types" or representatives of a particular kind. Kanter's work suggests that tokens are unaware of the negative constraints of tokenism until after the relative numbers shift and they are no longer tokens.

A factor as apparently simple as relative numbers, then, profoundly shapes our experiences in group and organizational life, determining how much of our "true selves" we can experience and express. But mitigating the impact of tokenism was not my only reason for wanting to create same-sex discussion groups on the river trip. I knew that women's groups help women define themselves with imagination and without constraint, and I was experienced both as a facilitator and as a member of such groups. Men, too, would be "more themselves" in a men's group, rather than in a group that included one woman. The seminar leader agreed to the same-sex group composition and I was satisfied. I forgot that tokens identify with the majority culture and thus I assumed, mistakenly, that the female participants would share my enthusiasm.

Just Like a Woman?

I was entirely unprepared for the resistance I encountered when my small group met for the first time. The women, feeling like lower-caste citizens excluded from the real action, demanded to know why this act of segregation had occurred. Although the men were satisfied to be together, the women felt ghettoized. Their negative comments about our group's composition implicitly set the men up and put the women (i.e., themselves and me) down.

When I reported on my small group experience during an evening staff meeting, my colleagues voiced no surprise. Surely women tend to prefer the company of men. Haven't women always been complicitous with sexist attitudes, viewing their own activities as inferior to what men do? From this perspective, the women were simply behaving "like women." What else is new?

But did my group's negativity reflect their gender or their position as tokens? Was I observing something "natural" and enduring about women, or was I observing the outcome of an unnatural (i.e., numerically skewed) context? Contrast the river seminar experience with an activity such as a feminist conference, where women, rather than being tokens, are the creators of the group culture and the leaders who sustain it. What happens when tokens become dominants?

Here's one example: My friend and colleague Marianne Ault-Riché and I co-directed a national women's conference at Menninger from 1983 to 1990. Because the format included small discussion groups, Marianne and I struggled over the years with the dilemma of group composition. How should we distribute the handful of tokens (in this case, men) who participated in the conference?

Because we were familiar with Kanter's work on tokenism, we were committed to putting no less than three men together in a discussion group. Our first conference included two mixed-gender groups and twice that many all-female groups. Complaints were voiced by the women in the mixed groups, who were disappointed and angry that they were not assigned to women's groups. In the next two conferences, we put all the men together in one small group led by two male adjunct faculty members. Now the women were satisfied but the men complained bitterly. Even though the conference brochure stated clearly that participants would be placed in same-sex discussion groups, the men felt cheated, marginalized, and removed from the center of learning and the heart of the emotional experience. As would be expected from their position of numerical scarcity, their behavior was like that of the women in the river seminar.

From my perspective, the women in the river seminar were not behaving "like women." Rather, they were behaving like *people in a particular context*, one in which they were numerically scarce, one in which their "own kind" held no power (the executive seminars were created and led by men), and one in which their group leader was the newest staff member as well as the least skilled and most anxious about navigating the rapids and the wilderness. The members of my small group did transcend their initial disappointment. But we can never fully transcend the impact of tokenism. Tokens themselves may not complain, and may even feel honored to be included among the dominants. But we cannot begin to know what tokens do "naturally" in groups until the relative numbers shift and they are tokens no more.

Tokenism is just one of the countless variables that affect how "naturally" we behave in group life and what we take to be true or real about ourselves and others. But it is hardly a new or startling idea that we are continually influenced by context and circumstance—by power or the lack of it. Why elaborate on the obvious?

Most of us fail to appreciate how profoundly we influence each other and how larger systems influence us. Instead, we learn to think in terms of individual characteristics, as if individuals are separable from the relationship systems in which they operate. Obviously, we do have aspects of the self that are relatively stable and enduring, predictable, and even rigidly patterned. And some aspects of the self are not negotiable under relationship pressures. We do not, however, have one "true self" that we can choose to either hide or authentically share with others. Rather, we have multiple potentials and possibilities that different situations will evoke or suppress, make more or less likely, and assign more or less positive or negative values to.

What Counts?

When I was on the river, I learned how it felt to be the least competent and most frightened person in a work group. I enlisted for this trip without any prior camping or whitewater experience, and I was entirely unprepared for the grit and skill required for wilderness living and whitewater rafting. I was particularly unprepared for how slowly I learned outdoor skills in comparison to the seminar participants, who were both more experienced and far quicker to learn.

I had difficulty mastering everything from tying the gear securely into the raft to understanding what commands I should shout ("Right!" "Left!" "Stop!" "Backpaddle!") to guide my raft safely down the rapids when it was my turn to captain. As the week progressed and the wilderness became my "real world," I imagined what it would be like to live out my life in this setting. How would my experience of myself and my self-worth change in this context? Back home, my particular skills were socially and economically valued, while skills requiring physical ability were typically assigned a lesser worth. In the wilderness, these values were reversed: my individual talents were irrelevant to adaptation and survival and, in fact, seemed just plain unimportant.

As I struggled to start a fire, or tie a knot, or control my anxiety, I thought about how closely our definition of "what counts" is linked to time and place. My feelings of inadequacy reminded me of how difficult it can be to value ourselves when our own special talents and abilities are not "what really counts." Of course, one could argue that I was failing to consider context in viewing myself as hopelessly incompetent in the great outdoors. A friend who runs wilderness trips for women reassures me that, in the right setting, I could learn both confidence and skills on the water. I'm not convinced, but I suspect I would do better than I think I might, and worse than she imagines. In any case, I know it wouldn't come easily.

My river experience, like my conversation with Sue about my award ceremony, pushed my thinking about what counts and about who *decides* what counts. In the wilderness, doing things well is far more important than talking or writing well. But in our everyday lives, who determines "the truth" about the relative importance of our talents, interests, and skills? Who decides whose work and experience is worthy of attention and economic reward—and whose is not?

All of us internalize the dominant group's values, transmitted through family and culture, about who and what count. We may, to take just one example, question our intelligence without asking who has defined "intelligence," who benefits from this definition, and what other definitions are possible. A particular view of "the truth"—created by a specific group of people—is presented as representative of the whole, or as relevant to all humankind.

In my mother's generation, for example, I watched countless women discount their remarkable intelligence (or question their "IQ") because they never asked, "Who says?" Who says that a man is brilliant when he solves mathematical problems but fails to notice that someone in the room is crying? Who says that the ability to grasp the nuances of a social interaction is a lesser measure of "intelligence" than the ability to grasp the principles of engineering? Who says that the complex skills women traditionally excel in reflect "intuition" rather than intelligence?

Intelligence comprises more factors than we can ever begin to quantify; it includes such complex skills as the capacity for friendship, for empathy, for being perceptive, caring, alert, and emotionally present in the world. But the construction of standardized intelligence tests, like the construction of much of our reality, tells a different story—one that reflects racial, class, and gender biases. There are no universal, ultimate, or fixed "truths" about what constitutes intelligence. Nor can individual intelligence ever be captured by so arid a concept as IQ.

How then do we expand the possibilities of knowing what is "true" about our selves and our world? Only by recognizing how partial, subjective, and contextual our "knowing" is can we even hope to begin to enlarge it. Only as we understand that a very small group of privileged human beings have defined what is true and real for us all can we begin to pay attention to the many diverse voices (our own, included) that we have been taught to ignore. Only by viewing human behavior in context, by placing ourselves in new contexts, and by trying out new behaviors in the old contexts, can we begin to move toward a more complex truth about ourselves and others.

Who Defines Truth . . . and for Whom?

Feminist consciousness raising began with white, middle-class women awakening to the fact that privileged, white, Euro-American males defined the nature of things, including the nature of women and human nature itself. Yet amazingly (or perhaps not surprisingly), modern feminism repeated and mirrored old errors. In creating new truths about "women," the voices of dominant women silenced a diversity of female stories, as men had silenced theirs.

One needn't be a feminist scholar to observe that women differ from one another by virtue of age, race, class, physical ability, ethnicity, sexual orientation, and other factors that combine to form a filter or vantage point from which we define what is real or true. Less obvious are the ways that dominant voices submerge others, and purport to define what is true or real for all. Nor is it necessary to harbor discriminatory intentions to erase another's authentic voice, or to elevate oneself at another's expense. The process may be automatic and covert, a matter of who is included, in what proportions, and who is paying attention. Errors of exclusion and tokenism run deep, as my own experience illustrates.

When Marianne Ault-Riché and I organized the first feminist women's conference at the Menninger Clinic, our goal was to create a safe space in which to critique theory and share personal experience. We knew that the freedom to speak honestly and openly required a conference setting that offered a radical departure from patriarchal structures. Our first conference was called "Women in Context." Subsequent conferences focused on such themes as "Women and Self-Esteem" and "Mothers and Daughters." Marianne and I were proud of creating and co-directing a successful feminist conference series in our workplace.

Our self-congratulatory stance, however, was tempered over time. Minority women began to challenge the white, middle-class, heterosexual "culture" of the conference. Initially, I felt defensive and said things to myself like "But we *are* a white institution," and "I don't really know women of color who could lecture on this subject," and "Won't the quality of the conference suffer if we try to invite speakers of every race, class, and creed?"

These are the same arguments that privileged men use to exclude women, but the parallel didn't register. Similarly, Marianne and I were attuned to the dilemma faced by token males in the women's conference, but we didn't recognize the dilemma of the token females. As I recall complaining to Marianne, we surely couldn't be expected to create a space for *everyone's* story. Wasn't it sufficient that we had added African Americans and lesbians to our conference staff? How could we begin to make room for the multiplicity of female voices: Native American, Hispanic (Latina, Chicana, Puerto Rican, Cuban), Mexican-American, Asian, old, poor, disabled . . . The list was endless. I could imagine only problems rather than benefits from such rich diversity.

In fact, there is nothing wrong with any group of people getting together with their own kind to teach and articulate their own truths. Nothing wrong, that is, as long as they make no pretense of representing anyone other than themselves. As the philosopher Elizabeth Kamarck Minnich points out, both clear thinking and truth-telling itself demand that we name our sample or reference group. This is what Marianne and I had failed to do. Ours was not, in fact, a conference "on women," but rather an exclusive gathering organized by, about, and for women who were just like us.

When we attend a conference on "African-American Mothers and Daughters," we understand that the subject matter is partial and particular. There is no pretense of putting forth truths for all womankind. The very presence of the prefix or marker "African-American" acknowledges the existence of others whose experience may be different but no less central. As Marianne said in her introductory comments at our final conference, "We should have called our first conference, 'White, Middle-Class, Heterosexual Women in Context.'"

The point is not to divide the human family into endless categories and minute subdivisions. Rather, as Minnich illustrates in her book *Transforming Knowlege*, truth-telling (indeed, democracy itself) falters when we pretend that one group represents the variety of humankind by claiming generality, let alone universality. Admittedly, she notes, it sounds funny when dominants "prefix" themselves ("I met the most charming white male heterosexual banker last night") because dominants (whether dominant by virtue of gender, class, color, culture, numerical frequency, or all of the above) take themselves and their experience to be what is whole, real, inclusive, true, and important.

Thus the brochure on my desk promotes an upcoming panel on "Black Women Writers at Work." If the panel consisted of white males, it would be called "Writers at Work." As Minnich observes, the number of prefixes, or "markers," increases as we move down the traditional hierarchy. One can study "Women's History" or "Black Women's History" or "Black, Third-World Women's History."

But what of the white Euro-American heterosexual privileged male? His history is simply "history." His writing is simply "literature." He alone is not prefixed. He then, Minnich notes, becomes the generic human, the defining center, the one whose partial and particular truths are generalized to the whole. Meanwhile, as feminist scholars point out, the prefixed groups become "alternative," "nontraditional," "special interest," and implicitly "lesser than." Although these groups together compose the majority of humankind, as women now compose the majority of students on American college campuses, it is assumed that they can be covered by a course here and there, or the addition of a few works written by women or minorities in an otherwise unexamined curriculum ("Just add women and stir").

Marianne and I unwittingly replicated this error. We falsely believed that sprinkling a few minority voices throughout the conference *as we had designed it* would make everyone happy. When we finally co-directed an inclusive conference, giving real space to those women's voices long silenced and oppressed, I felt anxious and threatened. We did not all sit in a circle, hold hands, and sing "We Are the World." Significant differences emerged, including criticisms of our leadership. Some questioned whether a conference held in a white institution under the leadership of two white women was fully inclusive. Others questioned the politics of white women "giving space" in *their* conference to black women and others. In keeping with the research on tokenism, these important challenges did not emerge (and probably wouldn't have been heard) until there were significant numbers of minority women among us.

I learned more about myself in that conference, albeit through my errors, than I had in any other. And I gained a deeper appreciation of the fact that truth-telling is not simply a matter of individual insight or courage. It is, first and foremost, a matter of context. For context determines not only what truths we will feel safe to voice, but also what truths we can discover and know about ourselves.

Truth-telling demands far more than "honesty" and good intentions, as these are conventionally defined. It also requires us to relinquish our habitual, patterned modes of reaction and thought, so that we can move toward an expanded vision of reality that is multilayered, complex, inclusive, and accurate. The process requires us to be in conversation with other women similar to and radically different from ourselves. And it requires that the *context* of this conversation be a safe space where everyone can be herself, where no woman feels she must leave behind a part of herself (the African-American part, the lesbian part, the Jewish part).

A Category Called Woman?

Can we even begin to speak of "a common female experience"? Are there truths "about women" that include us all? Perhaps it's too early to make universal pronouncements. When family therapist Rachel Hare-Mustin complained as a child to her mother, "Everyone hates me!" her mother replied, "Everyone hasn't met you yet." Like Rachel, we haven't heard yet from all women, or even from representatives from all categories of women.

Of course, we all generalize. We do need to talk about "us," as my own use (and misuse) of the collective and unprefixed "we" illustrates. Talking about "us" helps create unity, solidarity, belongingness, and group identity. The recognition of common female experience moves us beyond shame and guilt, beyond pathologizing widely shared problems that are evoked by subordination. When *we* generalize about us ("Black is beautiful") we create more accurate, affirming, and empowering messages than when *they* generalize about us. This is particularly so if "they" are the dominant group. In the history of dominant and subordinate groups, the "truths" that dominants create about subordinates invariably serve to justify and maintain the status quo.

Generalizations about any group (women, Irish, Methodists, firstborns, schoolteachers) are useful when they help us appreciate the particular sets of filters through which different categories of people tend to see the world. At the same time, we cannot be too cautious about the generalizations we speak and hear. Who is doing the generalizing? From what sample? Who is served or disempowered in the process? Who is prefixed and who isn't?

Generalizations are particularly hazardous if they purport to tell us what is right or wrong, good or bad, normal or unnatural, for individuals who may or may not fit the generalizations constructed about their particular kind. Generalizations are stories that we become if we believe them. "Beware of the stories you tell," one psychologist warns, "for you will surely be lived by them."

We need also to pay attention to how generalizations can erase the experience of other human beings. I once spotted a famous runner on an airplane and asked him for an autograph for my younger son. He responded warmly and wrote: "To Ben, Run for Jesus." My family is Jewish, and I was startled both by this man's assumptions and by my own inability to speak up at the time. Later, I regretted that I hadn't gathered the courage to tell him we were Jewish and to ask him for another autograph.

Dominant, un-prefixed groups tend to think like the runner. I've done it myself, albeit in more subtle forms. Shortly after this experience, I gave a lecture on the West Coast that I called "Mothers and Daughters: The Crucial Connection." When I took questions from the audience, an African-American woman raised her hand and pointed out that what I had said was not accurate to her experience, and certainly not for black women in general. I told her quite frankly that I had little experience with black mothers and daughters. She said, "Well, if you're talking about white mothers and daughters, why don't you say so?"

I felt defensive and initially put off by this public criticism. Later I thought how courageous she was to make this point in front of a predominantly white audience. I also recalled my airplane experience and recognized that she was correct. How many times a day, I wondered, do groups like lesbians and disabled women face precisely this experience? How often do I construct generalizations about women that render an entire group nonexistent? How could I be complicitous with dominant thinking when, as a woman, I know exactly what it's like to be educated by dominants who make generalizations that don't describe me, on the one hand, or that fail to recognize my existence, on the other?

What part can we play in creating a world with space for more women to tell and know a more honest story? Those of us who have enough privilege to, say, put together an un-pre-fixed program (for example, "Motherhood in the Nineties") can use our privilege responsibly. If we are a panel of dominants, we can prefix ourselves ("Our panel will speak to you from the perspective of white, middle-class, married mothers—one perspective of many"). Better yet, we can also put together programs—or create spaces—that are inclusive and diverse. This is a difficult challenge because we tend to feel most comfortable huddled together with folks "just like us."

To the extent that we can make room for a rich weave of women's stories and voices, we will be better able to identify those universal threads that do unite us as women. Such unity will not be based on the silence, suppression, and shedding of difference, but rather on the recognition and celebration of difference. The truths that we then construct about the "I" and the "we" will be more complex, encompassing, richer, and accurate, as will be our lives.

Epilogue

When the Lion Learns to Write

There is a fabled tale about a little boy who questioned how Tarzan could have defeated all the jungle animals, including the mighty lion. The child's mother replied, "My son, you'll get a different story when the lion learns to write." Contained in her response are two valuable lessons in truth-telling. First, there is always more than one version of the truth. Second, the one with the pen (Freudian symbolism intended) is at the defining center and can tell a story that is (mis)taken to be inclusive, real, and whole.

At the center of a woman's life is the quest to discover, speak, and live her own truths, to cease living a life dictated and defined by others—that is, a life lived in another person's story. I hope I have inspired readers to reflect on the many faces of deception in our lives, and to consider the lies, secrets, and silences—our own and others—that affect us. I hope too, that the reader has learned something about the slow, bumpy process of truth-telling. Like peacemaking, truth-telling does not just "happen," or burst forth in our midst. Rather, it must be worked toward, plotted, and planned.

The struggle toward truth-telling is at the center of our deepest longing for intimacy with others. The poet Adrienne Rich speaks to this point in her notes on women, honor, and lying. It is not, she writes, that we have to tell everything, or to tell all at once, or even to know beforehand all that we need to tell. But an honorable relationship, she reminds us, is one in which we are trying, all the time, to extend the possibilities of truth between us, of life between us. She acknowledges that it is painful and exhausting for a woman to begin to uncover her own truths in a culture that validates only male experience, but that the politics worth having, the relationships worth having, demand that we go this hard route.

For women to go the hard route is to fly in the face of all that has been prescribed for us regarding possibility and place, to say nothing of good manners. It also requires us to protest the exclusion of women from public life. When we collude with the objectification, diminishment, and invisibility of women, we compromise all manner of clarity, truth, and honor.

As a dominant group, men have created for themselves many dehumanizing forces that block them from acting and reacting from an authentic center. There are, however, many categories of pretending in which men will not participate. Men will not pretend, for example, that words like "she" or "chairwoman" could ever truly include them. Men will not pretend that the works of womankind represent humankind. Men will not fail to notice when they are excluded from a particular subject, event, discourse, or governing body. In fact, most men have the opposite problem; they assume that to speak of women *is* to exclude them. (I'm often asked by men, "Why do you write books for women? Why do you exclude men?")

Truth-telling cannot co-exist with inequality. Our vision of truth is profoundly eclipsed by the loss of diverse voices and visions that give complexity, texture, and depth to what we name reality. Thus, it is not sufficient for us to stop lying to each other, to stop concealing the facts. It is also necessary for us to *include* each other and to create space for those voices, including parts of the self, that have long been silenced.

This is part of what it means to be an honest woman, at this particular time, in this particular place: We can take, or leave, what others insist is true for us and for our own good. We can pay passionate attention to our own experience, to the stories of other women, and to the voices of those men we have learned "don't count." We can understand the insep-arability of the personal and the political, because deception and duplicity thrive when certain groups and individuals have the power to elevate their own truths by diminishing, silencing, even eradicating, others.

Women make up over half the world's population, yet as a group we wield virtually no economic or political power and have no social authority. We have been taught to pretend that our special role as wives to men and mothers to children somehow accounts for this fact, or makes it tolerable or even natural. When women are fully represented and valued in every aspect of language, politics, and culture, the world will have different visions of what's true and what matters.

There is never a resting place in the struggle for personal and political integrity. When anxiety is high, and resources appear scarce, some individuals and groups will always operate at the expense of others. But we can long for and work toward that unrealized world where the dignity and integrity of all women, all human beings, all life, are honored and respected. More to the point, we can live *today* according to the values that we wish would govern the world in the hypothetical future we are working for. To honor diversity, complexity, inclusiveness, and connection in our lives now is to widen the path for truth-telling for everyone.

Notes

1 Tony and the Martians

1   Thanks to Marla Beth Isaacs for our friendship that has lasted since the first grade.

2 Deception and Truth-Telling

9–11   Drawing from the theoretical perspective of Murray Bowen, Stephanie Ferrera has written an excellent paper that discusses human deception in the context of deception in nature. See "Deception in Nature and the Family" in *Midwest Symposium on Family Systems Theory and Therapy*, May 1991 (Center for Family Consultation, 820 Davis Street, Suite 221, Evanston, IL 60201).

11   The examples of deception in nature are reported from the *St. Louis Post-Dispatch*, Section D, March 12, 1991, p. 1. Among those authorities quoted on a biocultural approach to deception are the theologian Loyal Rue, the molecular biologist Ursula Goodenough, and the anthropologist Robert Sussman. Readers interested in deception in nature, see Robert Trivers, *Social Evolution* (Menlo Park, Calif.: The Benjamin/Cummings Publishing Company, 1985); and R. W. Mitchell and Nicholas S. Thompson, eds., *Deception:*

Perspectives on Human and Nonhuman Deceit (Albany: State University of New York Press, 1986).

11   Trainers, notes Vicki Hearne . . . : From Vicki Hearne, *Adam's Task* (New York: Vintage Books, 1987), pp. 8–9. Hearne, an English professor, poet, and professional animal trainer, has written a remarkable book on animal–human encounters which begins with a discussion of the anthropomorphic, morally loaded language of trainers and the conflicting world of intellectual and academic discourse.

3 To Do the Right Thing

17–18   Robert Wolk and Arthur Henley, *The Right to Lie* (New York: Peter H. Wyden, 1970), pp. 172–73.

21   If even one heroic male senator . . . : See Peter Breggin's article on the Hill/Thomas hearings: "Abuses of Privilege," *Tikkun* 7, no. 1 (1992): 17–22; June Jordon, "Can I Get a Witness?" *Progressive*, December 1991, pp. 12–13. See also Toni Morrison, ed., *Race-ing Justice, En-Gendering Power: Essays on Anita Hill, Clarence Thomas and the Construction of Social Reality* (New York: Pantheon, 1992).

21   Does the epidemic of lying . . . : Readers interested in ethical/philosophical considerations regarding lying, see Sissela Bok, *Lying: Moral Choice in Public and Private Life* (New York: Vintage Press, 1978).

24   Paul Ekman, *Telling Lies: Clues to Deceit in the Marketplace, Politics, and Marriage* (New York: Norton, 1985), p. 63. Story from the *San Francisco Chronicle*, January 9, 1982, p. 1.

25   Bok, *Lying*, p. 23.

27–30   The psychiatrist Nanette Gartrell and many others in my field have sharpened my consciousness regarding homophobia. On the freedom to openly love whom we choose, I am indebted to the passionate work of Minnie Bruce Pratt, Barbara Smith, Audre Lorde, Adrienne Rich, Suzanne Pharr, Holly Near, and June Jordan.

4 In the Name of Privacy

The philosopher Sissela Bok defines secrecy as intentional concealment, and privacy as "the condition of being protected from unwanted access by others—either physical access, personal information or attention." I am particularly grateful for her careful definitions, distinctions, and elaborations of the language of concealment. See *Secrets: On the Ethics of Concealment and Revelation* (New York: Vintage Press, 1989), pp. 10–11.

The distinction between privacy and secrecy is addressed in the family therapy literature. Mark Karpel distinguishes between privacy and secrecy by determining the relevance of the information to the person who doesn't know it. See "Family Secrets: I. Conceptual and Ethical Issues in the Relational Context. II. Ethical and practical Considerations in Therapeutic Management," *Family Process* 19 (1980): 295–306.

Regarding distinctions between privacy and secrecy, see also Evan Imber-Black, ed., *Secrets in Families and Family Therapy* (New York: Norton, 1993).

36   If I do not control my own body . . . : On "truth" and the abortion controversy, see Harriet Goldhor Lerner, "Whose Truth Counts?" in *New Woman*, October 1991, p. 34.

37   On "flight distance" and "social distance," see Edward O. Wilson, *Sociobiology* (Cambridge, Mass.: Harvard University Press, 1980), Chapter 12; also, Bok, *Secrets*, p. 11.

37–38 See Alida Brill, *Nobody's Business: The Paradoxes of Privacy* (New York: Addison-Wesley, 1990). In her prologue, Brill writes, "Privacy is granted to you by others, by their decency, by their understanding, by their compassionate behavior, by the laws of the land. It exists only when others let you have it—privacy is an accorded right." Brill pays careful attention to the privacy issues for disempowered groups and addresses the paradoxes of privacy regarding reproduction, sexual choice, and ways of dying.

41–44 For more on family secrets, see Chapter 10 notes.

44–45   Along with gender, differences in race, class, and culture
         shape beliefs about what must be kept private or secret. See
         Chapter 10 notes.

45   Many feminists have explored the connections between
         women's silence/privacy and patriarchy. See Robin Morgan,
         "The Politics of Silence," in *The Word of a Woman: Feminist
         Dispatches 1968–1991* (New York: Norton, 1992), and Tillie
         Olsen's *Silences* (New York: Delacorte Press, 1978). I am par-
         ticularly indebted to Adrienne Rich's work, *On Lies, Secrets,
         and Silence: Selected Prose 1966–1978* (New York: Norton,
         1979), which includes her essay, "Women and Honor: Some
         Notes on Lying," 1975, pp. 185–94. I am similarly indebted
         to all the work of poet and writer Audre Lorde, including
         her books, *The Cancer Journals* (San Francisco: Spinsters/
         Aunt Lute Books, 1980) and *Sister Outsider* (Freedom, Calif.:
         Crossing Press, 1984).
             The linguist Deborah Tannen's popular work on
         male–female communication also addresses the meanings of
         silence. See *You Just Don't Understand: Women and Men in
         Conversation* (New York: William Morrow, 1990); also, D.
         Tannen and M. Saville-Troike, eds., *Perspectives on Silence*
         (Norwood, N.J.: Ablex Publishing Corporation, 1990).
             Joan Laird has written an account of the many forms of
         silence in women's lives. See Joan Laird, "Women's
         Secrets—Women's Silences," in Imber-Black, ed., *Secrets in
         Families and Family Therapy*.

47   As one woman speaks . . . : Adrienne Rich wrote in 1975,
         "When a woman tells the truth she is creating the possibility
         for more truth around her" (*On Lies, Secrets, and Silence*,
         p. 191).

5 A Funny Thing Happened on the Way to the Orifice

Special thanks to Pauline Bart for the chapter title. See
Pauline Bart and Diana Scully, "A Funny Thing Happened
on the Way to the Orifice: Women in Gynecology
Textbooks," *American Journal of Sociology* 78, no. 4 (1973):
1045–50.

48–50   On pretending and protecting men, see Harriet Goldhor Lerner, *Women in Therapy* (New York: Harper & Row, 1989), Chapter 11, pp. 158–69.

49   Arlene Dahl, *Always Ask a Man* (Englewood Cliffs, N.J.: Prentice-Hall, 1965), p. 8.

On female strength going underground in adolescence, see Carol Gilligan, Nona Lyons, and Trudy Hanmer, eds., *Making Connections: The Relational Worlds of Adolescent Girls at Emma Willard School* (Cambridge, Mass.: Harvard University Press, 1990). Also, C. Gilligan, A. G. Rogers, and D. L. Tolman, eds., *Women, Girls and Psychotherapy: Reframing Resistance* (New York: The Haworth Press, Inc., 1991); also, Carol Gilligan, *In a Different Voice* (Cambridge, Mass.: Harvard University Press, 1984).

50   Carolyn Heilbrun writes, "It is perhaps only in old age, certainly past fifty, that women can stop being female impersonators, can grasp the opportunity to reverse their most cherished principles of 'femininity.'" From *Writing a Woman's Life* (New York: Ballantine Books, 1988), p. 126.

53–56   On the false and incomplete labeling of female genitalia, see Harriet Goldhor Lerner, "Parental Mislabeling of Female Genitals" in *Women in Therapy*, pp. 23–37. "Raising Vulva Consciousness" appeared as "And What Do Little Girls Have?" in *New Woman*, February 1991, pp. 110–11. (First published in *New Directions for Women*, May/June 1990, p. 10.)

Alice Walker's novel *Possessing the Secret of Joy* (New York: Harcourt Brace Jovanovich, 1992) deals with the catastrophic procedure of genital mutilation. The dedication reads: "With Tenderness and Respect to the Blameless Vulva." Audre Lorde also reminds us that female circumcision is a crime against black women; see Lorde, *Sister Outsider*, p. 120.

On genital mutilation, see Robin Morgan and Gloria Steinem, "The International Crime of Genital Mutilation," in Steinem's *Outrageous Acts and Everyday Rebellions* (New York: New American Library, 1983), pp. 292–300. Also in Gloria Steinem's *Revolution from Within: A Book of Self-Esteem* (Boston: Little, Brown, 1992), pp. 356–57.

53   Quote from K. Taylor, *Almost Twelve*, (Wheaton, Ill.: Tyn-
            dale House, 1972), italics mine.
                The historian Thomas Laqueur has written a well-
            researched book about the making and unmaking of sex over
            the centuries. See *Making Sex: Body and Gender from the
            Greeks to Freud* (Cambridge, Mass.: Harvard University
            Press, 1990).

57–58   On feigning orgasms, "lying still," and women's distorted
            relationship to their sexuality and powers of reproduction
            under patriarchy, see Rich, "Women and Honor: Some
            Notes on Lying"; also see Rich's classic text, *Of Woman Born*
            (New York: Norton, 1976) and her article, "Compulsory
            Heterosexuality and Lesbian Existence," in *Signs: Journal of
            Women in Culture and Society*, 5, no. 4 (1980): 631–60.
                See also Sonia Johnson, *Wildfire: Igniting the She/Volution*
            (Estancia, N. Mex.: Wildfire Books, 1990) and Sonia John-
            son, *The Ship That Sailed into the Living Room: Sex and Inti-
            macy Reconsidered* (Estancia, N. Mex.: Wildfire Books, 1991).
            Sonia Johnson's books and tapes can be ordered from Wild-
            fire Books, Star Route 1, Box 55, Estancia, NM 87016;
            phone (505) 384-2500.

57   Gynecological texts . . . : See Scully and Bart, "A Funny
            Thing Happened on the Way to the Orifice."

59   Adrienne Rich, in *On Lies, Secrets, and Silence*, p. 189, men-
            tions clitoridectomies for "lustful" nuns and "difficult" wives.

60   Virgina Woolf, *A Room of One's Own* (New York: Harcourt
            Brace Jovanovich, 1929), p. 37.

61–63   I am indebted to Carolyn Heilbrun's eloquent words on
            consciousness raising and the necessity for women to articu-
            late authentic experience in groups to protest the available
            fictions about female experience. See Heilbrun, *Writing a
            Woman's Life*, chapter 1. See also Teresa De Lauretis, *Alice
            Doesn't: Feminism, Semiotics, Cinema* (Bloomington, Ind.:
            Indiana University Press, 1984), p. 186.
                I have been a member of a women's group since 1976.
            Women's groups are free, and anyone can start one. See
            Harriet Goldhor Lerner, "Getting a Women's Group
            Started," *New Woman*, March 1992, p. 30. Also see Gloria

Steinem's "Helping Ourselves to Revolution" in *Ms.*
November/December 1992, pp. 24–29. Steinem, who offers
practical advice for starting women's groups, notes, "If two
white male alcoholics could start a network of free, leader-
less, accessible meetings, so can we."

62   Judith Lewis Herman, *Trauma and Recovery* (New York:
        Basic Books, 1992), p. 29.

64   Carolyn Heilbrun in *Writing a Woman's Life*, p. 47, notes,
        "There will be narratives of female lives only when women
        no longer live their lives isolated in the houses and the sto-
        ries of men."

64–65   On motherhood as institution and experience, see Adrienne
        Rich's essential book, *Of Woman Born*. See also the sociolo-
        gist Jessie Bernard's classic texts, *The Future of Marriage*
        (New York: Bantam, 1973) and *The Future of Motherhood*
        (New York: Dial, 1974).
            On female depression as a protest against women's
        "sacred calling," see Rich, *Of Woman Born* and Lerner,
        Women in Therapy, pp. 202–03.

65   Therapists could not begin . . . : See Heilbrun, *Writing a
        Woman's Life*.

65   Of course, any interpretation of experience . . . : Postmod-
        ern views challenge the notion of an objective "truth" and
        view interpretation in therapy as privileging one meaning or
        story (usually that in line with the dominant culture) over
        others. See, for example, Rachel Hare-Mustin and Jeanne
        Marecek, eds., *Making a Difference: Psychology and the Con-
        struction of Gender* (New Haven, Conn.: Yale University
        Press, 1990), pp. 22–64.
            The psychotherapy literature reflects a growing emphasis
        on a "narrative perspective" regarding human problems. In
        the words of the psychologist George S. Howard, this per-
        spective views identity as an issue of life-story construction;
        psychopathology as instances of life stories gone awry; and
        psychotherapy as exercises in story repair" ("Culture Tales:
        A Narrative Approach to Thinking, Cross-Cultural Psychol-
        ogy and Psychotherapy," *American Psychologist*, March 1991,
        p. 187). For a psychiatrist's description of his work helping

people create new, growth-enhancing stories, see James Gustafson, *Self-Delight in a Harsh World: The Main Stories of Individual, Marital and Family Psychotherapy* (New York: Norton, 1992).

66   "The master's tools. . . ": Lorde, *Sister Outsider*, p. 110.

Readers interested in feminist revisions of traditional views of women might begin with Jean Baker Miller's classic and accessible book, *Toward a New Psychology of Women* (Boston: Beacon Press, 1986).

Feminist thinkers continue to critique and transform psychoanalytic and family systems views of women. For a psychoanalytic perspective, see, for example, Judith Jordan, Alexandra Kaplan, Jean Baker Miller, Irene Stiver, and Janet Surrey, *Women's Growth in Connection: Writing from the Stone Center* (New York: Guilford Press, 1991). From a family systems perspective see, for example, Marianne Walters, Betty Carter, Peggy Papp, and Olga Silverstein (The Women's Project in Family Therapy), *The Invisible Web: Gender Patterns in Family Relationships* (New York: Guilford Press, 1988). See also Lerner, *Women in Therapy.*

Thanks to Rachel Hare-Mustin for her pioneering work in feminist family therapy.

6 We Are the Stories We Tell

I am deeply indebted to two critically important papers by Peggy McIntosh, "Feeling Like a Fraud, Part One," *Work in Progress*, The Stone Center Working Papers Series, No. 18 (1985); and "Feeling Like a Fraud, Part Two" *Work in Progress*, The Stone Center Working Papers Series, No. 37 (1989). These papers can be ordered directly from Peggy McIntosh, Wellesley College, Center for Research on Women, Wellesley, MA 02181.

67   Is there a "true story" of female experience?: Psychologist Carol Tavris has written a wise and engaging book examining popular myths about sex differences. See *The Mismeasure of Woman* (New York: Simon and Schuster, 1992). See also Hare-Mustin and Marecek, eds., *Making a Difference.*

69   Our differing ethnic backgrounds . . . : Ethnicity, like gender, is a key factor that shapes what one conceals and reveals about personal achievement. Thanks to family therapist Monica McGoldrick for her pioneering work on ethnicity and family therapy.

70–74   On the denial and erasure of ambition, adventure, and achievement from stories of women's lives, see Carolyn Heilbrun's acclaimed book, *Writing a Woman's Life*. Heilbrun illustrates how patriarchal culture has defined and limited what stories about women's lives could be scripted and told.

72–78   Feminist scholars from many disciplines have explored the forces that block women from success in the public sphere, or leave women feeling illegitimate, guilty, or self-doubting and out of place when they do rise in male-dominated hierarchies. In addition to the work of Peggy McIntosh and Carolyn Heilbrun, see the pioneering work of Jean Baker Miller, *Toward a New Psychology of Women*; see also Rosabeth Moss Kanter, *Men and Women of the Corporation* (New York: Basic Books, 1977).

        Also see, Harriet Goldhor Lerner, "Work and Success Inhibitions," in *Women in Therapy*, pp. 171–99; see also Irene Stiver, "Work Inhibitions in Women," *Work in Progress*, The Stone Center Working Papers Series, No. 3 (1982).

74   See McIntosh, "Feeling Like a Fraud, Part One," and "Feeling Like a Fraud, Part Two."

75   Quote from McIntosh, "Feeling Like a Fraud, Part One," p. 5.

77   The belief that "rugged individualism," "separateness," and independence define maturity or mental health has been challenged by new theories of female development that emphasize connection and context. Work by Jean Baker Miller, Carol Gilligan, Peggy McIntosh, and the writings from The Stone Center (See Jordan et. al., *Women's Growth in Connection*) reflect this new perspective. Psychotherapists and other interested readers can order working papers from The Stone Center, Wellesley College, Wellesley, MA 02181-8268; phone (617) 283-2838.

The capacity for connection and cooperation is no less essential for men. See Alfie Kohn, *No Contest: The Case against Competition* (Boston: Houghton Mifflin, 1987) and Mark Gerzon, *A Choice of Heroes: The Changing Faces of American Manhood* (Boston: Houghton Mifflin, 1992).

81   Dead-end jobs evoke dead-end dreams . . . : See the sociologist Rosabeth Moss Kanter's groundbreaking book about how jobs "create" people, *Men and Women of the Corporation.* See also Chapter 13 notes.

7 Our Family Legacies

83   From Liz (Elizabeth Sprague) Hoffmeister's self-published book, *The Crawdad Nest* (Topeka, Kans.: 1976).

87–88   Betty Carter quotation (author's italics) from *Mothers and Daughters* by Elizabeth (Betty) Carter, Peggy Papp, Olga Silverstein, and Marianne Walters, The Women's Project in Family Therapy Monograph Series, vol. 1, no. 1, (Washington, D.C., 1983), p. 16 (out of print).

88–92   Thanks to psychiatrist Jerry Lewis and other early researchers on family functioning. I am especially indebted to the work of Murray Bowen, the founder of Bowen family systems theory, who died October 9, 1990, at the age of seventy-seven. His theoretical contributions include his pioneering efforts to describe human emotional functioning from a multigenerational perspective, and his concepts of triangles, emotional reactivity, emotional cut-off, and differentiation of self. Bowen and his colleagues, especially Jack Bradt, also pioneered the use of the multigenerational family genogram. Despite important differences in our worldview, all three of my *Dance* books draw heavily from Bowen's work. For a review of Bowen theory see Michael Kerr, "Family Systems Theory and Therapy," in Alan Gurman and David Knistern, eds., *Handbook of Family Therapy* (New York: Brunner/Mazel, 1981), pp. 226–64.

Also, see Stephanie Ferrera's summary of anxious family functioning, "Deception in Nature and the Family," based on Bowen's theory, and Roberta Gilbert's book, *Extraordi-*

nary Relationships (Minneapolis, Minn: CHRONIMED Publishing, 1992). The address for CHRONIMED Publishing is P.O. Box 47945, Minneapolis, MN 55447-9727. Contact Georgetown Family Center for information on Bowen theory, therapy, or training at 4404 MacArthur Blvd. N.W., Suite 102, Washington, DC 20007; phone (202) 965-0730.

My greatest intellectual debt is to Katherine Glenn Kent whose generous sharing of ideas has greatly enhanced my understanding of the process of truth-telling in families. What I understand of Murray Bowen's theory comes from her teaching and our countless conversations over many years of friendship.

Family therapists and readers interested in the emotional challenges of family life, see the following important texts, which address gender issues. Betty Carter and Monica McGoldrick, eds., *The Changing Family Life Cycle: A Framework for Family Therapy*, 2nd ed. (Boston: Allyn & Bacon, 1988); Monica McGoldrick, Carol Anderson, and Froma Walsh, eds., *Women in Families: A Framework for Family Therapy* (New York: Norton, 1989); Walters, Carter, Papp, and Silverstein (The Women's Project in Family Therapy) *The Invisible Web*.

In addition to the above texts, Virginia Goldner, Rachel Hare-Mustin, and other scholars in family therapy have articulated how the fate of women in families is shaped largely (and invisibly) by gendered power arrangements. See, for example, Thelma Jean Goodrich, ed., *Women and Power: Perspectives for Family Therapy*, (New York: Norton, 1991.) Also see Evan Imber-Black, "Women, Families, and Larger Systems," in Ault-Riché, ed., *Women and Family Therapy* (Rockville, Md.: Aspen Systems Corporation, 1986), pp. 25–33.

91   The poet Lynn Sukenick coined the phrase "matraphobia," the fear of being one's mother. Also see Rich, *Of Woman Born*, p. 235.

92–93   Thanks to Betty Carter for her insights about a daughter as her mother's "apprentice" and for her inspiring teaching and work with families. For enriching my understanding of the mother-daughter relationship, and for locating this relationship in the broader context of culture, class, and gender, I also thank Olga Silverstein, Laura Silverstein, Monica McGoldrick, Evan Imber-Black, Marianne Walters, Lois Braverman, and many other family systems therapists I continue to learn from.

On relationships between African-American mothers and daughters see Patrica Bell–Scott et al. *Double Stitch: Black Women Write about Mothers and Daughters* (Boston: Beacon Press, 1992). For a scholarly feminist challenge to conventional theories about the mother-daughter relationship through an examination of media representations, popular culture, and image making, see Suzanna Danuta Walters, *Lives Together, Worlds Apart: Mothers and Daughters in Popular Culture* (Berkeley: University of California Press, 1992).

94   As early as 1970, Phillip Slater wrote about the hazards of motherhood as a "career" in a production-oriented society; see *The Pursuit of Loneliness: American Culture at the Breaking Point* (Boston: Beacon Press, 1970). I am also grateful for the pioneering feminist insights of psychoanalyst Robert Seidenberg, and for the early support of psychoanalyst Anthony Kowalski.

96   Because "in the camps". . . : From audiotape ("Feminist Jewish Women's Voices: Diversity and Community"), Eighth Annual National Women's Studies Convention, Fourth Plenary, National Women's Studies Association.

97–101   Our Mothers' Stories: For a detailed guide on opening up the lines of communication with family members, see Harriet Goldhor Lerner, *The Dance of Anger* (New York: Harper & Row, 1985) and *The Dance of Intimacy* (New York: Harper & Row, 1989).

99–101   Untimely loss poses the most difficult emotional challenge for families to cope with. Facts and feelings surrounding death frequently go underground. I am grateful to my friend Libby (Elizabeth) Rosen, nurse and child-birth educator, whose work in this area has inspired me. Also see Froma Walsh and Monica McGoldrick, eds., *Living Beyond Loss: Death in the Family* (New York: Norton, 1991); Freda Herz Brown, "The Impact of Death and Serious Illness on the Family Life Cycle," in Carter and McGoldrick, eds., *The*

Changing Family Life Cycle. Also see psychiatrist Sue Chance's plainspoken account of her emotional journey following her son's suicide, *Stronger than Death* (Norton, 1992).

8 Honesty versus Truth

102 Holly Near, a foremother of women's and political music is a rare performing artist who has never veered from speaking, singing, and living her own truths. Her music can be ordered from Redwood Cultural Work, 1222 Preservation Parkway, Oakland, CA 94612. See also her autobiography, *Fire in the Rain, Singer in the Storm* (New York: William Morrow, 1990).

105 Clark Moustakas, *Loneliness and Love* (Englewood Cliffs, N.J.: Prentice-Hall, 1972), p. 109.

106–12 The distinction between thinking and anxiety-driven reactivity is central to Bowen family systems theory and therapy.

112 Definition of "honesty" from *The American Heritage Dictionary* (Boston: Houghton Mifflin, 1985), p. 620.

9 Just Pretending

121 Pretending is a "soft" verb: *The American Heritage Dictionary*, p. 981; and *Random House Webster's College Dictionary* (New York: Random House, 1991), p. 1069.

129–32 The concepts of overfunctioning and underfunctioning are elaborated in Bowen family systems theory. For a helpful book on overfunctioning/overresponsibility, see Claudia Bepko and Jo-Ann Krestan, *Too Good for Her Own Good* (New York: HarperCollins, 1990).

132 On secrecy surrounding adoption, see Chapter 10 notes.

132–35 The pattern of pursuit and distance has been so widely described in the family literature that it is difficult to trace its origins. Philip Guerin and Katherine Guerin wrote about it as early as 1976. The concept of triangles is also central in the family therapy literature and has been carefully elaborated by Murray Bowen.

Part of the text on Jen and Michelle appeared in Harriet Goldhor Lerner, "My Mother-in-law Is Driving Me Crazy," *New Woman*, July 1992, p. 42, (mother-in-law triangle), and "He Won't Make a Commitment," *New Woman*, November 1992, p. 34 (pursuing and distancing). For more on these patterns, see Lerner, *The Dance of Anger*, chapter 8, and *The Dance of Intimacy*, chapter 10.

135   Quotation by Goethe and paraphrase by Joy in W. Brugh Joy, *Joy's Way*, (Los Angeles: Jeremy P. Tarcher, Inc., 1979), p. 63.

10 Family Secrets: A Disturbance in the Field

As the chapter notes indicate, I am especially grateful to family therapist Evan Imber-Black, for her book, *Secrets in Families and Family Therapy*, which pays careful attention to the wider context in which family secrets are embedded.

I know of two books for nonprofessional readers on the subject of family secrets: Harriet Webster, *Family Secrets*, (Reading, Mass.: Addison-Wesley Publishing Company, 1991); and Kittredge Cherry, *Hide and Speak: How to Free Ourselves From Our Secrets* (San Francisco: HarperCollins, 1991), a self-help guide about secrets.

136   Every family has secrets...: I am indebted to Peggy Papp for her work on secrecy between parents and children. See "The Worm in the Bud: Secrets Between Parents and Children" in Imber-Black, *Secrets in Families and Family Therapy*.

137   How do we distinguish...: On defining a "family secret," see Karpel, "Family Secrets," and Imber-Black, *Secrets in Families and Family Therapy*.

138   Evan Imber-Black, Marilyn Mason, Jo-Ann Krestan, Claudia Bepko, and other family therapists have addressed the connections between shame, stigma, and secrecy and the

broader societal context. See Imber-Black, *Secrets in Families and Family Therapy*.

On secrecy, stigma, and AIDS, see Gillian Walker, *In the Midst of Winter: Systemic Therapy with Families, Couples, and Individuals with AIDS Infection* (New York: Norton, 1991)—chapter 8 deals with issues of secrecy, confidentiality, and the duty to warn. Also see Lascelles Black, "AIDS and Secrets," in Imber-Black, *Secrets in Families and Family Therapy*.

140–45   Untimely and nonnormative loss commonly lead to secrecy and a shutdown of communication among family members regarding facts, feelings, and fantasies about who's to blame. See Chapter 7 notes.

142   Peggy Papp, in Imber-Black, *Secrets in Families and Family Therapy*.

145   On "locations" of family secrets: Janine Roberts, using some ideas of Evan Imber-Black, has expanded on Mark Karpel's original topology to include the location of secrets when therapists and larger systems are involved. See Janine Roberts, "On Trainees and Training: Safety, Secrets and Revelation," in Imber-Black, *Secrets in Families and Family Therapy*.

146   Letty Cottin Pogrebin, *Deborah, Golda, and Me* (New York: Crown Publishers, 1991), p. 13.

149   "Blow the whistle". . . : Peggy Papp describes a child or adolescent's symptomatic or acting-out behavior as an unconscious attempt to blow the whistle on a family secret. (In Imber-Black, *Secrets in Families and Family Therapy*.)

150–52   Family therapist Edwin Friedman takes the position that all family secrets have a profoundly negative effect on family life and should be revealed. Other family therapists (see Imber-Black, *Secrets in Families and Family Therapy*) emphasize that secrets have both pathological and adaptational value, and they stress the importance of assessing whether the opening of secrets will be healing or harmful. There are widely divergent views regarding the function, adaptational value, and therapeutic management of family secrets.

Therapists dealing with family secrets need to be informed about issues of race, culture, and class. Nancy Boyd-Franklyn, for example, illustrates how therapists working with African-American families must understand the history of slavery and racism and how it contributes to the process of secret-keeping within families. "Racism, Secret-Keeping, and African-American Families," in Imber-Black, *Secrets in Families and Family Therapy.*

Fiction writers such as Maxine Hong-Kingston and Amy Tan have dealt with the subject of secrets and silence between generations in Asian families. Writers from all marginalized groups invariably address the subject of shame, stigma, secrecy, and enforced silence as shaped by gender, generation, sexual orientation, and the specific history of culture, class, and race. See Cherrie Moraga and Gloria Anzaldua, eds., *This Bridge Called My Back: Writings by Radical Women of Color* (New York: Kitchen Table/Women of Color Press, 1983); Barbara Smith, ed., *Home Girls: A Black Feminist Anthology* (New York: Kitchen Table/Women of Color Press, 1983); Elly Bulkin, Minnie Bruce Pratt, and Barbara Smith, *Yours in Struggle: Three Feminist Perspectives on Anti-Semitism and Racism* (Ithaca, N.Y.: Firebrand Books, 1984); Claudia Tate, ed., *Black Women Writers at Work* (New York: The Continuum Publishing Corporation, 1983); and Pogrebin, *Deborah, Golda, and Me.*

151   A helpful guide for adoptive parents is Lois Ruskai Melina, *Making Sense of Adoption* (New York: Harper & Row, 1989). I also highly recommend Ann Hartman's important article, "Secrecy in Adoption," in Imber-Black, *Secrets in Families and Family Therapy.*

152–53 The case of Billy was reported by Peggy Papp in Imber-Black, *Secrets in Families and Family Therapy.* The example reported by Papp of the adopted child with a "selective math disability" is from Deborah Donovan and Denis McIntyre, *Healing the Hurt Child* (New York: Norton, 1990). Donovan and McIntyre note that family secrets lead a child to wear "cognitive blinders" that impede school performance.

153   On secrecy and addictions, see Jo-Ann Krestan and Claudia Bepko's "On Lies, Secrets, and Silence: The Multiple Levels

of Denial in Addictive Families," in Imber-Black, *Secrets in Families and Family Therapy*. Therapists see Krestan and Bepko, *The Responsibility Trap: A Blueprint for Treating the Alcoholic Family* (New York: Free Press, 1985).

153   One woman I saw in psychotherapy. . . : See Lerner, *Women in Therapy*, pp. 23–37.

154   When women publicly. . . : For more on women who comply with the cultural prescription to lie, joke, or keep secret about their age, see Harriet Goldhor Lerner, "Hiding Our Age," *New Woman*, October 1992, p. 37.

154–55   In the February 1992 *Lear's* report on incest by Heidi Vanderbilt, she notes that as recently as the early 1970s, experts in the psychiatric community estimated only one to five cases of incest per one million people.

In her book *Trauma and Recovery*, Judith Lewis Herman writes, "In the absence of strong political movements for human rights, the active process of bearing witness inevitably gives way to the active process of forgetting" (p. 9). See also her earlier book, *Father-Daughter Incest* (Cambridge, Mass.: Harvard University Press, 1981). I also want to thank Robin Morgan, Audre Lorde, June Jordon, Susan Brownmiller, and other theorists and activists who have offered a feminist analysis of the silence surrounding violence against women.

11 An Affair Is a Big Secret

159   Frank Pittman, *Private Lies: Infidelity and the Betrayal of Intimacy* (New York: Norton, 1989).

159–60   Pittman quotation from "Mending Broken Ties," *New Woman*, November 1990, p. 42.

164–65   I am indebted to Peggy Vaughan's excellent self-help book, *The Monogamy Myth* (New York: Newmarket Press, 1989).

On a radically different note, see Sonia Johnson's feminist challenge to monogamy. She rejects the notion of fidelity and sexual exclusivity: ". . . the red herring of numbers that focuses us on how many lovers we are taking naked to bed instead of what condition our souls are in and what is in our hearts as we lie with them." *The Ship That Sailed into the Living Room*, p. 112.

12 The Body Seeks Truth

176   Clark Moustakas, *Loneliness and Love*.

176   On techniques that detect deceit by reading body language, voice, and speech patterns, see Ekman, *Telling Lies*.

182   It is profit madness . . . : We must speak openly about the primary role of environmental contaminants in causing higher rates of breast cancer and other cancers in particular neighborhoods and communities. To do otherwise is to engage in the deadliest of deceptions. I am grateful for the work of Jay Gould, Benjamin Goldman, Terry Tempest Williams, Rita Arditti, Tatiana Schreiber, Judith Brady, and other individuals and groups documenting the connections between environmental contamination and cancer, and promoting activism and national debate.

I am grateful to my dear friend and colleague Emily Kofron for our many conversations about psychological theories regarding cancer patients and for her activism to increase funding for breast cancer research. Kofron has written an important article on breast cancer in the *The Family Therapy Networker*, January/February 1993. Also see Susan Sontag, *Illness as Metaphor and AIDS and Its Metaphors* (New York: Anchor, 1990) and Harriet Goldhor Lerner, "Can We Cause Our Own Cancer?", *New Woman*, January 1992, p. 28.

183–84 On women's anger and the complex forces that prohibit its expression, see the pioneering work of Teresa Bernardez, "Women and Anger: Conflicts with Aggression in Contemporary Women," in the *Journal of the American Medical Women's Association* 33 (1978): 215–19. See also Bernardez, "Women and Anger—Cultural Prohibitions and the Feminine Ideal. *Work in Progress*, The Stone Center Working

Papers Series, No. 31 (1988), and Lerner, *The Dance of Anger*. For a comprehensive overview on the uses and abuses of anger in truth-telling see Carol Tavris, *Anger: The Misunderstood Emotion* (New York: Simon and Schuster, 1983).

186   "Experience is the name everyone gives to their mistakes." Oscar Wilde, *Lady Windemere's Fan*.

187   Airline ticket quotation from David Reynolds's book, *Even in Summer the Ice Doesn't Melt*, excerpted in *Yoga Journal*, May/June 1992, p. 55. Reynolds is the founder of Constructive Living, based on the Japanese Morita and Naikan psychotherapies, and has authored numerous books.

187–88   Audre Lorde's *The Cancer Journals*, pp. 22–23. Lorde, who describes herself as a "black lesbian feminist warrior, poet" has written the first passionate, compelling feminist text on breast cancer and on the transformation of women's fear and silence into language and action. I also recommend *Chemo-Poet and other Poems*, by Helene Davis (Cambridge, Mass.: Alice James Books, 1989).

　　　　Audre Lorde died on November 17, 1992, in her home on St. Croix, U.S. Virgin Islands, after a fourteen-year struggle with breast cancer. She was fifty-eight years old. Lorde published seventeen volumes of poetry, essays, and autobiography. Her numerous honors include becoming the poet laureate of New York State in 1991 and receiving honorary doctorates from Hunter, Oberlin, and Haverford colleges. In her writing and political activism, Lorde spoke courageously and eloquently against racism, homophobia, and all forms of prejudice and violence. Her work has touched the hearts of countless women and men, worldwide.

　　　　In honor of Audre Lorde's life, a scholarship for black women writers has been established in her name. Donations, made payable to the Astrea Foundation/Audre Lorde Memorial Fund, can be sent to the Astrea Foundation, 666 Broadway, Suite 520, New York, NY 10012.

189   Sonia might happily agree. . . : "Since truth is reversed in patriarchy, to go out of our minds is to become most truly

sane." From the foreword of Sonia Johnson's book *From Housewife to Heretic* (Albuquerque: Wildfire Books, 1981). Johnson chronicles her run for president of the United States, along with her other political and emotional journeys.

189   My heartfelt gratitude to Jade Deforest and Sonia Johnson for their love, their wisdom, their lives, and their generous sharing of everything.

191   I first heard the term the "Irish grudge syndrome" from family therapist Monica McGoldrick.

193   On denial, repression, dissociation, and the recovery of history, memory, and connection for victims of sexual and domestic violence, see Herman, *Trauma and Recovery*. Her book also explores the experience of other traumatized people such as combat veterans and the victims of political terror. Also see the self-help guide *The Courage to Heal*, by Ellen Bass and Laura Davis (New York: HarperCollins, 1992).

194   For persons interested in spirituality and the psychic/sacred arts, I recommend workshops or other opportunities to learn from the psychologist Carolyn Conger. To be placed on her mailing list, call (800) 833-0611.

       There is a vast number of books on body/mind/spirit connections. For example, see Deepak Chopra, *Quantum Healing: Exploring the Frontiers of Mind/Body Medicine* (New York: Bantam Books, 1989), p. 33. See also Steinem, *Revolution from Within*, pp. 197–248.

194–95 On the subject of weight, dieting, and hunger, see Jane R. Hirschmann and Carol H. Munter's helpful book, *Overcoming Overeating* (New York: Fawcett Columbine, 1988). Regarding physical touch "in the moment," I am grateful to conversations with Jade Deforest and Sonia Johnson.

       Psychologist Carol Tavris challenges popular myths about women's bodies, sexuality, and "diseases" in *The Mismeasure of Woman*.

195   See, for example, Naomi Wolf, *The Beauty Myth: How Images*

of Beauty Are Used Against Women (New York: William Morrow, 1991). See also Steinem, *Revolution from Within*.

196   Lorde, *The Cancer Journals*, pp. 16, 64. See also Marsha Saxton and Florence Howe, eds., *With Wings: An Anthology of Literature by and about Women with Disabilities* (New York: The Feminist Press, 1987). A self-help video, *Chronic Illness: The Constant Companion*, features psychologist Meredith Titus, who is also its co-writer and producer; it is available from Menninger Video Productions, (800) 345-6036.

13 Will the Real Me Please Stand?

198   Pat Parker quotations come from a conversation with the poet Judy Grahn. See Dorothy Allison, "Memorial: Pat Parker 1944–1989," *Out/Look, National Lesbian and Gay Quarterly*, Fall 1989.

199–205   I am indebted to Rosabeth Moss Kanter's critically important work on the impact of tokenism and numerical scarcity in organizational life, *Men and Women of the Corporation* (see especially pages 206–42). Kanter's research illustrates how power, relative opportunity, and tokenism (numerical scarcity) shape the behavior and attitudes of men and women in the workplace. She provides an in-depth view of why "individual" or psychological models of change cannot address the "woman question" and she makes a compelling argument for the necessity of organizational reform (that is, policies and programs to balance numbers, enhance opportunities, and provide equal access to power).

200   Rosabeth Moss Kanter quotation, *Men and Women of the Corporation*, p. 161.

202   Do women have a "fear of success" or, rather, a fear of visibility that is characteristic of persons in token roles? See Kanter, *Men and Women of the Corporation*, p. 221.

203   Rosabeth Moss Kanter quotation, *Men and Women of the Corporation*, p. 209.

208–09   Part of this appeared in Harriet Goldhor Lerner, "Should I Find Out My IQ?" in *New Woman*, July 1991, p. 38.

210   I am grateful to Marianne Ault-Riché for her vision, courage, and hard work in creating and sustaining the "Women in Context" conference series at the Menninger Clinic (December 1983–November 1990). We both extend our heartfelt thanks to the conference staff who have enriched the conferences over many years.

211–13   On the matter of prefixing I am deeply indebted to the work of the philosopher and educator Elizabeth Kamarck Minnich. She writes, "we can add the prefixes, or markers . . . on the grounds that accurate scholarship, truth-telling itself, demands that we name our sample. If a course covers only white people, and/or is taught from the analytic perspectives developed within an exclusively white tradition, it should be so labeled and the perspective claimed as such. . . . Courses titled 'Man and His World' can still be taught, but now as courses in which gender analysis is central, not weirdly absent. Still, courses on 'Woman and Her World' are at this moment in history much more important to teach." From "The Circle of the Elite to the World of the Whole" in Carol Pearson, Donna Shavlik, and Judith Touchton, eds., *Educating the Majority* (New York: Macmillan, 1989), pp. 277–93 (a vital book for those interested in higher education).

           Elizabeth Kamarck Minnich's essential text, *Transforming Knowledge* (Philadelphia: Temple University Press, 1990) uncovers the ways in which our unexamined habits of language and thought perpetuate old exclusions, devaluations, and hierarchies.

           In 1973, Adrienne Rich wrote a visionary feminist essay, "Toward a Woman-Centered University," reprinted in *On Lies, Secrets, and Silence*, pp. 125–55.

212   "Just add women and stir.": A quotation from Charlotte Bunch, which originated in conversation and is frequently quoted among those in Women's Studies.

214–16   To appreciate the hidden power of false generalizations to influence how and what we think, see Minnich, *Transforming Knowledge*.

215   "Beware of the stories you tell. . . ": A paraphrase of Shakespeare by George S. Howard, "Culture Tales: A Narrative Approach to Thinking, Cross-cultural Psychology, and Psychotherapy," *American Psychologist* 46, no. 3 (March 1991), pp. 187–97, quotation, p. 196.

Carolyn Heilbrun notes, "Power consists to a large extent in deciding what stories will be told," *Writing a Woman's Life*, p. 44.

216   On wanting to huddle with folks "just like us," see Bernice Johnson Reagon, "Coalition Politics: Turning the Century," in Smith, *Home Girls*, pp. 356–68. Reagon reminds us that coalition work is difficult and if we prefer to feel safe and nurtured, we should return to a little village or barred room where we let in only people just like us. Reagon is an internationally acclaimed lecturer and scholar of African-American, community-based cultural life and history. She is also the founding member and leader of Sweet Honey in the Rock, an ensemble of African-American women whose sound is rooted in the African-American tradition of congregational choral style and its many extensions.

Epilogue: When the Lion Learns to Write

217   "My son, you'll get a different story. . . ": Quoted in Linda Webb-Watson, "The Sociology of Power," in Goodrich, *Women and Power*, p. 54.

218   See Rich, "Women and Honor: Some Notes on Lying" in *On Lies, Secrets, and Silence*.

218–19   Elizabeth Kamarch Minnich notes that the assumption that to talk about women is to exclude men, reverses the usual assumption that to talk about men is to include women.

219–20   Many feminist women of color have contributed to a more complex, diverse, and multilayered vision of human reality.

In addition to those writers already mentioned in my earlier chapter notes, I am grateful for the work of Joy Harjo, Maya Angelou, Angela Davis, bell hooks, Paula Giddings, Louise Erdrich, Sandra Cisneros, Toni Morrison, Toni Cade Bambara, Paula Gunn Allen, Luisah Teish, Michelle Cliff, Mary Crow Dog, Alexis De Veaux, Paule Marshall, and Mary Helen Washington. This is a very partial list. Thanks also to Barbara Smith, who is co-founder (with Audre Lorde) and current publisher of Kitchen Table/Women of Color Press.

The feminist community has challenged me to think more inclusively and accurately. I rely on feminist publications to prod and inform me, including *Ms.* magazine, *New Directions for Women*, *Sojourner*, *Women's Review of Books*, and *Belles Lettres*. I encourage others to support these and other vital feminist publications by subscribing.

I also rely on Redwood Cultural Work to tie music, culture, and politics together from a multicultural feminist perspective. For twenty years, Redwood has championed cultural rights and social justice, producing and presenting new music rooted in the folk traditions of the many cultures that exist today in the United States. To get their catalog or information about concerts, call (800) 888-SONG.

Index

Abuse/incest, 154, 162, 180, 193, 240*n*

Achievement, 67–74, 79

Adoption, 151, 236*n*

Affairs
  and anxiety, 158–59, 161, 163, 168
  and confrontation, 169
  excitement of, 167, 171
  and false myths about, 168
  and families, 157–63
  and guilt, 158–59, 162, 174–75
  and loss, 168
  and monogamy paradox, 167–71
  rationalization of, 160
  and reality, 156
  and relationships, 158–65, 173
  and secrets, 159, 165
  and self-deception, 168
  and trust, 169, 170
  and truth-telling, 171–73

Age, lying about, 196

Altruistic lies, 23–24

Always Ask a Man (Dahl), 49

Ambitions, of women, 67–69, 72–74, 80–81

Andrew (Jane's lover), 156–61, 163–65, 167

Angela (ambition), 80–81, 199

Angelou, Maya, 53–54, 244*n*

Anger, 104, 183–85

Animal kingdom, 11, 37, 217, 222*n*

Anna (Peg's mother), 109–10, 111

Anxiety
  and affairs, 158–59, 161, 163, 168
  and body signals, 185–89
  and children, 142, 175
  in families, 88–90, 96, 110
  and family secrets, 88, 138, 175
  and fear, 185–89
  interpretation of, 185–88
  responses to, 188–89
  survival, 142
  and triangles, 90, 168
  truth-telling vs., 99
  and waiting, 186

Anzaldua, Gloria, 236*n*

Arlene (parents' divorce), 138

Ault-Riché, Marianne, 205, 210–11, 231*n*, 242

Authority, and women, 74, 75, 77

Bart, Pauline, 224*n*, 226*n*

Bass, Ellen, 240*n*

Bea (mother-daughter), 84–86, 88, 90–92, 94, 95, 97–101, 111, 137

Bell-Scott, Patricia, 232*n*

Ben (son), 22, 120–121

Bepko, Claudia, 233*n*, 234*n*, 236*n*

Bernard, Jessie, 227n
Bernardez, Teresa, 92, 238–39n
Bess (Jane's sister), 166, 167
Beth (pretending), 119–20, 122
Betty (Vicki's daughter), 41–44
Beverly (Lenore's partner), 130–32
Bias, 209–16
Bill (Jane's lover), 156–65, 168
Billy (learning deficit), 152
Black, Lascelles, 235n
Body
  control of, 36, 58
  honest, 174–77
  love of, 194–97
  and memory, 193–94
  privacy of, 36, 39, 46–47
  and shame, 46, 51
  storing truth by, 193–94
Body language, 176
Body signals
  and affairs, 161–62
  and anger, 183–85
  and anxiety, 185–89
  and depression, 179, 180–81
  and guilt, 176
  and honesty, 104–5
  and hunger, 194
  and indecisiveness, 178–79
  interpretation of, 180–88, 194
  and pretending, 59
  and self-deception, 179–80
  and sleepiness, 177, 180
  and truth-telling, 175–76, 190–92
  and unconscious, 64–65, 161–62,
    179–80
Bok, Sissela, 25, 38, 222n, 223n
Bowen, Murray, 221n, 230–31n, 234n
Boyd-Franklin, Nancy, 236n
Bradt, Jack, 230n
Braverman, Lois, 232n
Breasts, 34–35, 39–40, 46, 47, 196
Breggin, Peter. 222n
Brill, Alida, 37, 223n
Brown, Freda Herz, 232n
Brownmiller, Susan, 237n
Bulkin, Elly, 236n
Bunch, Charlotte, 242n

Cancer, 3–5, 7, 8, 18, 142, 148, 181–82,
  187, 238n

environmental carcinogens, 181–182,
  196, 238n
Carter, Betty, 87–88, 228n, 230n, 231n,
  232n
Caste system, 113
Catherine (parent-child), 148–50
Chance, Sue, 232n
Change
  in relationships, 129
  resistance to, 115–16
  and social movement, 139, 155
Children
  and anxiety, 96, 142, 175
  as family members, 97, 151–52
  parents' relationships with, 85, 87, 96,
    131–32, 137, 148–50, 190–92
  secrets of, 137, 145
  symptoms of, 151–53
Chopra, Deepak, 240n
Clitoris, 51, 52, 54, 55, 56, 59, 153
Coalition work, 243n
Commonality of female experience, 45,
  46, 62, 63, 66, 214–16
Compartmentalization, 160
Competence, femininity vs., 49
Compromises, by women, 180
Conditioning
  and body love, 195
  and fear, 187
  feminists vs., 188–89, 197
  about men, 48–50, 154
  by patriarchy, 195, 219
  and pretending, 14, 48, 218
  and stereotyping, 219
  See also Myths
Conferences, for women, 205–6, 210–11
Confidantes, 157–58
Confrontation
  and affairs, 169
  and anger, 184
  and family secrets, 150–51
  truth-telling vs., 128, 150–51
  workplace, 107–8
Conger, Carolyn, 240n
Consciousness
  McIntosh/dual, 74–78
Consciousness raising
  and feminists, 61–63, 66, 209–16, 228n
  and truth-telling, 63, 64–66
Constructive lies, 17–18, 20

Context
    and anger, 184
    and culture, 8, 18, 20, 82
    and empathy, 8
    and gender differences, 200
    lies viewed in, 6–8, 33
    and perspective, 6–8, 79
    and pretending, 132–35
    and privacy, 47
    and safety, 213
    and self-esteem, 207
    stories created in, 81–82
    and therapists/therapy, 2–3, 154
    and tokenism, 205–6
    and true self, 200, 209
    truth-telling in, 213
Control
    and fantasy, 6
    of one's body, 36, 58
    of partner, 167
    and privacy, 39
Courage, 119–20, 124–29
Culture
    and context, 18, 20, 82
    differences in, 113–14
    and family background, 69
    myths prescribed by, 70
    norms of, 18–21, 23
    as patriarchy, 48, 60, 71, 218
    and pressures on women, 45, 52,
        66
    and therapists/therapy, 2–3, 154
    and tokenism, 202
    See also Conditioning
Cyrill (Maria's partner), 190–92

Dahl, Arlene, 49, 225n
Dance of Anger, The (Lerner), 72
Daughters
    father's relationships with, 3, 4, 7,
        43–44, 67–68, 92, 93, 94–95,
        126–28
    See also Mother-daughter relation-
        ships
Davis, Laura, 240n
Death
    as choice, 181
    and families, 83, 99–100, 141–145,
        162, 232n
    questions about, 142

Deception
    in animal kingdom, 11
    capacity to detect, 26
    denial of, 176–77
    by doctors, 3–4, 7, 8, 18
    ethnicity, 68, 69, 229n, 236n
    faking, 48–50
    fraudulence, 74–76
    language of, 9–11, 12
    motivation in, 9, 10, 32
    and pretending, 117–18
    privacy vs., 13, 122
    results of, 10, 29, 42
    as right thing, 17–21
    and silence, 5, 12–13, 15, 172–73
    and values, 175
    See also Lies, lying; Self-deception
Deforest, Jade, 240n
Denial, 25, 58, 176–77
Depression, 179, 180–81
Discrimination
    by dominants, 210–16
    as racism, 191–92
    and sexual orientation, 28–30
Distance
    as created by secrets, 144
    as created by truth, 69
Diversity, 113–14, 211, 216, 219
Divorce, 138, 167
Doctors, 3–4, 7, 8, 18, 77
Dominants, 63, 210–16
Donovan, Deborah, 236n
Dual consciousness, 74–78
Dumb, playing, 129–32

Ekman, Paul, 24, 238n
Emotions
    as barriers, 108
    and consciousness raising, 62–63
    expression of, 110–11
    and families, 88–92, 111, 191–92
    reality vs., 108–9
    thinking vs., 109–12, 163, 183
    and workplace, 106–8
Environment, and cancer, 182, 238n
Ethel (Molly's mother), 124–29
Ethics, 38, 57, 68
Evelyn G. (constructive lies), 17–18, 20,
    23
Evolution, 11

Exclusions, 218–19
Experience
    as compartmentalized, 160
    interpretation of, 65–66
    and reality, 153
    See also Female experience

Facts
    distortion of, 67–68
    fantasies vs., 165
Failure, and myth, 168
Families
    and affairs, 157–63
    anxiety in, 88–90, 96, 110
    background of, 69, 82, 98–99, 116
    children in, 97, 151–52
    and death, 83, 99–100, 141–145, 162, 232*n*
    and emotions, 88–92, 111, 191–92
    as first world, 83–84
    history of, 146
    honesty in, 85–86, 97, 112
    ideal, 85
    information flow in, 140
    intentions of, 87–88
    rigid roles in, 89, 90–92, 99–101, 140
    See also Family secrets; *specific relationship*
Family secrets
    and affairs, 158–61
    and anxiety, 88, 138, 175
    and confrontations, 150–51
    defined, 137–38
    insiders/outsiders of, 145–48
    price of, 42, 151
    and privacy, 42–44
    reality vs., 42, 153
    and relationships, 88, 139
    revelation of, 150–151, 163–166, 235–36*n*
    and shame, 146, 147
    stigma of, 138
    symptoms of, 148–52
    value of, 151
    See also specific relationship
Fantasies, 1–3, 6, 7, 142, 152, 165, 166, 171
Fathers
    daughter's relationship with, 3, 4, 7, 43–44, 67–68, 92, 93, 94–95, 126–28

and family secrets, 146–47
    son's relationship with, 95
    See also Parents
Fear
    and anxiety, 185–89
    of losing approval, 61
    power vs., 187
    and pretending, 59
    of rejection, 190–92
    and relationships, 61
    and silence, 187–88
    of success, 76, 78, 202
    of visibility, 202
    women taught to, 187
Female experience
    commonality of, 45, 46, 62, 63, 66, 214–16
    in context, 154
    distortion of, 55
    myths of, 45
    validation of, 60, 61
Female passivity, 49
Female sexuality, 56–57
Femininity, 49, 200
Feminists
    biases of, 209–16
    challenge of, 197
    conditioning vs., 188–89, 197
    and consciousness raising, 61–63, 66, 216–19, 228*n*
    and patriarchy, 61–63, 189
Fern (Linda's mother), 143–46
Ferrera, Stephanie, 221*n*, 230*n*
Fidelity. *See* monogamy
Flight distance, 37
Frank (Bea's father), 94–95
Frauds, 74–76
Freud, Sigmund, 52, 54
Friedman, Edwin, 235*n*
Friendship, 1–2, 6, 80–81

Gartrell, Nanette, 222*n*
Gender
    differences of, 26–27, 200
    and language, 10, 20–21
    stereotypes of, 200, 204, 219
    See also Tokenism
Generalization, 214–15
Generations, 91–92, 93, 94, 115, 128, 129
Genitalia, mislabeling of, 51–52, 53–56, 59, 153

Genograms, 141
Gerzon, Mark, 230*n*
Gilbert, Roberta, 230*n*
Gilligan, Carol, 225*n*, 229*n*
Goethe, 135, 234*n*
Goldner, Virginia, 231*n*
Goodenough, Ursula, 221*n*
Goodrich, Thelma Jean, 231*n*, 243*n*
Guilt
  and affairs, 158–59, 162, 174–75
  and body signals, 176
  lack of, 26
Gustafson, James, 228*n*
Gut feelings, 180–83

Hanmer, Trudy, 225*n*
Hare-Mustin, Rachel, 214, 227*n*, 228*n*, 231*n*
Harijan women, 113–14, 128–29
Harriet Goldhor Lerner Day (Kansas), 71, 74, 77
Hartman, Ann, 236*n*
Health
  as choice, 181
  and fantasies, 3, 7
Hearne, Vicki, 11, 222*n*
Heilbrun, Carolyn, 50, 64, 71, 225*n*, 226*n*, 227*n*, 229*n*, 243*n*
Helene (Jane's friend), 157–58, 161
Henley, Arthur, 17, 222*n*
Herman, Judith Lewis, 62, 227*n*, 237*n*, 240*n*
Hierarchies
  and fraudulence, 76, 77
  in Hindu society, 113
Hill, Anita, 18, 19, 21, 33
Hirschman, Jane, 240*n*
Hoffmeister, Liz, 83, 230*n*
Holocaust, 24, 96
Homophobia, 28–31
Honest body, 174–77
Honest woman, 219
Honesty
  beginning of, 97
  and body signals, 104–5
  complexity of, 31–32
  as compliment, 23
  in facts vs. feelings, 86
  in families, 85–86, 97, 112
  and judgment, 24–25
  and monogamy, 164–65, 170–71

  negative aspects of, 105
  and self-protection, 106–8
  and silence, 112
  spontaneous, 103–6
  timing of, 102–3, 162
  truth vs., 14, 102–16, 125
  views of, 86
  See also Truth-telling
Honesty quotient (HQ), 22–23, 32
Hong-Kingston, Maxine, 236*n*
Honorable lying, 21
Howard, George S., 227*n*, 243*n*
Howe, Florence, 241*n*
Hunger, 194

Imber-Black, Evan, 139–40, 223*n*, 231*n*, 232*n*, 234*n*, 237*n*
Imitation, 16
Immigrants, 7
Imposter syndrome, 76, 77, 78
India, 18–19, 113–14, 128–29
Infidelity. *See* Affairs
Information
  flow in families of, 140
  gathering of, 114
In-law triangles, 133–35
Integrity, erosion of, 22–23, 30–31
Intelligence, 208–9
Intercourse, as husband's right, 59
Internalization of cultural
  taboos. *See* Conditioning
Internalized values, 74, 105
Interpretation
  of anger, 183–85
  of anxiety, 185–88
  of body signals, 180–88, 194
  of experience, 65–66
  of truth, 26
IQ tests, 209
"Irish grudge syndrome," 191
Isaacs, Marla Beth, 1–3, 5, 8

Jan (ambition), 80–81, 199
Jane (affair), 156–61, 163–68, 170, 175
Jen (marriage), 132–33
Jobs, "creating" of people by, 199–200
Joey (Vicki's daughter), 41–44
John (Linda's father), 144
John (Rosa's husband), 168–70
Johnson, Sonia, 188–89, 226*n*, 237*n*, 238*n*, 239*n*, 240*n*

Jordan , Judith, 228*n*
Jordan, June, 222*n*, 237*n*
Joy, W. Brugh, 135, 234*n*
Judgment
    and honesty, 24–25
    moral, 14, 27, 31
Judy (sexism), 184–85

Kanter, Rosabeth Moss, 200, 202–3,
        205, 229*n*, 230*n*, 241*n*, 242*n*
Kaplan, Alexandra, 228*n*
Karpel, Mark, 223*n*
Kent, Katherine Glenn, 231*n*
Kerr, Michael, 230*n*
Kiltredge, Cherry, 234*n*
Kofron, Emily, 238*n*
Kohn, Alfie, 230*n*
Kowalski, Anthony, 232*n*
Krestan, Jo-Ann, 233*n*, 234*n*, 236*n*
Krista (faked orgasms), 50–52, 56–57,
        59–61

Labia, 54
Laird, Joan, 224*n*
Language
    body, 176
    of deception, 9–11, 12
    and gender, 10, 20–21
    and patriarchy, 54, 55
    and sexuality, 51, 52, 53–56
    and truth-telling, 55
Learning deficit, 152
Lena (airplane story), 27–32
Lenore (overfunctioner), 129–32
Lesbians, 27–32, 64
Lewis, Jerry, 230*n*
Lies, lying
    about age, 196
    altruistic, 23–24
    beginnings of, 6–7
    constructive, 17–18, 20
    context of, 6–8, 33
    and ethics, 68
    face-saving, 26
    honorable, 21
    multiple, 3
    outright, 12
    pretending vs., 8, 57–61, 118–19, 122
    reasons for, 20
    role of, 2–6
    and sex, 57–58

as signals, 168
social, 22–23, 26
subjective experience of, 26
types of, 12–13
    See also Deception; Orgasms
Linda (family secrets), 140–47
Listening, 113–14
Lorde, Audre, 66, 187–88, 196, 222*n*,
        224*n*, 226*n*, 227*n*, 231*n*, 239*n*,
        242*n*, 243*n*
Loss
    and affairs, 168
    by immigrants, 7
    threat of, 6
Luck, and success, 71–73
Lyons, Nora, 225*n*

Mason, Marilyn, 234*n*
Magic, and pretending, 6, 117
Marecek, Jeanne, 227*n*, 228*n*
Maria (interracial marriage), 190–92
Markers, 211–12, 216, 242*n*
Marla (friend), 1–3, 5, 8, 221*n*
Marriage
    focus on, 132–33
    and monogamy paradox, 167–71
    and myths, 87, 167–68, 179
Mary Anne (Jane's sister), 166–67
Masculinity, 200
Matraphobia, 91
McGoldrick, Monica, 229*n*, 231*n*, 232*n*,
        240*n*
McIntosh, Peggy, 74–78, 228*n*, 229*n*
McIntyre, Denis, 236*n*
Melina, Lois Ruskai, 236*n*
Memory, 193–94
Men
    conditioning about, 48–50, 154
    and myths, 52, 196
Menninger Clinic, 15, 64, 102, 201–2,
        205, 210–11
Mental flu, 174–75
Michelle (in-law triangle), 133–35
Miller, Jean Baker, 228*n*, 229*n*
Minnich, Elizabeth Kamarck, 211–12,
        242*n*, 243*n*
Molly (mother-daughter), 124–29
Monogamy, 164–65, 167–71
Moraga, Cherrie, 236*n*
Moral judgments, 14, 27, 31
Morgan, Robin, 224*n*, 225*n*, 237*n*

Morrison, Toni, 222n, 244n
Mother-daughter relationships
  Bea, 84–86, 88, 90–92, 94, 97–101,
    111, 137
  Catherine, 149
  and family legacies, 92–94, 231–32n
  Molly, 124–28
  Peg, 109–10, 111
  Vicki, 41–44
Motherhood, as career, 93–94
Mothers
  cancer of, 3–5, 7, 8, 18, 142
  death of, 83
  myth of good, 64–65, 66, 87–88, 94
  sons' relationships with, 134
  stories of, 97–101
  See also Mother–daughter relation-
    ships; Parents
Moustakas, Clark, 104–5, 176, 233n,
    238n
Multiple lies, 3
Munter, Carol, 240n
Myths
  and failure, 168
  of female experience, 45
  of good mother, 64–65, 66, 87–88,
    94
  and marriage, 87, 167–68, 179
  and men, 52, 196
  of motherhood as career, 93–94
  paradoxes in, 49–50
  protest against, 63, 66
  reality vs., 87–88
  and self-deception, 168
  of womanhood, 196
  of workplace, 70, 72

Nancy (mislabeled genitalia), 54–55
National Institutes of Health, 55
National Women's Business
    Association, 71
Near, Holly, 102, 222n, 233n
"Normal" sex, 56
Numerical scarcity, 201–6, 213

Olsen, Tillie, 224n
Orgasms, 48–52, 56, 57–58, 195
Outright lies, 12
Outsiders and insiders, and
  secrets, 41–44, 114, 136–37,
    139, 145–48, 214–16

Outward Bound, 201
Overfunctioners, 129–32

Papp, Peggy, 142, 152, 228n, 230n,
    231n, 234n, 235n, 236n
Paradox
  monogamy as, 167–71
  in myths, 49–50
Parents
  children's relationships with, 85, 87,
    96, 131–32, 137, 148–50, 190–92
  secrets of, 137, 145
Parker, Pat, 198, 241n
Partner, control of, 167
Passivity, 49
Patriarchy
  conditioning by, 195, 219
  culture as, 48, 60, 71, 218
  doctors' deceptions in, 7
  and expert opinion, 66
  and feminism, 61–63, 189
  and language, 54, 55
  pretense in, 14–15, 48–49, 122
  privacy vs., 44–45, 224n
  and sexual advances, 19–20
  and sexuality, 58–61
  and therapy, 65
  and workplace, 70
Paul G. (Evelyn's husband), 17–18, 23
Pearson, Carol, 242n
Peg (mother-daughter), 109–11
Penis/penis envy, 51, 52, 53, 54, 73, 153
Perspective
  and context, 6–8, 79
  of therapists, 79, 114–15
Pharr, Suzanne, 222n
Physical space, 35–37
Physical symptoms, 64–65, 104, 161–62
Pittman, Frank, 159–60, 237n
Plastic surgery, 195
Playing dumb, 129–32
Pogrebin, Letty Cottin, 146, 235n, 236n
Polarized relationships, 133
Power
  abuse of, 19–20, 21
  fear vs., 187
  and secrecy, 146, 171
  and tokenism, 201–6
  and women, 6, 74–75, 77, 219
Pratt, Minnie Bruce, 222n, 236n
Prefeminist teaching, 48–49

Prefixes, 211–12, 216, 242*n*
Prejudice, 28–30, 191–92, 210–16
Pretending
    and body signals, 59
    and conditioning, 14, 48, 218
    and context, 132–35
    and courage, 124–29
    and creativity, 117
    and deception, 117–18
    definition of, 120–21
    and fear, 59
    as imitation, 16
    intentions in, 118
    lying vs., 8, 57–61, 118–19, 122
    as magic, 6, 117
    moral judgments suspended in, 14
    others protected by, 14, 58, 59
    in patriarchy, 14–15, 48–49, 122
    and playing dumb, 129–32
    reality vs., 118, 123
    and self-presentation, 118
    sexual, 48–52, 58, 59
    and truth-telling, 13–16, 135
    by women, 121–24, 180
    See also Orgasms
Privacy
    of body, 36, 39, 46–47
    and context, 47
    and control, 39
    deception vs., 13, 122
    defined, 223*n*
    and ethics, 38
    and family secrets, 42–44
    functions/purpose of, 36, 39–40
    as human right, 35–38
    and insiders and outsiders, 41–44
    patriarchy vs., 44–45, 224*n*
    secrets vs., 34–41, 44–45, 223*n*
    and self-preservation, 37
    and silence, 13, 30, 38, 45
    of vulnerable groups, 37–38
    See also Secrets
Protection
    of father, 147
    pretending as, 14, 58, 59
    secrecy as, 39–40, 45
    See also Self-protection

Racism, 191–92
Rage, 65
Rape, 62

Reagon, Bernice Johnson, 243*n*
Reality
    ability to observe, 26
    and affairs, 156
    beginning of, 97
    emotions vs., 108–9
    expanded vision of, 213
    and experience, 153
    family secrets vs., 153
    as imposed by others, 47
    myth vs., 87–88
    new vs. old, 62
    pretending vs., 118, 123
Redwood Cultural Work, 233*n*,
        244*n*
Rejection, fear of, 190–92
Relationships
    and affairs, 158–65, 173
    changes in, 129
    erosion of, 22–23, 68
    and family secrets, 88, 139
    and fears, 61
    gender differences in, 27
    goals of, 108
    honorable, 218
    lies at center of, 4–5
    polarized, 133
    process in, 42, 44
    responsibility for, 164
    with spouse, 41–44
    See also specific relationship
Resistance
    to change, 115–16
    to truth-telling, 114, 115, 190–92
Re-storying, of self, 97
Reynolds, David, 239*n*
Rich, Adrienne, 30, 218, 222*n*, 224*n*,
        226*n*, 227*n*, 231*n*, 242*n*, 243*n*
River, seminar on the, 200–208
Roberts, Janine, 235*n*
Roles, in families, 89, 90–92, 99–101,
        140
Rosa (monogamy), 168–70, 172
Rosen, Libby, 232*n*
Rue, Loyal, 221*n*
Ruth (Bea's mother), 84–87, 91–92,
        97–101, 137

Safety, 111, 115, 213
Sally (self-protection), 106–8, 125
Sam (Molly's father), 126–28

Sam (Vicki's husband), 41–44
Saville-Troike, M., 224n
Saxton, Marsha, 241n
Scully, Diana, 226n
Secrecy, definition of, 39, 44, 223n
Secrets
    and affairs, 159, 165
    analysis of, 40
    burden of, 143–44
    of children, 137, 145
    and closeness, 159
    distance created by, 144
    from spouses, 34–35, 39–40, 46–47
    functions of, 39–40
    insiders and outsiders of, 41–44, 114,
        136–37, 139, 145–48, 214–16
    and intimacy, 159
    nature of, 38
    of parents, 137, 145
    and power, 146, 171
    privacy vs., 34–41, 44–45, 223n
    as protection, 39–40, 45
    and stigma, 138, 139
    revelation of, 163–66, 235–36n
    See also Family secrets; Orgasms
Seidenberg, Robert, 232n
Selective math disability, 152–53
Self
    in context, 200
    influences of and on, 206
    re-storying of, 97
    true, 198–208, 209
    and workplace, 199–200
Self-blaming fantasies, 152
Self-deception, 13, 40, 168, 179–80
Self-esteem, 60, 207
Self-help books, 46
Self-presentation, 79, 118
Self-preservation, 37
Self-protection, 106–8, 172
Seminar, about the true self, 200–208
Sex
    fantasies about, 165, 166, 171
    and lies, 57–58
    "normal," 56
    and pretending, 48–52, 58, 59
    See also Affairs; Orgasms
Sexism, 184–85
Sexual abuse, 154, 193
Sexual advances, unwanted, 19–20
Sexual honesty, 165–67

Sexuality
    female, 56–57
    and language, 51, 52, 53–56
    and patriarchy, 58–61
    repression of, 55, 58
    and silence, 51, 52, 55
Sexual orientation, 27–30
Shame, 45, 46, 51, 146, 147
Shavlik, Donna, 242n
Signals, 168. See also Body signals
Silence
    and abuse of power, 19–21
    as altruistic, 23–24
    and cancer, 7, 8, 148, 187
    and deception, 5, 12–13, 15, 172–73
    and fear, 187–88
    and honesty, 112
    and privacy, 13, 30, 38, 45
    and sexuality, 51, 52, 55
    and sexual orientation, 27–30
    and values, 190
    See also Family secrets; Secrets
Silverstein, Laura, 232n
Silverstein, Olga, 228n, 230n, 231n,
        232n
Sisters, 43
Slater, Phillip, 232n
Sleepiness, 177, 180
Smith, Barbara, 222n, 236n, 244n
Social distance, 37
Social lies, 22–23, 26
Social movement, as change agent, 139,
        155
Sons
    father's relationship with, 95
    mother's relationship with, 134
Sontag, Susan, 238n
Space, physical, 35–37
Spontaneous honesty, 103–6
Spouses
    and desire to please, 57–58
    relationships with, 41–44
    secrets from, 34–35, 39–40, 46–47
    See also Orgasms
Status quo, 149–50, 203
Steinem, Gloria, 225n, 226n, 227n,
        240n
Stereotypes, of gender, 200, 204,
        219
Stiver, Irene, 229n
Stone Center, 228n, 229n, 238n

Stories
    of achievement, 79
    choosing of, 78–79
    in context, 81–82
    and family background, 69, 82, 116
    of mothers, 97–101
    and truth-telling, 67–82, 88
    of women, 67–82
Success
    fear of, 76, 78, 202
    and luck, 71–73
    new definitions of, 77
    portrayal of, 78
Sue (status), 67–71, 73–74, 76–78, 121,
    208
Sukenick, Lynn, 91, 231n
Supreme Court, U.S., 23
Surrey, Janet, 228n
Survival anxiety, 142
Susan (sister), 4, 5–6, 117–18
Sybil (cancer), 181
Sylvia (Michelle's mother-in-law),
    133–35
Symptoms
    of children, 151–53
    physical, 64–65, 104, 161–62
    and status quo, 149–50
    See also Body signals

Tact, in truth-telling, 103, 108
Tan, Amy, 236n
Tannen, Deborah, 224n
Tate, Claudia, 236n
Tavris, Carol, 228n, 240n
Tests, intelligence, 209
Therapists, therapy
    consciousness raising vs., 62
    and cultural context, 2–3, 154
    goals of, 65
    perspective of, 79, 114–15
    role of, 150
    signals interpreted by, 180–83, 193
Thinking
    emotions vs., 109–12, 163, 183
    and memory, 193–94
Thomas, Clarence, 18, 33
Timing
    of honesty, 102–3, 162
    and truth-telling, 103, 108
Titus, Meredith, 241n
Togetherness, 91

Tokenism, 201–8, 210–11, 213
Tony and the Martians story, 1–8
Touchton, Judith, 242n
Trauma, memory of, 193
True selves, 198–208, 209
Trust
    capacity for, 24
    and monogamy, 169–70
    rebuilding of, 163–65
    and truth-telling, 87
Truth
    asking for, 167
    concealment of, 24
    different versions of, 217
    distance created by, 69
    honesty vs., 14, 102–16, 125
    inability to cope with, 25–26,
        172–73
    inadequacy of, 61
    interpretation of, 26
    naming of, 61–63
    nature of, 27
    revelation of, 24
    as sought by unconscious, 5, 64,
        160–63
    storing of, 193–94
Truth-telling
    and affairs, 171–73
    anxiety vs., 99
    beginning of, 97
    and body signals, 175–76, 190–92
    caution in, 189
    as challenge, 14–15
    confrontation vs., 128, 150–51
    and consciousness raising, 63, 64–66
    in context, 213
    and diversity, 219
    gender differences in, 27
    and language, 55
    to oneself, 47
    preparing for, 114, 126–28, 151,
        192
    and pretending, 13–16, 135
    as process, 111, 113–16, 128, 217–18
    questions in, 113–14
    resistance to, 114, 115, 190–92
    and safety, 115
    and stories, 67–82, 88
    timing and tact in, 103, 108
    and trust, 87
    See also Deception; Honesty

Unconscious
    and body signals, 64–65, 161–62,
        179–80
    and fantasies, 3, 142
    and memory, 194
    motives, 9
    truth sought by, 5, 64, 160–63
Unity, of women, 216
"Untouchable" women, 113–14, 128–29

Vagina, 53, 54, 153
Values
    and behavior, 161, 176
    and deception, 175
    internalized, 74, 105
    and sexual honesty, 165–67
    and silence, 190
    and true self, 199
    in wilderness, 207–8
Vaughan, Peggy, 164–65, 170, 237n
Vicki (insiders), 41–42, 139
Violence, by males, 62, 154
Visibility, fear of, 202
Vulnerable groups, privacy of, 37–38
Vulva, 54, 55, 153

Walker, Alice, 225n
Walker, Gillian, 235n
Walsh, Froma, 232n
Walters, Marianne, 228n, 230n, 231n
Walters, Suzanna Danuta, 232n
Webb-Watson, Linda, 243n
Webster, Harriet, 234n
Wellesley College Center for Research
    on Women, 74

Wilderness, values in, 207–8
Wilson, Edward O., 223n
Wolf, Naomi, 240n
Wolk, Robert, 17, 222n
Womanhood, myths about, 196
Woman of the Year, 71
Women
    ambitions of, 67–69, 72–74, 80–81
    and authority, 74, 75, 77
    as a category, 214–16
    compromises by, 180
    cultural pressures on, 45, 52
    as frauds, 74–76
    as guardians of family secrets,
        146
    Harijan ("Untouchable"), 113–14,
        128–29
    honest, 219
    male violence against, 62, 154
    minority, 210–11
    and power, 6, 74–75, 77, 219
    pretending by, 121–24, 180
    self-betrayal of, 52
    status of, 68
    stories of, 67–82
    as taught to fear, 187
    unity of, 216
"Women in Context," 210–11, 242n
Women's conferences, 205–6, 210–11
Women's groups, 226–27n
Women's Liberation movement, 61
Women's Project in Family Therapy,
    228n, 231n
Woolf, Virginia, 60, 226n
Workplace, 70, 72, 106–8, 199–200